KEY MATHS

Edexcel

GCSE

Summary and
Practice

INTERMEDIATE

- ► **Paul Hogan**
- ► **Barbara Job**
- ► **Diane Morley**

Published in 2002 by:
Nelson Thornes Ltd
Delta Place
27 Bath Road
CHELTENHAM
GL53 7TH
United Kingdom

02 03 04 05 06 / 10 9 8 7 6 5 4 3 2 1

A catalogue record for this book is available from the British Library.

ISBN 0 7487 6771 1

Cartoons by Clinton Banbury
Illustrations by Oxford Designers & Illustrators
Page make-up by Tech Set Ltd

Printed in China by Midas Printing International Ltd.

Acknowledgements

The authors and publishers are grateful to Edexcel for permission to reproduce
questions from their past examination papers. Any answers and mark schemes
included have not been provided by the examining boards, they are the
sole responsibility of the authors and may not necessarily constitute the only
possible solutions.

The publishers wish to thank the following for permission to reproduce copyright
material:
Britstock-IPA: 50 (Walsh), 56 (Walsh); Getty Images: 1 (Tony Stone Images/Will and
Deni McIntyre), 2 (Will and Deni McIntyre); Martyn Chillmaid: 8, 26, 32;
Stockmarket: 80; Topham Picturepoint (Press Association): 122; Alton Towers: 212;
John Walmsley Photography: 146; Still Pictures: 164 (David Hoffman).
All other photographs Nelson Thornes Archive.

The publishers have made every effort to contact copyright holders but apologise if
any have been overlooked.

Contents

Introduction

Key Maths GCSE Edexcel Summary and Practice Intermediate, is one of a brand new series of three books to support your work for the Edexcel Specification and examinations. Each book has been designed to be used throughout your course or for practice and revision in preparation for the examinations.

It contains the following features that are sure to substantially support you in your work:

- Summaries in every chapter focus on the essential concepts and skills that you need to cover

- A range of questions provide for comprehensive practice of all these core areas

- Two pages per chapter of worked examination questions with hints and tips for comprehensive examination preparation

- All the worked examination questions are provided by an examiner for Edexcel

All the highly popular features of Key Maths are included throughout the book to assist with your learning and understanding.

Also available from Nelson Thornes:

Key Maths GCSE Edexcel Summary and Practice Foundation 0 7487 6770 3

Key Maths GCSE Edexcel Summary and Practice Higher 0 7487 6772 X

1 Transformations

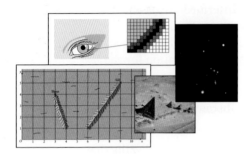

You need to know about:

- using co-ordinates
- equations of horizontal and vertical lines
- describing a reflection
- describing a rotation
- describing an enlargement
- combined transformations

Co-ordinates

Co-ordinates are used to give the position of a point.
The x co-ordinate (horizontal movement) is written first.
The y co-ordinate (vertical movement) is written second.

The co-ordinates of P are $(-2, 3)$. Don't forget the brackets.

All points on the red line have an x co-ordinate of 2.
The equation of the line is $x = 2$.

All points on the blue line have a y co-ordinate of -3.
The equation of the line is $y = -3$.

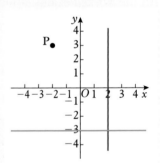

Transformation

A **transformation** can change the size and position of a shape.

Translation

A **translation** is a movement in a straight line.
The best way to describe a translation is to use a column vector.

This is a translation of $\begin{pmatrix} 3 \\ -5 \end{pmatrix}$.

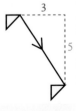

It means a translation of 3 units to the right and 5 units down.

The top number tells you the horizontal movement.
The bottom number tells you the vertical movement.

Reflection

A **reflection** flips a shape over a straight line called the mirror line. To describe a reflection you need to describe the mirror line or give its equation.

This is a reflection in the line $x = 1$.
Notice that the image of point A is labelled A′, the
image of point B is labelled B′ and so on.

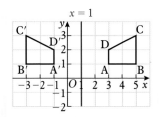

Rotation

A **rotation** turns a shape through a given angle around a fixed
point called the centre of rotation.

To describe a rotation you need to give the angle that the
shape has turned through, the direction of turn (clockwise
or anticlockwise) and the centre of rotation.

This is a rotation of 90° clockwise about O.

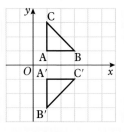

Translations, reflections and rotations do not change the size
of the shape.
The object and the image are always congruent for these
transformations.
Congruent means exactly the same size and shape.

Enlargement

An **enlargement** changes the size of an object.

To describe an enlargement you need to give the scale
factor and the centre of enlargement.

This is an enlargement of scale factor 2,
centre of enlargement C.

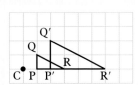

Inverse

The **inverse** of a transformation gets you back from the image to
the shape you started with.

The inverse of a translation of $\begin{pmatrix} 3 \\ -2 \end{pmatrix}$ is a translation of $\begin{pmatrix} -3 \\ 2 \end{pmatrix}$.

The inverse of a reflection is the same reflection.
The inverse of a rotation is the same rotation but in the opposite direction.
The inverse of an enlargement with scale factor 3 is an enlargement with the same
centre and scale factor $\frac{1}{3}$.

You can do more than one transformation on an object. Sometimes the result of
doing two transformations is the same as doing a single transformation. For
example, reflection in the x axis followed by rotation of 180° about the origin is the
same as reflection in the y axis.

1 **a** Describe each of these translations using a column vector.

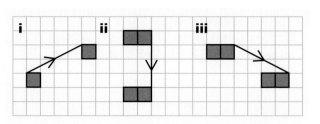

b Draw a line to show a translation of **i** $\begin{pmatrix} -4 \\ 3 \end{pmatrix}$ **ii** $\begin{pmatrix} 0 \\ -5 \end{pmatrix}$ **iii** $\begin{pmatrix} -2 \\ -3 \end{pmatrix}$

2 Copy the diagram.

a Reflect rectangle A in the y axis. Label the rectangle B.

b Rotate rectangle B 90° clockwise about O. Label the rectangle C.

c Reflect rectangle C in the x axis. Label the rectangle D.

d Reflect D in the y axis. Label the rectangle E.

e Write down the single transformation that maps rectangle C onto rectangle E.

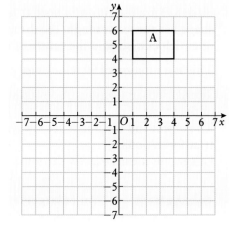

3 Copy the diagram.

a Enlarge shape A with scale factor 2. Use O as the centre of enlargement. Label the new shape B.

b Write down the transformation that will map B onto A.

c Reflect B in the y axis. Label the reflection C.

d Rotate shape C 90° anticlockwise about $(1, 2)$. Label the new shape D.

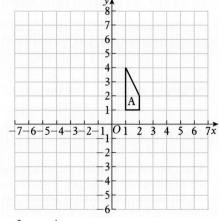

4 Write down the inverse of each of these transformations:

a rotation of 270° clockwise about $(2, -4)$

b translation 5 units to the left and 1 unit down

c reflection in the line $x = 6$

d enlargement, scale factor $\frac{1}{4}$, centre $(0, 6)$.

1 **a** Reflect triangle A in the *x* axis.
Label the triangle B. **(1 mark)**

   b Rotate triangle B 90° clockwise about
the origin.
Label the triangle C. **(1 mark)**

   c Write down the single transformation
that will map A on to C. **(2 marks)**

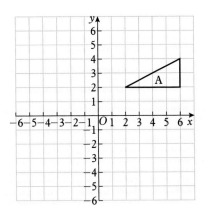

*Use tracing paper to help you do the
transformations.*

*To describe the single transformation from A to
C the first step is to identify the type of
transformation. Is it a translation, enlargement,
rotation or reflection?*

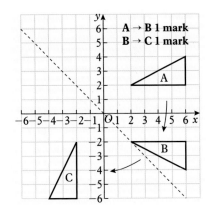

*Use the tracing paper to carefully map A onto
C, and check through each of these*

Translation: NO, the orientation has changed.
Enlargement: NO, there is no change in size.
Rotation: NO, 90° clockwise produces a shape the wrong way around.
Reflection: YES, in the dashed mirror line. The dashed line is y = −x.

The description of the transformation is:

   a reflection in the line *y* = −*x*
   1 mark   **1 mark**

1 **a** Describe fully the single
transformation which takes shape **A**
onto shape **B**.   **(2 marks)**

    b Describe fully the single
transformation which takes shape **A**
onto shape **C**.   **(3 marks)**
                     [S2001 P4 Q11]

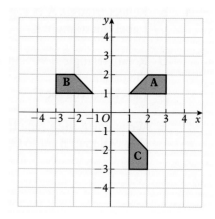

2

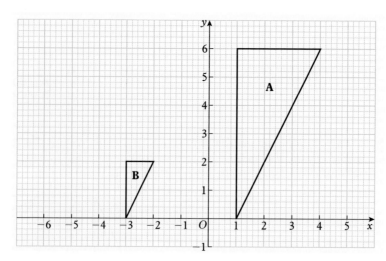

Describe fully the single transformation which maps triangle **A**
to triangle **B**.
                                  (3 marks)
                               [N1999 P3 Q18]

3 The shape **P** has been drawn on the grid.

    a Reflect the shape **P** in the y axis.
Label the image **Q**.   **(1 mark)**

    b Rotate the shape **Q** through 180°
about (0, 0).
Label this image **R**.   **(1 mark)**

    c Describe fully the single
transformation which maps the shape
P to the shape **R**.   **(2 marks)**
               [N1998 P3 Q12]

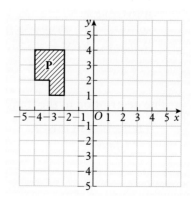

4 On the grid, draw the reflection of triangle PQR in the line AB.

(**2marks**)

[S1999 P3 Q2]

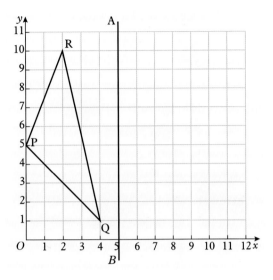

5 **a** Describe fully the single transformation that maps shape **P** onto shape **Q**. (**2 marks**)

b Rotate shape **P** 90° anticlockwise about the point A(1, 1). (**2 marks**)

[S2000 P3 Q22]

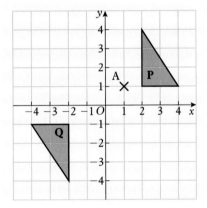

6 Rotate the triangle through 90° **clockwise** about the point (0, 0).

Draw the triangle in its new position. (**3 marks**)

[N2000 P4 Q7]

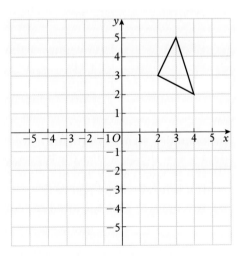

2 Numbers: approximating and rounding

You need to know about:

- place value in numbers
- using < and > signs
- rounding to the nearest 10, 100, 1000
- rounding to 1 significant figure
- estimating an answer
- changing a fraction into a decimal
- changing a decimal into a fraction
- putting fractions and decimals in order of size

	M	HTh	TTh	Th	H	T	U
Look at this number:	5	7	3	4	6	1	9

The value of the 7 is **seven hundred thousand**. The value of the 6 is **six hundred**.

> **means greater than.** For example, 398 > 172.
< **means less than.** For example, 19 < 23.

The number 57 is nearer to 60 than to 50.
57 is rounded to 60 to the nearest 10.

345 is halfway between 340 and 350. It is rounded to 350 to the nearest 10.

718 is nearer to 700 than 800. It is rounded to 700 to the nearest 100.

3500 is halfway between 3000 and 4000. It is rounded to 4000 to the nearest 1000.

Significant figure

In any number the first **significant figure** is the first digit that isn't a 0.
For most numbers this is the first digit.
The first significant figure is the red digit.

724.5   2.746   91.036   5078   0.327   0.00045

To **round to 1 significant figure**:
(1) Look at the digit after the first significant one.
(2) If it is 5, 6, 7, 8 or 9 add one on to the first significant digit.
    If it is 0, 1, 2, 3 or 4 ignore it.
(3) Be careful to keep the number about the right size.

63.8 is 60 to 1 sf. It is *not* 6.   467.9 is 500 to 1 sf.
0.302 is 0.3 to 1 sf.   0.0571 is 0.06 to 1 sf.

To **round to any number of significant figures**:
(1) Look at the first unwanted digit.
(2) Use the normal rules of rounding.
(3) Be careful to keep the number the right size.

364.5 is 360 to 2 sf.   5.7653 is 5.77 to 3 sf.   0.003 856 21 is 0.003 856 to 4 sf.

Estimating an answer

You can estimate by

(1) rounding to 1 sf.
An estimate for 682×22 is $700 \times 20 = 14\,000$.

or (2) looking for factors to cancel

An estimate for $\dfrac{33.9 \times 18.71}{6.41 \times 9.38}$ is $\dfrac{30 \times 18}{6 \times 9} = \dfrac{30}{6} \times \dfrac{18}{9}$

$= 5 \times 2 = 10.$

To estimate square roots look for the nearest square number.
An estimate for $\sqrt{48.46}$ is $\sqrt{49} = 7$. So $\sqrt{48.46}$ is a little less than 7.

To turn the fraction $\dfrac{a}{b}$ into a decimal you divide a by b.

When you do this you will always get *either* a decimal that stops, called a terminating decimal,

or a recurring decimal. This is a decimal that does not stop, it repeats.

Every terminating decimal can be written as a fraction.

0.7 is 7 tenths $= \dfrac{7}{10}$ because the 7 is in the tenths column.

0.56 is 56 hundredths $= \dfrac{56}{100}$ because the 6 is in the hundredths column.

0.713 is 713 thousandths $= \dfrac{713}{1000}$ because the 3 is in the thousandths column.

To put fractions and decimals in order of size change all the fractions into decimals then put the decimals in order.

Example   Put these in order. Start with the smallest. $\dfrac{3}{5}$, 0.49, $\dfrac{4}{9}$, 0.46

$\dfrac{3}{5} = 0.6$ and $\dfrac{4}{9} = 0.444\,44\ldots$ so the order is $\dfrac{4}{9}$, 0.46, 0.49, $\dfrac{3}{5}$.

1   Write down the value of the **red** digit in each of these numbers
   a 498   **b** 24 520   **c** 2587   **d** 0.5634   **e** 0.002

2   Sam is using the digits 7, 3, 1, 0 and 4.
   a What is the smallest five digit number that Sam can make?
   b What is the largest five digit odd number that Sam can make?
   c Sam uses all the digits to make up this sum ... − ... × ... = 95
      He uses each digit once only. Fill in the missing numbers.

3   Round each of these numbers.
   a 357 to the nearest 10   **c** 451 to 1 sf   **e** 0.053 76 to 3 sf
   b 4549 to the nearest 100   **d** 999 to 1 sf   **f** 0.807 35 to 2 sf

4   For each part: **i** Estimate the answer by rounding each number to 1 sf.
            ii Work out the answer using a calculator.
               Give your answer to 3 sf.

   a 783×64.38 **b** $\dfrac{42.76 \times 19.32}{3.918}$ **c** $\sqrt{11.21 \times 3.76}$

5   For each part: **i** Estimate the answer by rounding so that numbers will
            cancel.
            ii Work out the answer using a calculator.
               Give your answer to 3 sf.

   a $\dfrac{37.1 \times 14.25}{5.893 \times 6.99}$ **b** $\dfrac{18.921 \times 23.99}{5.74 \times 4.88}$ **c** $\dfrac{39.21 \times 29.154}{34.287}$

6   Write these fractions as decimals.

   a $\dfrac{2}{5}$ **b** $\dfrac{13}{100}$ **c** $\dfrac{5}{8}$ **d** $\dfrac{2}{3}$ **e** $\dfrac{5}{12}$

7   Write these decimals as fractions.
   Write each fraction in its simplest form.
   a 0.9   **b** 0.351   **c** 0.25   **d** 0.008   **e** 0.23

8   Write these decimals and fractions in order of size. Start with the
   smallest.

   $\dfrac{3}{8}$,   0.41, $\dfrac{2}{5}$, $\dfrac{1}{2}$,   0.62

These questions would appear on a non-calculator paper.

1 a Write down a decimal that lies between $\frac{1}{3}$ and $\frac{1}{2}$.

   b Which of these two fractions is the larger: $\frac{3}{4}$ or $\frac{2}{3}$?   **(4 marks)**

In both of these questions it is easier to write the fractions as decimals so that you can compare them.

a $\frac{1}{3} = 0.333\ldots$ $\frac{1}{2} = 0.5$ **(1 mark)**

You need a decimal between 0.333 . . . and 0.5

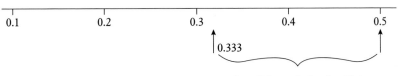

Any of these decimals will do.

Any one of 0.34, 0.35, ..., 0.4, 0.45 will do.   0.37   **1 mark**

b $\frac{3}{4} = 0.75\ldots$ $\frac{2}{3} = 0.666\ldots$ **1 mark**

So the larger fraction is $\frac{3}{4}$.   **1 mark**

The answer is the fraction $\frac{3}{4}$. Don't give the decimal equivalent.

2 Find an estimate for $\dfrac{45.98 \times 56.56}{3.24 \times 24.8}$.   **(3 marks)**

When rounding off the numbers you should look for factors.

3 is a factor of 45.   *24 and 56 both have a factor of 8.*

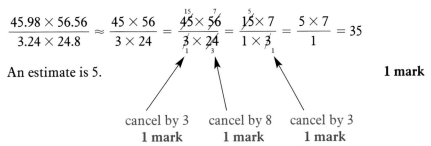

$$\frac{45.98 \times 56.56}{3.24 \times 24.8} \approx \frac{45 \times 56}{3 \times 24} = \frac{\overset{15}{\cancel{45}} \times \overset{7}{\cancel{56}}}{\underset{1}{\cancel{3}} \times \underset{3}{\cancel{24}}} = \frac{\overset{5}{\cancel{15}} \times 7}{1 \times \underset{1}{\cancel{3}}} = \frac{5 \times 7}{1} = 35$$

An estimate is 5.   **1 mark**

            cancel by 3   cancel by 8   cancel by 3

             1 mark   **1 mark**   **1 mark**

1   Write down **two** different fractions that lie between $\frac{1}{4}$ and $\frac{1}{2}$.

                                                   (2 marks)

                                                  [S2000 P3 Q2]

2

> **BUY £20 000**
>
> **WORTH OF**
>
> **PREMIUM BONDS**
>
> **AND**
>
> **ON AVERAGE**
>
> **YOU'LL WIN**
>
> **13**
>
> **PRIZES A YEAR**

On average, someone with £20 000 in Premium Bonds should win 13 prizes each year.

Flora has £7700 in Premium Bonds.

  a   Work out the number of prizes she should win, on average, each year.

                                                   (2 marks)

Premium Bonds are sold in multiples of £10.
Rajesh works out that he is likely to win 9 prizes next year.

  b   Work out an estimate for the amount of money Rajesh has in
       Premium Bonds.   **(3 marks)**

                                                [S2000 P4 Q13]

3   Ann wins £160. She gives

     $\frac{1}{4}$ of £160 to Pat,
     $\frac{3}{8}$ of £160 to John
     and £28 to Peter.

What fraction of the £160 does Ann keep?
Give your fraction in its simplest form.   **(4 marks)**

                                                [N2000 P4 Q3]

4 The formula

$$Q = \frac{f^2 + 2g^2}{f - 3g}$$

can be used to calculate the value of Q.

$f = 9.04$ and $g = 1.8$.

Jane uses the formula to estimate the value of Q without using a calculator.

i Write down approximate values for f and g that Jane could use to estimate the value of Q.

ii Work out the estimate for the value of Q that these approximate values give. **(3 marks)**

[N1999 P3 Q17]

5 Tom uses his calculator to multiply 17.8 by 0.97. His answer is 18.236.

a **Without** finding the exact value of 17.8×0.97, explain why his answer must be wrong. **(1 mark)**

Sally estimates the value of $\dfrac{42.8 \times 63.7}{285}$ to be 8.

b Write down three numbers Sally could use to get her estimate.

$$\frac{\text{............} \times \text{............}}{\text{............}}$$

(2 marks)

[N1998 P3 Q10]

3 Dealing with data

You need to know about:

- drawing pie-charts
- drawing scatter graphs
- drawing histograms and frequency polygons
- writing questionnaires
- drawing stem and leaf diagrams

A **pie-chart** is a circle marked off in sectors.
The 360° angle at the centre of the circle represents all the data.
The angle of each sector represents the number of items in that sector.
A pie-chart is not useful for reading off accurate figures.
It also does not show up small differences very clearly.

Type of transport

A **scatter graph** is used to see if there is a connection between two sets of data.

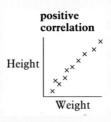

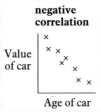

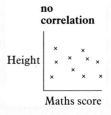

If the points on a scatter graph lie roughly in a straight line then a **line of best fit** is drawn through the middle of the points.
You can use this line to estimate a value of one of the variables if you know the value for the other variable.

Ben scored 32 in Maths but missed the Science test.
You can use the red lines to estimate his Science score as 34.

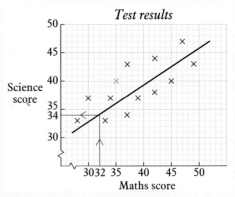

A **histogram** looks like a bar-chart but there are several important differences.

- It can only be used to show continuous data.
- There must not be any gaps between the bars.
- The data is always grouped.
  The widths of all the groups must be the same.
- Both axes are labelled like graph scales.

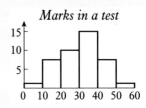

Marks in a test

You draw a **frequency polygon** by joining the mid-points of the top of each bar with straight lines. The **red** lines show the frequency polygon.

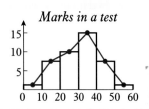

Marks in a test

Frequency polygons are often used to compare two sets of data.

It is possible to draw a frequency polygon without drawing the histogram.
You work out the mid-point of each group and then plot the frequencies against the mid-points. The points are then joined with straight lines.

The frequency polygon shows the **trend** of the data. The **trend** shows how the data is changing.

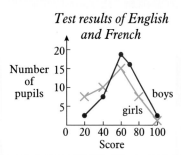

Test results of English and French

When using **questionnaires** you need to get a good spread of people so that your results represent a wide range of views.
A small group of people that represent a much larger group of people is called a **sample**.

When writing a questionnaire you need to make sure that the questions are not biased.
A question is **biased** if it makes you think that one particular answer is right.
A question that does this is called a **leading question**.
Questions should also not offend people and should be easy to answer.

Surveys that have a sensible sample size are called **reliable**.
This means that the sample is likely to represent the views of all the people.
More reliable surveys have smaller **margins of error**.

A **stem and leaf diagram** shows the shape of a set of data.
It is like a bar-chart but the actual data is used to form the bars.
The data must be numbers. Each number is split into a stem and a leaf.
A key must always be drawn to show how each number has been split.

Weekly attendance

Stem	Leaf
1	69 78
2	50 65 65 91
3	4 51

Key: 2|65 means 265

Some stem and leaf diagrams have a small number of stems and a lot of leaves.
For this type of diagram you can split each stem number into two rows.
The first row contains the leaves 0, 1, 2, 3 and 4.
The second row contains the leaves 5, 6, 7, 8 and 9.

Weekly attendance

Stem	Leaf
6	1 2 3 3
6	5 6 7 8 8 9
7	0 2 2 3 3 4
7	5 6 7 7 8
8	1 1 4
8	6 8 9 9

Key: 7|2 means 72

1 Harmeet asked the members of her hockey club for the colour of their car. Here are her results.

Car colour	Red	Silver	Black	Green	White	Blue
Number of members	5	9	3	4	2	7

Draw a pie-chart to show this data.

2 Hayley is looking at the relationship between the height and the arm span of members of her family. For each person she records the height and the arm span.

Height (cm)	165	145	170	175	130	135	151	155	185
Arm span (cm)	160	144	172	180	132	142	151	166	176

a Plot a scatter graph to show this data.

b What type of correlation does your graph show?

c Draw a line of best fit on your graph.

d Use your line to estimate the arm span of a person with height 160 cm.

3 At the school's sports day, Simon recorded all the times for the egg and spoon race. This is his data.

Times (nearest second)	0–30	30–60	60–90	90–120	120–150
Number of pupils	4	6	9	7	1

a Draw a histogram for this data.

b Use your histogram to draw a frequency polygon for the data.

4 Matthew records the results of all his French tests in one year. These are the marks that he scored.

64	82	66	98	73	78	83	73	91
79	65	79	54	91	74	52	41	75

Draw a stem and leaf diagram to show this data.

1 Sean has collected stamps from four
countries.
The table shows how many stamps
he has collected.

Draw a pie-chart to represent this
information.

Country	Number of stamps
France	33
Germany	49
Spain	31
UK	67

(6 marks)

*To work out each angle of the pie-chart you need to calculate the angle for
1 stamp.*

The total number of stamps collected is $33 + 49 + 31 + 67 = 180$.
So angle for 1 stamp $= 360° \div 180 = 2°$.   **1 mark**

So the angles are

France: $33 \times 2° = 66°$ Germany: $49 \times 2° = 98°$ **1 mark**

Spain: $31 \times 2° = 62°$ UK: $67 \times 2° = 134°$ **1 mark**

To draw the pie-chart draw each angle in turn:

 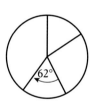

You will normally
be given the circle
in which you
should draw your
pie-chart.

Angles have to be drawn to an accuracy of $\pm 2°$

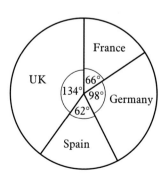

First angle: **1 mark**
Other angles: **1 mark**
Labels: **1 mark**

Write the angles in the pie-chart – this shows what you have worked out.

*You **must** also write the labels in each of the sectors from the table. It is these
that give you the final mark.*

2 The scatter graph shows the literacy and numeracy scores of ten students.

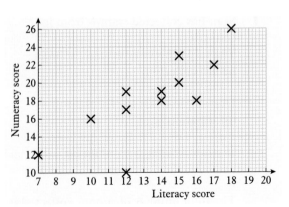

a Describe the relationship between the literacy and numeracy marks. **(1 mark)**
b Describe the correlation. **(1 mark)**
c Draw a line of best fit on the scatter graph. **(1 mark)**
d Use your line of best fit to estimate a literacy score for a student who has a numeracy score of 23. **(1 mark)**

a *The description needs to mention the change in literacy and numeracy:*
'A high literacy score gives a high numeracy score'. **0 marks**
'A higher literacy score would give a higher numeracy score'. **1 mark**

b *State the type of correlation; do **not** give a description of the relationship:*
Positive correlation **1 mark**

c *A line of best fit needs to*
(1) follow the direction of the points
(2) go through the middle of the points
(3) have approximately half the points one each side of the line
*(4) be a **single** straight line the full width of the graph.*

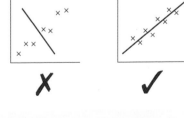

The red line on the graph is the line of best fit. **1 mark**

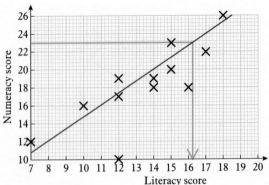

d *Read off from 23 on the numeracy axis.*
Draw the line shown in blue on the graph to show your method.
The answer is 16.3.
*Make your reading as accurate as you can. Do **not** round off.* **1 mark**

1 40 passengers at Gatwick Airport were asked which country they were flying to. Here is a frequency table which shows that information.

Country	Number of passengers
USA	14
France	10
Spain	11
Greece	5

Draw an accurate pie chart to show this information. Use the circle below.

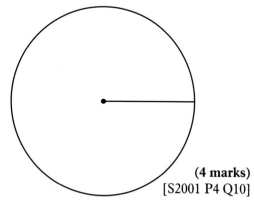

(4 marks)
[S2001 P4 Q10]

2 The table shows the hours of sunshine and the rainfall, in mm, in 10 towns during last summer.

Sunshine (hours)	650	455	560	430	620	400	640	375	520	620
Rainfall (mm)	10	20	15	29	24	28	14	30	25	20

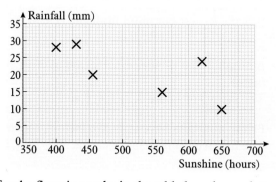

The points for the first six results in the table have been plotted in a scatter diagram.
a Plot the other four points to complete the scatter diagram. **(1 mark)**
b Describe the relationship between the hours of sunshine and the rainfall. **(1 mark)**
c Draw a line of best fit on your scatter diagram. **(1 mark)**
d Use your line of best fit to estimate
 i the rainfall when there are 450 hours of sunshine,
 ii the amount of sunshine when there are 18 mm of rainfall. **(2 marks)**
[S2001 P3 Q15]

4   Patterns: lining up

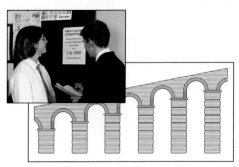

You need to know about:

- special types of numbers
- lowest common multiples
- highest common factors
- recurring and terminating decimals
- number sequences
- finding a formula for a number sequence
- using a formula to find any term of a number sequence

Odd numbers	The **odd numbers** are 1, 3, 5, 7, 9, 11, …
Even numbers	The **even numbers** are 2, 4, 6, 8, 10, 12, ….
Multiples	The **multiples** of 3 are 3, 6, 9, 12, 15, 18, 21, 24, … The **multiples** of 4 are 4, 8, 12, 16, 20, 24, 28, 32, …
Common multiples	The multiples 12 and 24 appear in both lists. They are called **common multiples**. You can find more common multiples by writing more multiples of 3 and 4.
Lowest common multiple	12 is the lowest of all the common multiples. It is the **lowest common multiple (LCM)**.
Factor	A number that divides exactly into another number is called a **factor**. The factors of 12 are 1, 2, 3, 4, 6 and 12.
Prime numbers	**Prime numbers** have only two factors, themselves and 1. The first ten prime numbers are 2, 3, 5, 7, 11, 13, 17, 19, 23, 29, …
Prime factor	The factors of 30 are 1, 2, 3, 5, 6, 10, 15 and 30. The factors 2, 3 and 5 are also prime numbers. They are called **prime factors** of 30.

A number can be written as a product of its prime factors.
You can use a factor tree to do this.

$60 = 2 \times 2 \times 3 \times 5$

This can be written $2^2 \times 3 \times 5$.

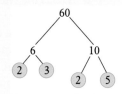

The factors of 24 are 1, 2, 3, 4, 6, 8, 12 and 24.
The factors of 30 are 1, 2, 3, 5, 6, 10, 15 and 30.

The **common factors** of 24 and 30 are 1, 2, 3 and 6.
The **highest common factor (HCF)** is 6.

Square numbers

The **square numbers** are 1, 4, 9, 16, 25, 36, 49, 64, ...

Triangle numbers

The **triangle numbers** are 1, 3, 6, 10, 15, 21, 28, 36, ...

Number sequence

A **number sequence** is a list of numbers that follow a rule.

Term

Each number in a sequence is called a **term**.
The sequence 4, 14, 24, 34, 44, 54, . . . has the rule 'add 10'.
The next term is the 7th term. it is $54 + 10 = 64$.

nth term

The term in a sequence with term number n is called the **nth term**.
The nth term in the sequence 3, 6, 9, 12, 15, 18, ... is $3n$.
The nth term in the sequence 10, 20, 30, 40, 50, ... is $10n$.

The formula for the nth term is also called the formula for the sequence.
Sometimes the formula has two parts.

Look at this sequence.   6, 10, 14, 18, 22, ...
it goes up in 4s but it is not the multiples of 4. It is related to the sequence $4n$.

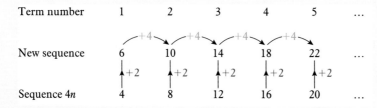

Compare the terms of the two sequences.
You need to **add 2** to the sequence $4n$ to get the new sequence.
The formula for the new sequence is $4n + 2$.

You can use the formula for the nth term to find any term in the sequence.
A sequence has the formula $5n − 3$.

The 1st term is $5 \times 1 − 3 = 2$,
the 2nd term is $5 \times 2 − 3 = 7$,
the 12th term is $5 \times 12 − 3 = 57$ and so on.

1 Look at the numbers 1, 2, 3, 4, 5, 14, 15, 16, 19, 45, 51, 60, 63, 81 and 100.
Write down the numbers that are:

a odd numbers

b factors of 16

c multiples of 7

d prime numbers

e *prime factors of 20*

f square numbers

g triangle numbers

h the common multiples of 5 and 3.

2 Write each of these numbers as a product of their prime factors.

a 120   **b** 180   **c** 1485   **d** 1470

3 **a** Write 224 as a product of its prime factors.

b Write 1260 as a product of its prime factors.

c Use the answers to **a** and **b** to calculate the HCF of 224 and 1260.

4 For each of these sequences write down the next two terms.

a 3, 5, 7, 9, ..., ...

b 3, 9, 27, 81, ..., ...

c 60, 56, 52, ..., ...

d 4, 9, 16, 25, ..., ...

e 1, 8, 27, ..., ...

5 Work out the 10th term in the sequence whose formula is:

a $3n + 4$ **c** $2n - 1$ **e** $6n + 7$

b $2n + 5$ **d** $5n + 3$ **f** $n^2 + 3n$

6 Write down the formula for each of these sequences.

a 4, 7, 10, 13, ..., ...

b 5, 12, 19, 26, ..., ...

c 7, 11, 15, 19, ..., ...

d 12, 9, 6, ..., ...

7 The nth term of a sequence is $4n + 3$.

a Write down the first six terms of the sequence.

b Which term has the value of 43?

These questions could appear on a non-calculator paper.

1 When 56 is written as the product of its prime factors we get $56 = 2^3 \times 7$.

   a Write 126 as the product of its prime factors.   **(2 marks)**

   b Write down 126×56 as a product of prime factors.   **(2 marks)**

   c Write down the square root of your answer to **b** as a product of prime factors.   **(1 mark)**

  a   2)126   So $126 = 2 \times 3 \times 3 \times 7$

       3) 63 $= 2 \times 3^2 \times 7$ **1 mark**

       3) 21   **1 mark**

         7 ⟵ *Make sure you show the method you use. You could use a factor tree.*

  b *For 126×56 use the prime factors that have already been found.*

             $126 = 2 \times 3^2 \times 7$, $56 = 2^3 \times 7$

     So $126 \times 56 = 2 \times 3^2 \times 7 \times 2^3 \times 7$ **1 mark**

               $= 2^4 \times 3^2 \times 7^2$ **1 mark**

  c *To find the square root, you halve the power.*

     So $\sqrt{2^4 \times 3^2 \times 7^2} = 2^2 \times 3 \times 7$ **1 mark**

2 A pattern is made of sticks.

Number of squares	1	2	3
Number of sticks	4	7	10

1 square   2 squares   3 squares

   a **i** Find the number of sticks needed to make a pattern with 10 squares.

      ii Explain how you worked out your answer.   **(2 marks)**

   b Write down an expression, in terms of n, for a pattern with n squares.   **(2 marks)**

   a **i** *You can find the answer by continuing the number series in the table:*

         4   7   10   ... up to 31   **1 mark**

           +3   +3   +3   *Make sure you show these differences, either in your working or under the table.*

      ii *Your explanation could describe how you continued the table, for example, by adding on 3 each time until you come to the 10th square.*   **1 mark**

   b As the number difference is $+3$ the expression will contain a $3n$.   **1 mark**

     $3n$ gives the sequence 3, 6, 9. The sequence here is 4, 7, 10. This is 1 more each time. So the full expression is $3n + 1$.   **1 mark**

1 The number 175 can be written as a product of its prime factors

$$175 = 5^2 \times 7$$

Write as a product of its prime factors

i 50   **ii** 50^2 **(4 marks)**

[N2001 P3 Q20]

2 A series of patterns is drawn using dots.

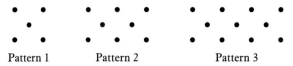

Pattern 1   Pattern 2   Pattern 3

a Draw patterns to show the number of dots needed for

    i pattern 4   **ii** pattern 5   **(2 marks)**

The table shows the number of dots needed for different patterns.

Pattern	1	2	3	4	5	6	7
Number of dots	5	8	11				

b Complete the table.   **(1 mark)**

c Explain how you would work out the number of dots needed for pattern 12.   **(2 marks)**

[N1998 P4 Q4]

3 The diagrams show patterns made out of sticks.

Pattern number   1   2   3

a Draw a diagram to show pattern number 4.   **(1 mark)**

The table below can be used to show the number of sticks needed for a pattern.

Pattern number	1	2	3	4	5	6	7
Number of sticks	3	5					

b Complete the table.   **(2 marks)**

c **i** Work out the number of sticks needed for pattern number 15.

    ii Explain how you obtained your answer.   **(4 marks)**

d Write down a formula which can be used to calculate the number of sticks, S, in terms of the pattern number, n.   **(2 marks)**

[S1998 P4 Q1]

4 Here are some patterns made of crosses.

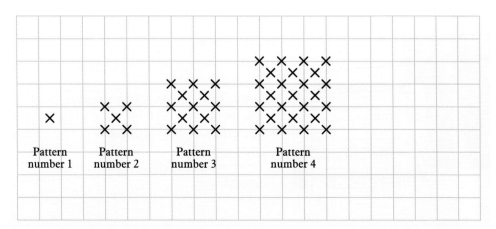

Pattern number 1   Pattern number 2   Pattern number 3   Pattern number 4

    a Draw pattern number 5.   **(1 mark)**
    b Complete the table.   **(1 mark)**

Pattern number	1	2	3	4	5
Number of crosses	1	5	13		

    c Work out the number of crosses in pattern number 8.   **(2 marks)**
    [S2001 P3 Q1]

5 Chetna makes patterns using sticks.

Pattern Number 1   Pattern Number 2   Pattern Number 3

Complete the table for pattern number n.

Pattern number	Number of lollipop sticks
1	4
2	5
3	6
4	7
n	

    (1 mark)
    [S2000 P3 Q1]

5 Negative numbers

LEADERBOARD

Player	Score
David Arnold	−5
Robert Elswit	−3
Allan Cameron	−1
Anthony Waye	0
Bruce Firstein	0
Michael G. Wilson	1
Roger Spottiswoode	2
Albert R. Broccoli	4

You need to know about:

- adding and subtracting negative numbers
- multiplying and dividing negative numbers
- squaring and cubing negative numbers
- substituting negative numbers into formulas

Adding a negative number is the same as taking away.

$$7 + -3 = 7 - 3 = 4$$

Taking away −3 is the same as adding 3.

$$7 - -3 = 7 + 3 = 10$$

When you multiply or divide numbers of the **same** sign you get a **positive** answer.

$$-6 \times -2 = +12 \qquad 3 \times 4 = 12$$
$$-10 \div -5 = 2 \qquad 18 \div 6 = 3$$

When you multiply or divide numbers of **different** signs you get a **negative** answer.

$$-3 \times 4 = -12 \qquad 7 \times -2 = -14$$
$$16 \div -8 = -2 \qquad -24 \div 4 = -6$$

When you square a negative number the answer is always positive.

$$(-3)^2 = -3 \times -3 = 9$$

When you cube a negative number the answer is always negative.

$$(-2)^3 = -2 \times -2 \times -2 = -8$$

You can substitute negative numbers into formulas.

Example Use the formula $s = ut + 5t^2$ to find s when $u = 5$ and $t = -4$.

$$s = ut + 5t^2 \qquad ut = u \times t = 5 \times -4 = -20$$
$$5t^2 = 5 \times t^2 = 5 \times (-4)^2 = 5 \times 16 = 80$$
$$s = -20 + 80 = 60$$

---

1 Work these out.

a $4 - 9$ e $3 - -7$ i $-14 \div 7$

b $-3 + 15$ f $-6 - -4$ j $-7.4 \div 2$

c $-7 - 11$ g 3×-2 k $15 \div -3$

d $16 + -3$ h -4×6 l $(-3)^2$

2 Use the formula $A = 14c - 20$ to find A when:

a $c = 2$ b $c = -2$ c $c = 0.5$

3 Use the formula $P = 14.2(6 + 4.13x)$ to find P when:

a $x = 3.43$ b $x = -2.81$ c $x = 8.17$

4 Write down the next three numbers in each of these.

a $-6, -4, -2, \ldots, \ldots, \ldots$

b $12, 9, 6, 3, \ldots, \ldots, \ldots$

c $-15, -12.5, -10, \ldots, \ldots, \ldots$

d $-8, 16, -32, 64, \ldots, \ldots, \ldots$

5 Put the correct symbol between each pair of numbers.
Choose from $<$ or $>$.

a $4 \quad -3$ b $-7 \quad -12$ c $-2 \quad 3$

6 On a cold winter's night the temperatures were recorded in towns around Britain. The table shows these temperatures.

Town	Temperature (°C)
Chester	-2
Cambridge	-4
London	3
Manchester	1
Glasgow	-12
Bournemouth	8

a Write down the name of the coldest town.

b Write the temperatures in order. Start with the smallest.

c By midday on the following day the temperature in Cambridge had risen by 8°C.
Write down the temperature in Cambridge at midday on the following day.

1 The table shows the temperature (in °C) in four cities at midday.

London	Moscow	Helsinki	Melbourne
3	−8	−12	23

  a What are the differences in temperature between
    i Helsinki and Melbourne?
    ii Helsinki and Moscow?   **(2 marks)**

  b By midday the following day the temperature in London has risen to 5°C, and the temperature in Moscow has risen by 2°C. What is the difference in temperature between London and Moscow the following day?   **(2 marks)**

  c One week later the temperature in Moscow is −2°C, London is 3°C warmer than Moscow, and Helsinki is 8°C colder than London. What is the temperature in Helsinki?   **(2 marks)**

  a **i** −12°C to 23°C is 35°C.   **1 mark**
     ii −12°C to −8°C is 4°C.   **1 mark**

  b Moscow: −8 + 2 = −6°C   **1 mark**
     London to Moscow: 5 to −6 = 11°C   **1 mark**

  c Moscow: −2°C, London: −2 + 3 = 1°C   **1 mark**
     Helsinki: 1 − 8 = −7°C   **1 mark**

2 These formulas link F, the temperature in °F, and C, the temperature in °C:

$$F = \frac{9C + 160}{5} \qquad C = \frac{5(F - 32)}{9}$$

Use these formulas to change
  a −20°C to °F   **(3 marks)**
  b −13°F to °C   **(3 marks)**

  a $F = \dfrac{(9 \times -20) + 160}{5}$ **1 mark**   **b** $C = \dfrac{5(-13 - 32)}{9}$ **1 mark**

Show how the numbers are substituted before you do any calculation.
Then work out the brackets first.

$$F = \frac{-180 + 160}{5} \qquad \text{1 mark} \qquad C = \frac{5 \times -45}{9} \qquad \text{1 mark}$$

$$F = \frac{-20}{5} = -4°F \qquad \text{1 mark} \qquad C = \frac{-225}{9} = -25°C \qquad \text{1 mark}$$

1 Find the value of
  i $-7 - (-3)$,   **ii** -2×4.   **(3 marks)**
                                            [N1999 P3 Q10]

2 The table shows the maximum and minimum temperatures for five
  cities during one year.

City	Maximum	Minimum
Chicago	30°C	−15°C
Bombay	37°C	12°C
London	34°C	−12°C
Montreal	26°C	−17°C
Reykjavik	17°C	−14°C

  a Which city had the lowest temperature?   **(1 mark)**
  b Work out the difference between the maximum temperature and the
     minimum temperature for Chicago.   **(2 marks)**
                                             [N1998 P4 Q6]

3 At midday the temperature in Moscow was −6°C.
  At midday the temperature in Norwich was 4°C.

  a How many degrees higher was the temperature in Norwich than the
     temperature in Moscow?   **(2 marks)**

  At midnight the temperature in Norwich had fallen by 7 degrees from 4°C.

  b Work out the midnight temperature in Norwich.   **(2 marks)**
                                             [N1998 P3 Q2]

4 At 6 o'clock on January 1st the temperature was −3°C. By midnight the
  temperature had fallen by 6°C.

  a Write down the temperature at midnight.   **(1 mark)**

  By midday of January 2nd, the temperature had risen to 4°C.

  b Calculate the increase in temperature between midnight and midday.

                                                  (1 mark)
                                             [N1995 P4 Q3]

5 The lowest temperatures recorded in Manchester each night for a week
  are given below.

        7°C,   −4°C,   3°C,   1°C,   −2°C,   0°C,   −1°C

  a Write down the temperatures in order.
     Start with the lowest temperature.   **(2 marks)**

  b Work out the difference between the highest and lowest
     temperatures.   **(2 marks)**
                                             [N1997 P4 Q1]

6 **a** $p = -8$ and $q = -3$. Work out the value of

$$p - 2q$$ **(2 marks)**

b Work out

$$\frac{-14 + 2}{-0.2}$$ **(2 marks)**

c Work out

$$\frac{5}{7} - \frac{1}{3}$$ **(2 marks)**

[N2000 P3 Q14]

7 The air temperature, $T°C$, outside an aircraft flying at a height of h feet is given by the formula

$$T = 26 - \frac{h}{500}$$

An aircraft is flying at a height of 27 000 feet.

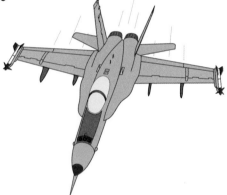

a Use the formula to calculate the air temperature outside the aircraft. **(2 marks)**

The air temperature outside an aircraft is $-52°C$.

b Calculate the height of the aircraft. **(3 marks)**

[S1995 P3 Q20]

8 $v^2 = u^2 + 2as$

a Calculate the value of v when $u = -6$, $a = 5$, $and\ s = 0.8$. Give your answer to one significant figure. **(2 marks)**

b Make u the subject of the formula $v^2 = u^2 + 2as$. **(3 marks)**

[S1996 P4 Q12]

9 $E = \frac{1}{2}m(v^2 - u^2)$

Calculate the value of E when $m = 15$, $v = -3$ and $u = 4$. **(2 marks)**

[N1995 P3 Q16]

10 $y = ab + c$

Calculate the value of y when

$$a = \frac{3}{4}, \quad b = \frac{7}{8} \quad \text{and} \quad c = -\frac{1}{2}$$

Give your answer in the form $\dfrac{p}{q}$ where p and q are integers.   **(3 marks)**
[N1997 P4 Q22]

11 Use the formula

$$y = \frac{x - t}{\sqrt{(1 - v^2)}}$$

to calculate the value of y given that

$$x = 50, t = 2.5 \text{ and } v = 0.6$$

Give your answer correct to 1 decimal place.
Show all necessary working.   **(5 marks)**
[S1994 P4 Q20]

12 The temperature during an Autumn morning went up from $-3°C$ to $6°C$.

a By how many degrees did the temperature rise?   **(2 marks)**

During the afternoon the temperature then fell by 8 degrees from $6°C$.

b What was the temperature at the end of the afternoon?   **(2 marks)**
[N1994 P4 Q1]

13 This formula is used in science

$$d = L(1 + at)$$

$$L = 97 \qquad a = 0.000\,023 \qquad t = 72$$

Calculate the value of d.
Write down all the figures on your calculator display.   **(3 marks)**
[N1995 P3 Q12]

6 Simplifying and solving

You need to know about:

- collecting algebraic terms
- multiplying terms and brackets
- solving equations
- using trial and improvement to solve equations

To **collect terms** together they must have exactly the same letters in them. Any powers must also be the same.

In h^3, the power 3 tells you how many hs are multiplied together. So $h^3 = h \times h \times h$.

Example   Simplify these by collecting terms if possible.

a $4s + 3t - 3s + t$ **b** $2x^2 - 7x + 4 + 8x + x^2 - 7$ **c** $2ab^2 + 5a^2b$

a $4s + 3t - 3s + t = s + 4t$ because $4s - 3s = 1s = s$
                                      and $3t + t = 3t + 1t = 4t$

b $2x^2 - 7x + 4 + 8x + x^2 - 7$ because $2x^2 + x^2 = 2x^2 + 1x^2 = 3x^2$
       $= 3x^2 + x - 3$ and $-7x + 8x = 1x = x$
                                       and $+4 - 7 = -3$

c $2ab^2 + 5a^2b$ cannot be simplified.   Both terms involve a and b and squared, but the power 2 is on a different letter in each term.

When you **multiply terms together** you deal with any numbers first then each letter in turn.

Example   Simplify these by multiplying

a $4d \times 6d$ **b** $3x \times 5y$ **c** $8y^2 \times 2y$ **d** $(x^2)^3$

a $4d \times 6d = 24d^2$ because $4 \times 6 = 24$ and $d \times d = d^2$

b $3x \times 5y = 15xy$ because $3 \times 5 = 15$ and $x \times y = xy$

c $8y^2 \times 2y = 16y^3$ because $8 \times 2 = 16$ and $y^2 \times y = y \times y \times y = y^3$

d $(x^2)^3 = x^6$ because $(x^2)^3 = x^2 \times x^2 \times x^2 = x^6$

To **multiply out a bracket** you multiply everything inside the bracket by the term outside.

Example   Multiply out these brackets.

a $4(2c + 3)$ **b** $w(5 - 6y)$ **c** $5k(7k^2 + k)$

a $4(2c + 3) = 8c + 12$ because $4 \times 2c = 8c$ and $4 \times 3 = 12$

b $w(5 - 6y) = 5w - 6wy$ because $w \times 5 = 5w$ and $w \times 6y = 6wy$

c $5k(7k^2 + k) = 35k^3 + 5k^2$ because $5k \times 7k^2 = 5 \times k \times 7 \times k \times k$

$$= 5 \times 7 \times k \times k \times k$$
$$= 35k^3$$

and $5k \times k = 5 \times k \times k = 5 \times k^2 = 5k^2$

You **solve an equation** by finding the value of the unknown letter.
If the letter appears on both sides, you need to get the letter on one side only.
Multiply out any brackets and collect terms before you start.

Example   Solve $2(3x - 1) + 7 = 25 - 4x$.

Multiply out the bracket: $6x - 2 + 7 = 25 - 4x$
Collect terms on each side: $6x + 5 = 25 - 4x$
Add $4x$ to both sides: $10x + 5 = 25$
Take 5 from both sides: $10x = 20$
Divide by 10 $x = 2$

To solve an equation by **trial and improvement** you have to guess the answer.
You check this answer and then make a better guess depending on the result.

Example   Solve this equation, giving your answer to one decimal place.

$$x^3 - 5x = 13\,480$$

value of x	value of $x^3 - 5x$	
20	$20^3 - 5 \times 20 = 7900$	too small
25	$25^3 - 5 \times 25 = 15\,500$	too big
24	$24^3 - 5 \times 24 = 13\,704$	too big
23	$23^3 - 5 \times 23 = 12\,052$	too small
23.8	$23.8^3 - 5 \times 23.8 = 13\,366.272$	too small
23.9	$23.9^3 - 5 \times 23.9 = 13\,532.419$	too big
23.85	$23.85^3 - 5 \times 23.85 = 13\,447.166\,63$	too small

The answer lies between 23.85 and 23.9.
Any number in this range would round to 23.9 to one decimal place so the answer is
$x = 23.9$.

1   Simplify these by collecting terms.

   a $b + b + b$ **d** $2r + 4r + 4s - 5s$

   b $t + t + t - s - s$ **e** $6ab + 3ab - 4ab$

   c $4g + 5g + 6g$ **f** $7x^2 + 4x^2 - 3x^2$

2   Simplify these by multiplying

   a $2s \times 4s$ **b** $-3t \times 5t$ **c** $2a \times 4a \times 5a$

3   Multiply out these brackets.

   a $4(x + 6)$ **c** $2y(3y + 2)$

   b $-3(2x - 1)$ **d** $a^2(a + b)$

4   Solve these equations.

   a $2x + 3 = 9$ **d** $4x + 6 = x + 24$

   b $3x + 7 = 19$ **e** $5x - 11 = 3x + 9$

   c $2x + 1 = x + 5$ **f** $7x - 6 = 4x - 15$

5   Solve these equations.

   a $4(3x + 2) = 68$ **d** $\dfrac{x}{6} = 3$

   b $2(4x - 1) = 18$ **e** $\dfrac{20}{x} = 2$

   c $10(2x - 3) + 6 = 2(4x - 9)$ **f** $\dfrac{16}{2x} = -3$

6   Solve these equations by trial and improvement.
Draw a table to help you find each solution.
Give each answer to 1 decimal place.

   a $x^3 = 58$

   b $x^3 + 2x = 712$

   c $x^2 + \dfrac{1}{x} = 31$

1 Simplify   **a** $x^2 + x^2$ **c** $3a + 3c - a - 5c + 4$ **e** $3x^5y^2 \times 2x^2y^3$

           b $d + d + d$ **d** $x^2 \times x^2$ **(5 marks)**

a $x^2 + x^2 = 2x^2$ *A common mistake is to write*   **1 mark**
this incorrectly as x^4 *or* $2x^4$.

b $d + d + d = 3d$ *A common mistake is to write*   **1 mark**
this incorrectly as d^3.

c $3a + 3c - a - 5c + 4 = 2a - 2c + 4$ **1 mark**

d $x^2 \times x^2 = x \times x \times x \times x = x^4$ *A common mistake is to write*   **1 mark**
this incorrectly as $2x^2$ *or* $2x^4$.

e $3x^5y^2 \times 2x^2y^3 = 6x^7y^5$ *Multiply the numbers and*   **1 mark**
     $as\ 3 \times 2 = 6,\ x^5 \times x^2 = x^7\ and\ y^2 \times y^3 = y^5$ *the like terms separately.*

2 Solve: $\dfrac{15 - x}{4} = 3 - x$ **(3 marks)**

Multiply both sides by 4. $\dfrac{(15 - x) \times 4}{4} = 4 \times (3 - x)$ **1 mark**
Put the $3 - x$ *in brackets.*
Then multiply out the brackets.

Add x *to both sides.* $15 - x = 12 - 4x$ **1 mark**
Take 12 from both sides. $15 = 12 - 3x$

Divide both sides by -3. $3 = -3x$
                                $x = -1$ **1 mark**

3 Use a trial and improvement method to find a solution to the equation $x^3 + x = 40$. Give your answer correct to one decimal place.   **(4 marks)**

      Try $x = 3$ $3^3 + 3 = 30$ **1 mark**
      Try $x = 4$ $4^3 + 4 = 68$

A solution lies between 3 and 4.   *Always show how you have*
      Try $x = 3.5$ $3.5^3 + 3.5 = 46.375$ *worked it out, and the answer*   **1 mark**
      Try $x = 3.4$ $3.4^3 + 3.4 = 42.704$ *to the calculations. You can use*
      Try $x = 3.3$ $3.3^3 + 3.3 = 39.237$ *a table to set out your work.*

A solution lies between 3.3 and 3.4, probably nearer 3.3.
      Try $x = 3.33$ $3.33^3 + 3.33 = 40.256$ **1 mark**
      Try $x = 3.32$ $3.32^3 + 3.32 = 39.914$

The solution lies between 3.32 and 3.33.   *The solution is the value of* x
So a solution, to one decimal place, is 3.3.   *that has been used,* **not** *the*   **1 mark**
                                        value of $x^3 + x$.

1 **a** Simplify $5x + 3x - x.$ (1 mark)

    b Simplify $4y - 3 + 3y - 2.$ (2 marks)
[N1999 P4 Q4]

2 **a** $x = -4$
$y = 5$
Work out the value of $3x + 2y$ (2 marks)

    b Simplify fully
$$7p - 4(p - q)$$ (2 marks)
[S2001 P4 Q5]

3 **a** Simplify
$$2x - 1 + x + 4 + x$$ (2 marks)

    b Solve the equation
$$5(2p - 3) = 50$$ (2 marks)

    c Solve the equation
$$\frac{16 - q}{3} = 3$$ (3 marks)
[N2000 P4 Q9]

4 **a** Solve the equation
$$4r - 1 = 7$$ (2 marks)

    b Solve the equation
$$7s + 2 = 5 - 3s$$ (2 marks)

    c Solve the equation
$$5(x + 2) = 3x + 7$$ (3 marks)
[S2001 P4 Q13]

5 **a** Solve $4p + 6 = 26$ (2 marks)

    b Solve $5(2q + 6) = 25$ (2 marks)

    c Solve $18y - 27 = 10y - 25$ (2 marks)
[N1999 P4 Q7]

6 Solve the equations

    a $4a + 3 = 9$ (2 marks)

    b $5b - 7 = 2b + 5$ (2 marks)

    c $3(c - 6) = 10 - 2c$ (2 marks)
[N1998 P3 Q9]

7 Use the method of trial and improvement to solve the equation

$$x^3 + x = 26$$

Give your answer correct to one decimal place.

You must show **all** your working. **(4 marks)**

[S2001 P4 Q17]

8 Use the method of trial and improvement to solve the equation

$$x^3 - 2x = 37$$

Give your answer correct to two decimal places.
You must show ALL your working. **(4 marks)**

[N1998 P4 Q14]

9 The equation $x^2 + 2x = 13$ has a solution for x between 2.7 and 2.8.

Use trial and improvement methods to find this solution correct to two decimal places.

Show all the trials clearly. **(4 marks)**

[N1994 P4 Q13]

10 Use trial and improvement, or otherwise, to find the positive value of x for which

$$x^2 - x = 144$$

Use the table below to show your working.
You may not need to use all the rows of the table.
Give your answer correct to 1 decimal place.

Trial number	Trial value	$x^2 - x$	Comment
1	5	20	too low
2			

(4 marks)

[N1995 P4 Q16]

7 Ratio and proportion

You need to know about:

- setting up a ratio
- simplifying a ratio
- changing a ratio to the form $n : 1$ and $1 : n$
- dividing in a given ratio
- the link between ratios and fractions
- direct proportion and best value for money

Ratios can be used to compare two measurements.

Example Paul is three times as old as Mia. Write this as a ratio.

Paul's age : Mia's age $= 3 : 1$

You can **simplify a ratio** if you can find a number that divides exactly into each part of it.

Example Simplify these ratios if possible.

a $20 : 8$ **b** $5 : 9$

a 4 divides into 20 and 8 exactly.

$20 \div 4 = 5$ and $8 \div 4 = 2$ so $20 : 8 = 5 : 2$

b No whole number divides exactly into 5 and 9 so $5 : 9$ can't be simplified.

Example **a** Write the ratio $11 : 5$ in the form $n : 1$.

b Write the ratio $8 : 3$ in the form $1 : n$.

a To get the right hand side of the ratio to be 1 you need to divide by 5, so divide both sides of the ratio by 5:

$$11 : 5 = \frac{11}{5} : \frac{5}{5} = 2.2 : 1$$

b To get the left hand side of the ratio to be 1 you need to divide by 8:

$$8 : 3 = \frac{8}{8} : \frac{3}{8} = 1 : \frac{3}{8}$$

Ratios are used to describe how **something is divided up**.

Example   Divide £50 in the ratio 3 : 7.

First find the total number of parts: Total number of parts $= 3 + 7 = 10$

Find the value of one part: Value of one part $= £50 \div 10 = £5$

Find the value of 3 parts: $3 \times £5 = £15$

Find the value of 7 parts: $7 \times £5 = £35$

Check the two amounts add up to £50: $£15 + £35 = £50$ ✓

The amounts are £15 and £35.

Ratios are really just another way of thinking of fractions.
You can easily swap between **ratios and fractions**.
It is very important to work out the total number of parts first.

Example   Purple paint is made from blue and red paint in the ratio 5 : 3.
What fraction of the paint is blue and what fraction is red?

Find the total number of parts. $5 + 3 = 8$

The total number of parts gives the denominator.   The fraction of blue $= \dfrac{5}{8}$

The fraction of red $= \dfrac{3}{8}$

Example   Green paint is made from blue and yellow paint in the ratio 2 : 7.
How much green paint do you get if 20 ml of blue paint is used?

For the blue paint 2 parts $= 20$ ml, so 1 part $= 10$ ml.
For the green paint there are $2 + 7 = 9$ parts, so 9 parts $= 9 \times 10 = 90$ ml
The amount of green paint is 90 ml.

If one pen costs £2.50 then two pens will cost twice as much, three pens three times as much, and so on. This is called **direct proportion**.

You can use direct proportion to find the **best value for money**.

Example   Nuts are sold in two sizes.
The 450 g pack costs 89p and the 1 kg pack costs £1.85
Which pack is better value?

Find the cost of 100 g for the 450 g pack:
Cost of 100 g in the smaller pack $= 89 \div 4.5$
$= 19.777\,777\,77 \ldots$
$= 19.8\text{p (1 dp)}$

Change 1 kg to grams and £1.85 to pence:
1 kg $= 1000$ g and £1.85 $= 185$p

Find the cost of 100 g for the 1 kg pack
Cost of 100 g in the larger pack $= 185 \div 10 = 18.5$p

The larger pack is better value as you pay 18.5p for 100 g compared with 19.8 (1 dp) for 100 g in the smaller pack.

1   Simplify these ratios
    a   18 : 6   d   14 : 49
    b   24 : 4   e   144 : 60
    c   10 : 25   f $\frac{1}{3} : \frac{2}{3}$

2   Simplify these ratios. Make sure that the units are the same first.
    a   3 m : 25 cm   c   4 mm : 5 cm   e   40 ml : 3 litres
    b   15 min : 1.5 h   d   3 kg : 200 g   f   2 km : 50 m

3   A fruit drink is made by mixing orange juice, lemon juice and lemonade
    in the ratio 2 : 1 : 6.
    a   How much orange juice is needed to make 900 ml of the fruit drink?
    b   How much lemonade is needed to make 3 litres of the fruit drink?

4   The four angles of a quadrilateral are in the ratio 2 : 3 : 5 : 8.
    Calculate the size of each angle.

5   Mr Fisher has four children. Each week he shares £30 pocket money
    between them.
    They share the money in the ratio of their ages, 2 : 7 : 9 : 12.
    Calculate how much money each child receives.

6   Scrumptious chocolate bars cost £3.12 for 6 bars and £4.80 for 10 bars.
    a   Work out the cost of 1 bar in the 6 bar pack.
    b   Work out the cost of 1 bar in the 10 bar pack.
    c   Which pack is better value?

7   An omelette for 1 person uses 3 eggs and 40 g of cheese.
    a   How much cheese would be needed to make omelettes for 8 people?
    b   How many eggs would be needed to make omelettes for 3 people?
    c   Francis has only 15 eggs. How many omelettes can he make?

8   Shinyhair shampoo comes in three sizes. The sizes and costs are shown
    in the table.

Size	Cost
200 ml	£2.27
300 ml	£3.56
450 ml	£4.82

    Which size is the best value for money?
    Show all your working.

1 Janet and Tina share a flat and pay all their bills in the ratio 1 : 2.

    a The telephone bill is £75. How much does Janet pay?   **(2 marks)**

    b Janet's share of the electricity bill is £42.
      How much is Tina's share?   **(2 marks)**

    a *£75 has to be divided in the ratio 1 : 2.*

      $1 + 2 = 3$ parts, so 1 part is £75 ÷ 3 = £25.   **1 mark**

      Janet's share is $1 \times £25 = £25$.   **1 mark**

    b 1 : 2
      £42 : £?   Tina's share is twice as much.
                           £42 × 2   =   £84
                           1 mark   **1 mark**

2 A car travels 450 km on 30 litres of petrol.
How far should it travel on 20 litres of petrol?   **(2 marks)**

                            450 km takes 30 litres

*Find how far the car
travels on 1 litre.*   450 ÷ 30 = 15 km per 1 litre   **1 mark**

*Then work out how far the
car travels on 20 litres.*   15 km × 20 = 300 km for 20 litres   **1 mark**

3 A tin of beans costs 43p, and has a weight of 224 g.
A larger tin of beans costs 89p, and has a weight of 454 g.
Which size of tin gives the best value for money?
Show your working with the answer.   ←   *This tells you the answer will get
no marks without the working.*

Small tin: 224 g for 43p is the same as $\dfrac{224\,\text{g}}{43}$ for 1p = 5.209 g for 1p
                                                        1 mark

Large tin: 454 g for 89p is the same as $\dfrac{454\,\text{g}}{89}$ for 1p = 5.101 g for 1p
                                                        1 mark

Since 5.209 > 5.101, the smaller tin is better value, since it gives you
slightly more beans for each 1p.   **1 mark**

1 Robert used these ingredients to make 24 buns.

> 100 g of butter
>
> 80 g of sugar
>
> 2 eggs
>
> 90 g of flour
>
> 30 ml of milk

Robert wants to make 36 similar buns.
Write down how much of each ingredient he needs for 36 buns.

butter .... g

sugar .... g

eggs ....

flour .... g

milk .... ml

(3 marks)
[N2000 P3 Q8]

2 Rashid has 35 sweets.
He shares them in the ratio 4 : 3 with his sister.
Rashid keeps the larger share.

How many sweets does Rashid keep? **(3 marks)**
[S2000 P3 Q12]

3 This is a recipe for making Tuna Bake for **4** people.

Tuna Bake

Ingredients for **4** people.

400 g of tuna

400 g of mushroom soup

100 g of grated cheddar cheese

4 spring onions

250 g of breadcrumbs

Work out the amounts needed to make a Tuna Bake for **10** people.

.... g of tuna

.... g of mushroom soup

.... g of grated cheddar cheese

.... spring onions

.... g of breadcrumbs

(3 marks)
[S2001 P3 Q12]

4 Tracey and Wayne share £7200 in the ratio 5 : 4
Work out how much each of them receives.   **(3 marks)**
[N2000 P4 Q14]

5 Recipe for Bread and Butter Pudding.

  6 slices of bread

  2 eggs

  1 pint of milk

  150 g raisins

  10 g margarine

This recipe is enough for 4 people.

  a Work out the amounts needed so that there will be enough for 6 people.

  .... slices of bread

  .... eggs

  .... pints of milk

  .... g raisins

  .... g margarine   **(3 marks)**

There are 450 g in 1 pound.
There are 16 ounces in 1 pound.

  b Change 150 g into ounces.
  Give your answer correct to the nearest ounce.   **(3 marks)**
[S1999 P4 Q11]

6 Stephen and Joanne share £210 in the ratio 6 : 1
How much more money does Stephen get than Joanne?   **(3 marks)**
[S2001 P4 Q4]

7 Anna, Beth and Cheryl share the total cost of a holiday in the ratio
6 : 5 : 4. Anna pays £294.
  a Work out the total cost of the holiday.   **(2 marks)**
  b Work out how much Cheryl pays   **(2 marks)**
[S2000 P4 Q15]

8 Jack shares £180 between his two children Ruth and Ben.
The ratio of Ruth's share to Ben's share is 5 : 4.
  a Work out how much each child is given.   **(3 marks)**

Ben then gives 10% of his share to Ruth.
  b Work out the percentage of the £180 that Ruth now has.   **(3 marks)**
[S1999 P3 Q10]

8   Graphs: a bit steep

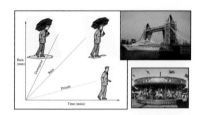

You need to know about:

- gradients of lines
- equations of straight lines
- recognising equations of parallel lines
- using graphs to solve problems
- graphs of linear equations

Gradient

The **gradient** of a line tells you how steep the line is.

Example

Find the gradient of this line.

First mark two points on the line as far apart as possible.
You need to be able to read the co-ordinates of the points accurately.
Using your two points draw the triangle shown in red.
Mark in the vertical and horizontal changes.
Substitute these changes into the formula

$$\text{gradient} = \frac{\text{vertical change}}{\text{horizontal change}} = \frac{9}{3} = 3$$

Lines that slope upwards have positive gradients.

Lines that slope downwards have negative gradients.

The **equation of a straight line** can be written in the form $y = mx + c$
m is the gradient of the line, c is where the line cuts the y axis.

Example

Write down the gradient of this line and where it crosses the y axis.

$$y = 7 - 2x$$

The gradient is the number multiplying the x.
The gradient is -2.

The line cuts the y axis at 7.

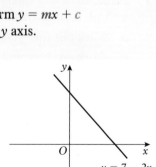

$y = 7 - 2x$

Parallel lines have the same gradient.

The lines $y = 4x - 9$ and $y = 4x + 1$ both have a gradient of 4 so the lines are parallel.
The lines $y = 5x - 8$ and $y = 4 - 5x$ have different gradients so they are not parallel.

Example

  a Write down the gradient of the line $y = 5x - 4$.

  b Does the point $(-3, -20)$ lie on the line?

a Look for the number multiplying x. The gradient of the line is 5.

b Substitute $x = -3$ into the equation:

$$\begin{aligned} y &= 5x - 4 \\ &= (5 \times -3) - 4 \\ &= -15 - 4 \\ &= -19 \end{aligned}$$

For the point to be on the line, y should be -19, so the point does not lie on the line.

Linear equation   An equation that can be written as $ax + by = c$ is called a **linear equation**. $y = mx + c$ is a linear equation.

The graph of a linear equation is always a straight line.

$2x - 5y = 6$ is linear with $a = 2, b = -5$ and $c = 6$

$y = 3x + 5$ can be written $-3x + y = 5$ so it is linear with $a = -3, b = 1$ and $c = 5$.

$4x^2 + 3y = 2$ is not linear. Neither is $6x - \dfrac{3}{y} = 2$.

Example   Draw the graph of $3x + 5y = 15$.

The equation is linear so the graph is a straight line.
You need to find the co-ordinates of two points on the line.
Find the intercepts with the axes like this:

When $x = 0$ $(3 \times 0) + 5y = 15$

So $5y = 15$

                     $y = 3$

The point $(0, 3)$ lies on the line.

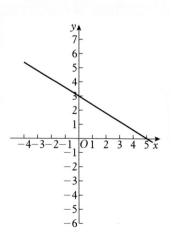

When $y = 0$ $3x + (5 \times 0) = 15$

So $3x = 15$

                    $x = 5$

The point $(5, 0)$ lies on the line.

Now use these two points to draw the line.

1 Find the gradient of the line passing through each pair of points.

   a (4, 9) and (12, 33)   **b** (0, 10) and (4, 5)

2 Write down the gradients of each of these lines.

   a $y = 5x + 6$ **b** $y = 3x - 9$ **c** $y = 6 - 7x$

3 Write down where each line crosses the y axis.

   a $y = 3x + 7$ **b** $y = 2x - 4$ **c** $y = 11 - 3x$

4 Write down the equation of the line with:

   a gradient 4, y intercept 6   **b** gradient -2, y intercept 3

5 **a** Write down the equation of a line that is parallel to $y = 5x + 6$.

   b Write down the equation of a line that is parallel to $y = 5x + 6$ and has y intercept -2.

6 Write down the equations of these lines.

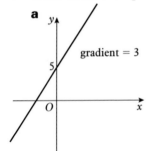 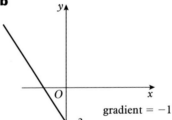 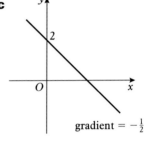

7 Write down the equation of each red line.

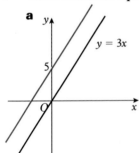 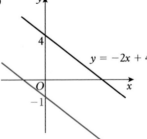 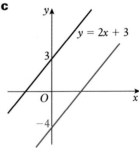

8 Draw the graph of $3x + 4y = 12$.

9 Find the equation of the line passing through the points (0, 7) and (6, 19).

1 a Write down the equation of the line given on the grid. **(2 marks)**

b Write down the equation of the line that passes through $(0, -2)$ and is parallel to the line on the grid. **(1 mark)**

c i Draw the line $2y - x = 3$.

ii Find the gradient of the line. **(3 marks)**

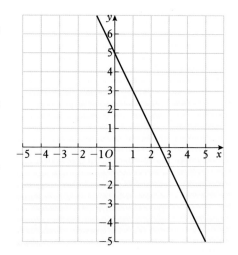

a *This is a straight line, so the equation is of the form* $y = mx + c$.
The intercept with the y axis is at 5, so $c = 5$.

$$\text{gradient} = \frac{\text{vertical change}}{\text{horizontal change}} = \frac{-5}{2.5} = -2, \text{ so } m = -2$$

The equation is $y = -2x + 5$. **1 mark for 5 or −2**
1 mark for complete equation

b *Passing through $(0, -2)$ gives* $c = -2$.
As it is parallel, the gradient m *is still* -2.
So the equation is $y = -2x - 2$. **1 mark**

c The equation can be rearranged like this:

$$2y = x + 3, \text{ so } y = \tfrac{1}{2}x + 1\tfrac{1}{2}$$

i *Find where the line cuts each axis by putting* $x = 0$ *and then* $y = 0$.
The line passes through $(0, 1\tfrac{1}{2})$ and $(-3, 0)$. **1 mark for each point**

ii If $y = \tfrac{1}{2}x + 1\tfrac{1}{2}$, the gradient is $\tfrac{1}{2}$. **1 mark**

2 A is the point $(-3, 4)$, B is the point $(4, 2)$.
A line AB is drawn from A to B.
Find the co-ordinates of the mid-point of the line AB. **(2 marks)**

The co-ordinates of the mid-point are given by the mid-point of both x
and y *co-ordinates.*

The mid-point using $x = -3$ and $x = 4$ is $x = \tfrac{1}{2}$. **1 mark for $\tfrac{1}{2}$ or 3**

The mid-point using $y = 4$ and $y = 2$ is $y = 3$.

So the co-ordinates of the mid-point are $(\tfrac{1}{2}, 3)$ **1 mark for coordinates**

1 a Complete this table of values for $y = 2x + 3$.

x	-3	-2	-1	0	1	2
y		-1				

(2 marks)

b Draw the graph of $y = 2x + 3$ on the grid opposite.

(2 marks)

c Use your graph to find
  i the value of y when $x = 1.5$,
  ii the value of x when $y = -0.5$.   (2 marks)
              [S1999 P4 Q8]

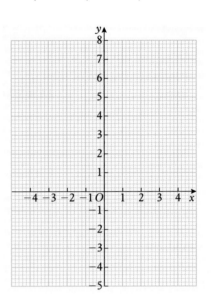

2 a Complete the table of values for $y = 2x - 1$.

x	-2	-1	0	1	2	3
y						

(2 marks)

b Draw the graph of $y = 2x - 1$.

(2 marks)

c Use your graph to find
  i the value of y when $x = -1.4$,
  ii the value of x when $y = 3.8$.   (2 marks)
              [N1998 P4 Q8]

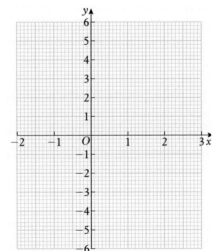

3 **a** Complete this table of values for $y = 3x - 1$.

x	-3	-2	-1	0	1	2	3
$y = 3x - 1$	-10		-4			5	

(2 marks)

b On the grid below, draw the graph of $y = 3x - 1$.

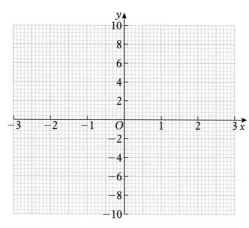

(2 marks)

c Use your graph to find the value of x when $y = 6.5$. **(1 mark)**

[N2000 P4 Q4]

4 **a** On the grid opposite draw the graphs of

   i $y = \frac{1}{2}x + 1$,

   ii $x = -2$. **(4 marks)**

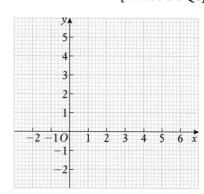

A straight line, **L**, has been drawn on the grid opposite.

b Find an equation of the line **L**. **(2 marks)**

[N1999 P4 Q14]

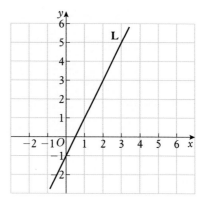

49

9   Fractions, decimals and percentages

You need to know about:

- using fractions
- the link between fractions and percentages
- the link between percentages and decimals
- the link between ratio and percentage
- finding the percentage of a quantity
- writing a number as a percentage of another
- working out percentage change

You can make **equivalent fractions** by multiplying the numerator and denominator by the same number.

$$\frac{2}{3} \overset{\times 5}{=} \frac{10}{15}$$

$\frac{2}{3}$ and $\frac{10}{15}$ are equivalent fractions.

To **add or subtract fractions** the denominators must be the same.

$$\frac{3}{8} + \frac{2}{8} = \frac{5}{8} \qquad \frac{4}{5} - \frac{3}{5} = \frac{1}{5}$$

If the denominators are different you need to make them the same before adding or subtracting.

$$\frac{4}{5} - \frac{2}{3} = \frac{12}{15} - \frac{10}{15} = \frac{2}{15}$$

If there are whole numbers, deal with them separately.

$$7\frac{5}{8} + 11\frac{1}{2} = 18 + \frac{5}{8} + \frac{1}{2}$$
$$= 18 + \frac{5}{8} + \frac{4}{8}$$
$$= 18 + \frac{9}{8}$$
$$= 18 + 1\frac{1}{8}$$
$$= 19\frac{1}{8}$$

You can tell **which fraction is bigger or smaller** when they have the same bottom number.

Example   Which is bigger, $\frac{5}{8}$ or $\frac{9}{16}$?

$\frac{5}{8} = \frac{10}{16}$, so $\frac{5}{8}$ is bigger than $\frac{9}{16}$ because $10 > 9$.

To **multiply fractions**:

First, change any mixed numbers to top heavy fractions.

$$5\frac{1}{2} \times \frac{4}{5} = \frac{11}{2} \times \frac{4}{5}$$

Next, multiply the two top numbers and the two bottom numbers. Then simplify the fraction if you can.

$$= \frac{44}{10}$$
$$= 4\frac{2}{5}$$

To **divide fractions** you turn the second fraction over and multiply.

$$\tfrac{3}{8} \div \tfrac{2}{5} = \tfrac{3}{8} \times \tfrac{5}{2} = \tfrac{15}{16} \quad \text{and} \quad 4\tfrac{1}{2} \div \tfrac{1}{5} = \tfrac{9}{2} \times \tfrac{5}{1} = \tfrac{45}{2} = 22\tfrac{1}{2}$$

To **multiply or divide a fraction by a whole number**, write the whole number as a fraction with denominator 1.

Example   Work these out.   **a** $\tfrac{2}{3} \times 4$ **b** $\tfrac{3}{8} \div 2$

   a $\tfrac{2}{3} \times 4 = \tfrac{2}{3} \times \tfrac{4}{1} = \tfrac{8}{3} = 2\tfrac{2}{3}$

   b $\tfrac{3}{8} \div 2 = \tfrac{3}{8} \div \tfrac{2}{1} = \tfrac{3}{8} \times \tfrac{1}{2} = \tfrac{3}{16}$

To change a **percentage to a fraction** you put the percentage over 100.

$$35\% = \tfrac{35}{100} = \tfrac{7}{20}$$

To change a **percentage to a decimal** you first write it as a fraction.

$$26\% = \tfrac{26}{100} = 0.26$$

To change a **decimal to a percentage** you multiply it by 100.

$$0.83 \times 100 = 83\%$$

To change a **fraction to a percentage** you first write it as a decimal.

$$\tfrac{5}{8} = 5 \div 8 = 0.625 = 62.5\%$$

To find the **percentage of an amount** change the percentage to a decimal and then multiply.

$$26\% \text{ of } £360 = 0.26 \times £360 = £93.60$$

To **increase** or **decrease** an amount by a percentage you work out the percentage as normal and then either **add to** or **subtract from** the original amount.

Example   Decrease 500 ml by 35%.
   35% of 500 = 0.35 × 500 = 175
   500 − 175 = 325 ml

To find **one number as a percentage of another**, first write the numbers as a fraction, then multiply by 100%.

Example   Express 45p as a percentage of £9.
   You need to make sure the units are the same: $\tfrac{45}{900} \times 100\% = 5\%$

You always work out the **percentage change** using the starting value:

$$\text{Percentage change} = \frac{\text{actual change}}{\text{starting value}} \qquad \text{Percentage profit} = \frac{\text{actual profit}}{\text{cost price}} \qquad \text{Percentage loss} = \frac{\text{actual loss}}{\text{cost price}}$$

Example   Find the percentage loss when a racquet is bought for £150 and sold for £90.

Loss = £150 − £90 = £60   Percentage loss = $\tfrac{60}{150} \times 100 = 40\%$

1 Work these out.

a $\frac{2}{8} + \frac{5}{8} - \frac{6}{8}$ **c** $\frac{13}{16} - \frac{3}{8}$ **e** $3\frac{3}{8} - 1\frac{3}{4}$

b $\frac{3}{8} + \frac{1}{4}$ **d** $1\frac{3}{4} + \frac{1}{8}$ **f** $2\frac{1}{2} + 3\frac{1}{4} - 1\frac{1}{8}$

2 Write these in order of size. Start with the smallest.

a $\frac{3}{16}, \frac{3}{8}, \frac{1}{2}, \frac{1}{4}$ **b** $\frac{2}{3}, 65\%, 0.62, \frac{6}{10}$

3 Work these out.

a $\frac{2}{3}$ of $\frac{1}{2}$ **b** $2\frac{1}{2} \times 1\frac{1}{3}$ **c** $1\frac{1}{3} \div 1\frac{1}{5}$

4 Copy these. Fill in the gaps.

a $\dfrac{2}{x} = \dfrac{...}{5x}$ **b** $\dfrac{20}{4x} = \dfrac{5}{...}$ **c** $\dfrac{3}{2x} = \dfrac{15}{...}$

5 **a** Write $\frac{16}{100}$ as a percentage.   **c** Write 5% as a fraction.

b Write $\frac{7}{20}$ as a decimal.   **d** Write 0.32 as a percentage.

6 Find the value of each of these.

a 20% of 55   **b** $33\frac{1}{3}\%$ of 75 kg

7 A jumper is reduced by 30% in a sale. Before the sale, the jumper cost £36. How much is saved by buying the jumper in the sale?

8 Luke earns £20 on Saturday. He spends £8 on a visit to the cinema.

a What fraction of his money does he spend at the cinema?

b What percentage of his money does he spend at the cinema?

9 **a** Increase 480 by 30%   **b** Decrease £150 by 25%.

1 A machine tool is made from two parts, the lengths of which are shown in the diagram.

   a Work out the total length of the machine tool. **(3 marks)**

   b Work out the difference in length between the two parts. **(3 marks)**

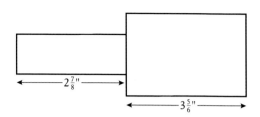

In both cases give your answer in its simplest form.

a $2\frac{7}{8} + 3\frac{5}{6} = 5 + \frac{42 + 40}{48} = 5 + \frac{82}{48} = 5 + 1\frac{34}{48} = 6\frac{34}{48} = 6\frac{17}{24}$ *Show all your working.*

   Common denominator   *Change vulgar to mixed fraction*   *Cancel*

    1 mark   **1 mark**   **1 mark**

b $3\frac{5}{6} - 2\frac{7}{8}$ *Subtract the whole numbers first:*

   $1\frac{5}{6} - \frac{7}{8} = \frac{11}{6} - \frac{7}{8} = \frac{88 - 42}{48} = \frac{46}{48} = \frac{23}{24}$ *Each step of the calculation should be shown.*

    1 mark   **1 mark**   **1 mark**

2 A shop sells jackets and shirts. Shirts are sold at a price of £8.00 plus VAT at $17\frac{1}{2}\%$.

   a What is the cost of buying one shirt, including the $17\frac{1}{2}\%$ VAT?

                                                                (2 marks)

There are 120 jackets and shirts in the ratio 5 : 3.

   b Work out the number of jackets. **(3 marks)**

   c Calculate the percentage that are shirts. **(2 marks)**

a £8.00 × $\frac{17.5}{100}$ = £1.40, £8.00 + £1.40 = £9.40 *Show all your working.*

                               1 mark   **1 mark**

   OR £8.00 × 1.175 = £9.40

b 5 : 3 is 8 parts so 1 part is 120 ÷ 8 = 15. For jackets: 15 × 5 = 75

     1 mark   **1 mark**   **1 mark**

c The ratio tells you that 3 out of 8 or $\frac{3}{8}$ are shirts. *Use the given figures rather than your own from part **b**.*
   As a percentage: $\frac{3}{8}$ × 100 = 37.5%

       1 mark

1   Write these numbers in order of size.
    Start with the smallest number.

    $\frac{7}{8}$ 80%   0.9 $\frac{8}{9}$ **(2 marks)**
                                                                           [N1998 P3 Q1]

2   Write these numbers in order of size.
    Start with the largest number.

    0.8   70% $\frac{7}{8}$ $\frac{3}{4}$ **(2 marks)**
                                                                           [N2000 P3 Q2]

3   30%, $\frac{1}{4}$,   0.35, $\frac{1}{3}$, $\frac{2}{5}$,   0.299

    Write this list of six numbers in order of size.
    Start with the smallest number.   **(3 marks)**
                                                                           [S2001 P4 Q3]

4   A school buys a trampoline.
    The school is given a discount of $\frac{1}{8}$ of the price.

    a   Write $\frac{1}{8}$ as
        i   a decimal,   **ii**   a percentage.
    The price of the trampoline is £3218.   **(2 marks)**

    b   Work out the amount the school actually has to pay.   **(3 marks)**
                                                                           [S1999 P4 Q3]

5   Class 11A has 30 pupils.
    18 of these pupils are girls.
    What percentage of the class is girls?   **(2 marks)**
                                                                           [S1999 P3 Q1]

6   Work out 20% of 1800.   **(2 marks)**
                                                                           [S2001 P3 Q2]

7
Calculators are Us	Top Calculators
Model HX 130	Model HX 130
£7.50	£8.75
VAT not included	VAT included

Two shops sell the same make of calculator.
At **Calculators are Us,** the price of a calculator is £7.50 plus VAT.
At **Top Calculators,** the price is £8.75. This includes VAT.
VAT is charged at a rate of 17.5%.
Work out the difference in cost between the two prices.   **(3 marks)**
                                                                           [S1998 P4 Q2]

8 Mrs Dolan wants to buy a washing machine. She can buy the washing machine by using Credit Plan A or by using Credit Plan B.

Credit Plan A
A deposit of £135
plus
6 equal payments of $\frac{1}{8}$ of £380

Credit Plan B
A deposit of 20% of £380
plus
12 equal payments of £28.90

Work out the difference between the cost if she uses Credit Plan A and the cost if she uses Credit Plan B. **(7 marks)**

[S2001 P4 Q8]

9 A shop buys Indian rugs from a factory.

In July, the cost to the shop of buying a rug was £100.
The shop bought 800 rugs in July.

In August, the cost to the shop of buying a rug increased by 10%.
The number of rugs bought by the shop decreased by 25%.

Find the difference between the total cost to the shop of all the rugs bought in July and the total cost of all the rugs bought by the shop in August. **(4 marks)**

[N2001 P3 Q18]

10 Sue buys a pack of 12 cans of cola for £4.80.

She sells the cans for 50p each.

She sells all of the cans.

Work out her percentage profit.

(3 marks)

[S2000 P3 Q11]

10 Basically probability

You need to know about:

- drawing probability scales
- whether an experiment is fair
- probabilities adding up to 1
- equally likely events
- finding probabilities

| **Probability** | **Probability** tells you how likely something is to happen. Something that is impossible has a probability of 0. Something that is certain to happen has a probability of 1. |

You can mark probabilities on a **probability scale**. The value of a probability can only lie between 0 and 1.

```
|--------------------------------|
0                                1
```

Probabilities can only be given as fractions, decimals or percentages.

For this spinner P(getting a red) is $\frac{3}{5}$ or 0.6 or 60%.

Probabilities always add up to 1.

Example

Damion leaves his form room to go to his first lesson.
The probability that Damion will be early for his first lesson is 0.05
The probability that he will be on time is 0.36
Find the probability that he will be late.

$$P(\text{Damion is late}) = 1 - (0.05 + 0.36)$$
$$= 1 - 0.41$$
$$= 0.59$$

Example

The probability that the traffic lights are red is $\frac{1}{4}$.
Find the probability that they are not red.

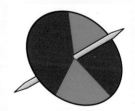

$$P(\text{not red}) = 1 - \frac{1}{4} = \frac{3}{4}$$

| **Event** | An **event** is something that can happen. |

Equally likely

Events are **equally likely** if they have the same chance of happening.

You can use equally likely events to work out probabilities.

Probability of an event A

$$= \frac{\text{the number of ways that the event A can happen}}{\text{the total number of things that can happen}}$$

You can get data from tables to find probabilities.
This table shows the contents of a box of coloured shapes.
A shape is chosen at random.
Find the probability that the shape is a red circle.

	square	circle
red	3	4
blue	5	6

$$P(\text{red circle}) = \frac{4}{3 + 5 + 4 + 6} = \frac{4}{18} = \frac{2}{9}$$

You can carry out experiments to find probabilities.

Frequency

The **frequency** of an event is the number of times that it happens.

Relative frequency

$$\textbf{Relative frequency} \text{ of an event} = \frac{\text{frequency of the event}}{\text{total frequency}}$$

The relative frequency gives an **estimate** of the probability.
This estimate gets better as you do more trials.

Example

Tom is a goalkeeper. His manager records the numbers of shots he saves. Estimate the probability that Tom will save the next shot.

	tally	frequency
saves	ⵏⵏⵏ ⵏⵏⵏ ⵏⵏⵏ IIII	19
doesn't save	ⵏⵏⵏ ⵏⵏⵏ I	11

$$P(\text{Tom saves the next shot}) = \frac{19}{19 + 11} = \frac{19}{30}$$

There are three **methods of finding probability**:

Method 1   Use equally likely outcomes
e.g. to find the probability of getting a 6 with a fair dice.

Method 2   Use a survey or do an experiment
e.g. to find the probability that a piece of toast will fall butter side down.

Method 3   Look back at data
e.g. to find the probability that it will snow in Spain this year look back at data for previous years.

1   The probability that Louise will go shopping tomorrow is 0.45
    What is the probability that Louise will not go shopping tomorrow?

2   The probability that Southampton lose or draw their next match is 0.4 or
    0.15 respectively.
    Find the probability that they win their next match.

3   A bag contains 20 coloured beads. Of these, 14 are red. Jennifer picks a
    bead at random from the bag. Write down the probability that the bead
    is:

    a red   **b** not red

4   The table shows the favourite pet owned by a class of 30 pupils.

Pet	Dog	Cat	Hamster	Rabbit	Pony	Guinea Pig
Number of boys	5	4	1	2	0	1
Number of girls	3	6	2	3	1	2

    A pupil is chosen at random from the class. Find the probability that the
    pupil will be:

    a a boy   **c** a boy who owns a dog
    b a girl who owns a hamster   **d** a boy who does not own a cat

5   Marco is interested in the colour of cars. He records the colour of 100
    cars entering the car park. The table shows his results.

Colour	Red	Silver	Black	Yellow	White
Frequency	24	16	31	10	19

    Use Marco's results to estimate the probability that the colour of the
    next car to enter the car park is:

    a red   **b** yellow   **c** not white

6   The letters of the word EQUILATERAL are written on cards.
    The cards are put into a box and one card is then chosen at random.
    Find the probability that the letter on the chosen card is:

    a Q   **b** A   **c** not a vowel

7   Look at these numbers: 1, 4, 8, 23, 25, 100
    A number is chosen from these at random. Find the probability that the
    number chosen is:

    a prime   **b** a multiple of 25   **c** an even number

1 Martin bought a packet of 50 mixed flower seeds. The seeds produce flowers which are red, blue, white or yellow.
The probability of a flower seed producing a flower of a particular colour is given in the table.

Colour	Red	Blue	White	Yellow
Probability	0.6	0.15		0.15

a Write down the most common flower colour. **(1 mark)**

Martin chooses a flower seed at random from the packet.

b Work out the probability that the flower produced will be
  i white **ii** orange. **(2 marks)**
c How many red flowers would you expect to grow? **(2 marks)**

a *The highest probability is red, so red is therefore the most common colour.* **1 mark**

b i *White is the missing probability:*
  $1 - (0.6 + 0.15 + 0.15) = 1 - 0.9 = 0.1$ **1 mark**
  ii There are no orange flowers, so the probability is 0. **1 mark**
c $50 \times 0.6 = 30$ *For this question the answer is a quantity*
  1 mark **1 mark** *(a number) and not a probability.*

2 Two fair spinners are used for a game.
The game score is the red score − the blue score.
The game score shown is $5 - 2 = 3$

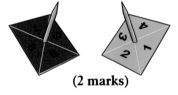

a Complete the table to show all the possible game scores for the two spinners. **(2 marks)**

		red spinner			
		5	6	7	8
blue spinner	1	4	5	6	7
	2	3	4	5	6
	3	2	3	4	5
	4	1	2	3	4

b What is the probability of the game score being an even number?

a *missing values are shown in red.* **1 mark for first six values**
1 mark for second six values

b There are 16 games scores altogether.
There are 8 scores that are even. **1 mark**
The probability is $\frac{8}{16}$. **1 mark**

Note: *Acceptable answers are $\frac{8}{16}$, $\frac{4}{8}$, $\frac{1}{2}$, or equivalents (e.g. 50%, 0.5, 0.50).*
Unacceptable answers include 8 in 16, 8 out of 16, 8 : 16, 1 : 2, etc.

1   Asif has a box of 25 pens.

12 of the pens are blue.
8 of the pens are black.
The rest of the pens are red.

Asif chooses one pen at random from the box.
What is the probability that Asif will choose.

i   a blue pen,

ii   a red pen?

(2 marks)
[S2001 P3 Q7]

2   Shreena has a bag of 20 sweets.

10 of the sweets are red.
3 of the sweets are black.
The rest of the sweets are white.

Shreena chooses one sweet at random.
What is the probability that Shreena will choose

a   a red sweet,

(1 mark)

b   a white sweet?

(1 mark)
[S1999 P4 Q7]

3   Ben has some coloured cubes in a bag.

The table shows the number of cubes of each colour.

Red	Blue	Yellow	Brown
7	4	8	6

Ben is going to take one cube at random from the bag.
Write down the probability that Ben

i   will take a yellow cube,

ii   will **not** take a brown cube.

(4 marks)
[N1999 P3 Q8]

4   Asif's bus could be on time or late or early.

The probability that his bus will be on time is 0.9.
The probability that his bus will be late is 0.03.

Work out the probability that Asif's bus will be early.

(2 marks)
[N1998 P3 Q7]

5 All female chaffinches have the same patterns of laying eggs. The probability that any female chaffinch will lay a certain number of eggs is given in the table below.

Number of eggs	0	1	2	3	4 or more
Probability	0.1	0.3	0.3	0.2	x

    a Calculate the value of x.   **(2 marks)**

    b Calculate the probability that a female chaffinch will lay less than 3 eggs.   **(3 marks)**

    c Calculate the probability that two female chaffinches will lay a total of 2 eggs.   **(4 marks)**

                                      [N1996 P4 Q16]

6 There are 20 bubble gums in a bubble gum machine.
The colour of each bubble gum can be red or green or yellow or white.

This pictogram shows the number of bubble gums of each colour in the bubble gum machine.

Red	● ●
Green	● ● ● ● ●
Yellow	● ● ●
White	● ● ● ● ● ● ● ● ● ●

Bob gets one bubble gum at random from the machine.

    a Write down the probability that he will get

        i a **white** bubble gum,

        ii a **black** bubble gum,

        iii either a **red** or a **green** bubble gum.   **(3 marks)**

    b Write down the probability that he will **not** get a **green** bubble gum.

                                        (2 marks)

                                      [S2001 P4 Q1]

11 The bigger picture

You need to know about:

- enlargements
- similar shapes
- the effect of enlargement on perimeter
- finding the centre of enlargement
- scale drawing
- constructing triangles

The **scale factor** of an enlargement can be a fraction.

The diagram shows a triangle enlarged with scale factor $1\frac{1}{2}$, centre of enlargement C.

All the lengths are $1\frac{1}{2}$ times longer in the enlarged shape.

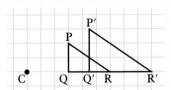

An enlargement with a scale factor less than 1 will make a shape smaller.

This rectangle has been enlarged with scale factor $\frac{1}{3}$, centre C.

All the lengths are $\frac{1}{3}$ times as long in the enlarged shape.

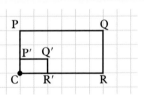

The **angles** of the original shape are not changed by an enlargement.

| Similar | Two diagrams are **similar** if one is an enlargement of the other. They have the same shape but different sizes. You can use the scale factor to find missing lengths. |

Example

These two trapeziums are similar. Find the missing lengths.

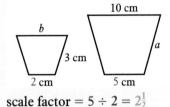

First find the scale factor of the enlargement by using a pair of corresponding sides.

scale factor $= 5 \div 2 = 2\frac{1}{2}$

Now find length a by multiplying by the scale factor.

$a = 3 \times 2\frac{1}{2} = 7.5$ cm

You need to divide by the scale factor to get length b.

$b = 10 \div 2\frac{1}{2} = 4$ cm

If a shape is enlarged by a scale factor n then the perimeter will also be enlarged by a scale factor n.

Example The perimeter of a parallelogram is 21 cm. The parallelogram is enlarged by scale factor 4. Find the perimeter of the enlarged parallelogram.

New perimeter = old perimeter × scale factor = 21 × 4 = 84 cm

To **find the centre of enlargement** join corresponding points on the object and image. These lines will all meet at the centre of enlargement.

Example Find the centre of enlargement for these two triangles.

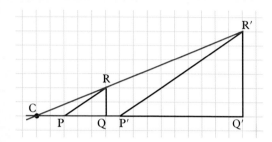

The red lines join corresponding points.
They meet at C.
C is the centre of enlargement.

Models, scale drawings, plans and maps are all exact copies of something drawn to a smaller scale.
They are all enlargements of each other.
The scale of a map is the scale factor of the enlargement from the map to the real world.

Example A road map is drawn to the scale 1 : 50 000.
  a How many kilometres are represented by 1 cm on the map?
  b The distance between two towns is 35 km.
    What is this distance on the map?

  a The scale factor of the enlargement is 50 000, so 1 cm represents
    50 000 cm = 500 m = 0.5 km.
  b To find the distance on the map you divide by the scale factor.
    Change kilometres to centimetres before you do the division.
    35 km = 35 000 m = 3 500 000 cm
    Distance on the map = 3 500 000 ÷ 50 000 = 70 cm

You need a pair of compasses to construct a triangle when you know the lengths of all three sides.

Example Construct a triangle with sides 5 cm, 4 cm and 3 cm.
  First draw the 5 cm side.
  Then set your compass to 4 cm.
  Place the compass point at one end
  of the 5 cm line and draw an arc.
  Now set the compass to 3 cm and
  draw an arc with the compass point
  at the other end of the line.
  The two arcs should cross at a point.
  This point is the third vertex of the triangle.
  Finally, join this point to the ends of the 5 cm line.

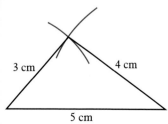

1   Copy this shape on to squared paper.
    Enlarge the shape using a scale factor of 2.
    Use C as the centre of enlargement.

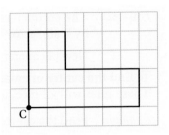

2   a Copy this shape on to squared paper.
    b Enlarge the shape using a scale factor
       of $\frac{1}{3}$ and centre of enlargement $(6, 6)$.
    c Write down the co-ordinates of the
       vertices of the enlarged shape.

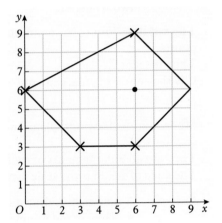

3   These two triangles are similar. Find the missing lengths a and b.

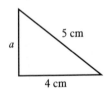   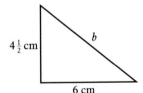

4   A shape has a perimeter of 18 cm. The shape is enlarged by a scale factor
    of 2.5. Write down the perimeter of the enlarged shape.

5   A map is drawn to the scale 1 : 20 000.
    a How many kilometres are represented by 1 cm on the map?
    b How many kilometres are represented by 7 cm on the map?

6   Construct each of these triangles.

    a   b

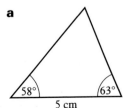   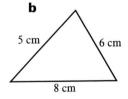

1 Qasim made a scale model of a car on a scale of 1 to 12.5.
The height of the model car is 10 cm.

   a Work out the height of the real car. **(1 mark)**

The length of the real car is 5 m.

   b Work out the length of the model car. Give your answer in
centimetres. **(1 mark)**

The angle the windscreen makes with the bonnet on the real car is 140°.

   c What angle does the windscreen make with the bonnet on the model
car? **(1 mark)**

   a *Going from small to large so multiply by the scale factor:*
10 cm × 12.5 = 125 cm **1 mark**

   b *Going from large to small so divide by the scale factor:*
5 m ÷ 12.5 = 0.4 m
0.4 m × 100 = 40 cm **1 mark**

   c *When something is enlarged or reduced in size, the angles remain the same.*
The angle is still 140°. **1 mark**

2 **a** Find UV.

   b Find AE   **(3 marks)**

*To find the scale factor you match up two sides that are in the same position,
and that you know the lengths of:*

Show how you found the scale factor.

$$\text{Scale factor} = \frac{ST}{AB} = \frac{7}{4} = 1.75$$ **1 mark**

*This means that to go from the smaller shape to the larger shape you have to
multiply a length by 1.75*

   a *To find UV you will have to **multiply** the corresponding side on the smaller
shape (CD) by 1.75*

       CD = 5 cm, so UV = 5 × 1.75 = 8.75 cm **1 mark**

   b *To find AE you will have to **divide** the corresponding side on the larger shape
(SW) by 1.75, since you are now going from large to small.*

       SW = 10.5 cm, so AE = 10.5 ÷ 1.75 = 6 cm **1 mark**

1

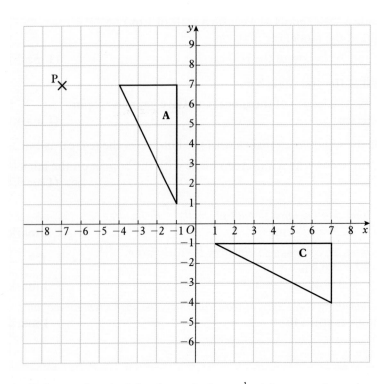

  a Enlarge triangle **A** by the scale factor $\frac{1}{3}$ with centre the point
    $P(-7, 7)$ **(2 marks)**
  b Describe fully the single transformation which maps triangle **A** onto
    triangle **C**.   **(2 marks)**
                             [N2000 P3 Q16]

2   Diagram **NOT**
accurately drawn

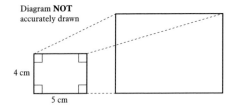

4 cm

5 cm

The diagram represents two photographs.
  a Work out the area of the small photograph.
    State the units of your answer.   **(2 marks)**

The photograph is to be enlarged by scale factor 3.
  b Write down the measurements of the enlarged photograph. **(2 marks)**
  c How many times bigger is the area of the enlarged photograph than
    the area of the small photograph?   **(2 marks)**
                             [S1998 P4 Q3]

3 Shape **A** is shown on the grid.

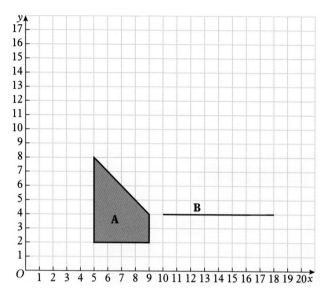

Shape **A** is enlarged, centre (0, 0), to obtain shape **B**.
One side of shape **B** has been drawn for you.

  a Write down the scale factor of the enlargement. **(1 mark)**

  b On the grid, complete shape **B**.

The shape **A** is enlarged by scale factor $\frac{1}{2}$, centre (5, 16) to give the shape **C**.

  c On the grid, draw shape **C**. **(2 marks)**

[N2001 P3 Q13]

4 A shaded shape is shown on grid A.

Draw an enlargement, scale factor 2, of the shaded shape. **(2 marks)**

[S1999 P4 Q4]

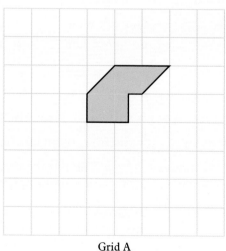

Grid A

12 **Power rules**

You need to know about:

- square roots and cube roots
- reciprocals
- the rules of indices
- negative powers
- BODMAS

The x^2 key on your calculator can be used to work out square numbers.

To find 15^2 use the keys **1** **5** **x^2** **=**.

The calculator will show the answer 225.

The square root key **$\sqrt{\ }$** undoes what the **x^2** key does.

You can use the **x^y** or **y^x** key on your calculator to work out any power.

To find 3^5 key in **3** **x^y** **5** **=** or **3** **y^x** **5** **=**.

The calculator will show the answer 243.

You can use the **$\sqrt[x]{\ }$** or **$\sqrt[y]{x}$** on your calculator to work out any root.

To find $\sqrt[3]{64}$ key in **3** **$\sqrt[x]{\ }$** **6** **4** **=** or **3** **$\sqrt[y]{x}$** **6** **4** **=**.

The calculator will show the answer 4.

In 3^5, 3 is called the **base** and 5 is called the **index**.

Any number with an **index of 0** is equal to 1.　　　　$19^0 = 1$.

When you multiply you **add** the indices:　　$7^2 \times 7^4 = 7^{2+4} = 7^6$
When you divide you subtract the indices:　　$3^9 \div 3^5 = 3^{9-5} = 3^4$

Example　　　　Simplify these.

　　a　$3a^2b \times 5a^3b^{-5}$　　　**b**　$8x^6y^{-3} \div 4xy^{-5}$

　　a　$3a^2b \times 5a^3b^{-5} = 15a^{2+3}b^{1+-5} = 15a^5b^{-4}$

　　b　$8x^6y^{-3} \div 4xy^{-5} = 2x^{6-1}y^{-3--5} = 2x^5y^2$

The square root of x is written $\sqrt{x}$. It can also be written $x^{\frac{1}{2}}$, so $25^{\frac{1}{2}} = 5$.

The cube root of x is written $\sqrt[3]{x}$. It can also be written $x^{\frac{1}{3}}$, so $8^{\frac{1}{3}} = 2$.

$(a^3)^5$ is the same as $a^{3 \times 5} = a^{15}$. $(a^{\frac{1}{2}})^6$ is the same as $a^{\frac{1}{2} \times 6} = a^3$.

When you remove the brackets you multiply the indices.

BODMAS　　　　**BODMAS** tells you which operation to do first. Brackets first, then powers **O**f, **D**ivision and **M**ultiplication next, then finally **A**ddition and **S**ubtraction.

---

1 Use your calculator to find the value of:

    a 14^2 **c** $\sqrt{529}$ **e** 3^6

    b 11^3 **d** $\sqrt[3]{512}$ **f** 2^8

2 Write each of these using powers:

    a $5 \times 5 \times 5$ **c** $4 \times 4 \times 4 \times 4$ **e** $9 \times 9 \times 9 \times 9 \times 9 \times 9$

    b 3×3 **d** $7 \times 7 \times 7 \times 7 \times 7$ **f** $6 \times 6 \times 6 \times 6$

3 Write down the exact values of:

    a 3^{-1} **d** $25^{\frac{1}{2}}$ **g** $\left(\frac{2}{3}\right)^{-1}$ **j** $\left(1\frac{9}{16}\right)^{-1}$

    b 6^0 **e** $16^{\frac{1}{2}}$ **h** $27^{\frac{1}{3}}$ **k** $8^{\frac{2}{3}}$

    c 4^{-2} **f** $\left(\frac{1}{4}\right)^{-1}$ **i** 27^0 **l** $16^{\frac{3}{4}}$

4 Simplify:

    a $b^6 \times b^2$ **d** $b^4 \times 2b^2$ **g** $4h^2 \times 5h^3$ **j** $4h^2 \times 5k^5$

    b $c^3 \times c$ **e** $4x^6 \times 3x$ **h** $6x^3 \times 2y^2$ **k** $6x^3 \times 2y^2$

    c $3d^2 \times d^3$ **f** $3p^4 \times 2p^2$ **i** $5p^3 \times 2q^2$ **l** $3xy^2 \times 2x^2y^2$

5 Simplify:

    a $(3x^2)^3$ **c** $(4y^3)^2$ **e** $(2a^2b^2)^3$ **g** $14x^6 \div 2x^3$

    b $x^6y^2 \div x^4y$ **d** $4a^3b^3c \div 2ab^2c$ **f** $(a^2)^{-3}$ **h** $\left(x^{\frac{1}{3}}\right)^{-1}$

6 Find the value of x in each of these:

    a $2^x = 16$ **c** $27^x = 3$ **e** $4^x = 2$

    b $64^x = 8$ **d** $1000^x = 10$ **f** $5^x = 625$

7 Work these out without using a calculator:

    a $7 \times 5 + 4$ **c** $49 \div 7 - 2$ **e** $5 \times (6 + 9)$ **g** $6^2 \times 4$

    b $3 \times 4 + 2 \times 6$ **d** $25 \div 5 + 44 \div 11$ **f** $(3 \times 5) + 25$ **h** $4 + 6 \times 2^2$

8 Work these out using a calculator.
Give the answer to 1 dp.

    a $\dfrac{4.96 - 2.35}{5.1}$ **b** $\dfrac{6^3 + 5.45}{3.78 - 1.26}$ **c** $\dfrac{15.67 - 6.82}{3.87} + 5.67$

9 Use the formula $A = 2b\sqrt{4a^2 - 3c}$ to find A for each part.
Give your answers to 1 dp.

    a $a = 16$ $b = 5.3$ $c = 2.9$

    b $a = 15.4$ $b = 110$ $c = 41.6$

1 Work out:

   a $12 + 9 \div 3$ **(1 mark)**

   b $7 \times 2 - 2 \times 6$ **(1 mark)**

   c $\dfrac{38.5 \times 82.7}{2.02 \times 1.95}$, giving your answer to 3 significant figures   **(3 marks)**

   d $\dfrac{24 + \sqrt{12.5 - 2.25}}{3.2 + 5.4}$, giving your answer to 1 decimal place   **(3 marks)**

*In all these calculations you are expected to use your calculator: **do not** change any of the figures to estimates.*

You will need to do the operations in the correct order. You may need to put brackets in to help you to get the order right.

   a $12 + 9 \div 3 = 12 + (9 \div 3) = 12 + 3 = 15$ **1 mark**

   b $7 \times 2 - 2 \times 6 = (7 \times 2) - (2 \times 6) = 14 - 12 = 2$

                                                                   1 mark

   c $\dfrac{38.5 \times 82.7}{2.02 \times 1.95} = \dfrac{3183.95}{3.939} = 808.314\,293 = 808 \text{ (to 3 sf)}$

*Make sure you work out the top and the bottom separately **and** write the full number down.*	*Write the answer to the full calculation before rounding.*	*Round the answer as asked in the question.*
1 mark	**1 mark**	**1 mark**

   d $\dfrac{24 + \sqrt{12.5 - 2.25}}{3.2 + 5.4} = \dfrac{24 + \sqrt{10.25}}{3.2 + 5.4} = \dfrac{24 + 3.201\,56}{3.2 + 5.4} = \dfrac{27.20156}{8.6}$

                                                           1 mark   **1 mark**

        $= 3.162\,97 = 3.2 \text{ (to 1 dp)}$

            1 mark

   Write down the accurate answer before you round it.   *Make sure you write out all the numbers at each stage of the calculation.*

2 Simplify: **a** $(x^2)^3$ **b** $4x^2y \div 2xy^3$ **(2 marks)**

   a $(x^2)^3 = x^2 \times x^2 \times x^2 = x^6$ **1 mark**

   b $4x^2y \div 2xy^3 = \dfrac{4x^2y}{2xy^3} = \dfrac{\overset{2}{4}x^2y}{\underset{}{2}xy^3} = \dfrac{2xy}{y^3} = \dfrac{2x}{y^2}$ **1 mark**

It is sometimes useful to write the division in algebra as a fraction for cancelling.

1   Find the value of

$$\sqrt{2 \times 2 \times 3 \times 3 \times 5 \times 5}$$

(2 marks)
[N2000 P3 Q13]

2   Use your calculator to evaluate

$$\frac{560.3 \times 20.3}{(0.2 + 4.5)^2}$$

Write down all the figures on your calculator.   **(3 marks)**
[N1997 P4 Q14]

3   In this question you **MUST** use your calculator and you **MAY** write down any stage in your calculation.

Evaluate

$$\frac{(23.4 + 35.6) \times 5.7}{200.3 \times (16.2 - 8.15)}$$

(2 marks)
[S1996 P3 Q7]

4   Use your calculator to evaluate

$$\frac{2.8 \, (3.75 - 1.53)}{17.74 - 3.96}$$

(2 marks)

[N1996 P3 Q12]

5   Calculate the value of

$$\frac{21.7 \times 32.1}{16.20 - 2.19}$$

Give your answer correct to 3 significant figures.   **(3 marks)**
[S1998 P4 Q10]

6   Use your calculator to work out the exact value of

$$\frac{14.82 \times (17.4 - 9.25)}{(54.3 + 23.7) \times 3.8}$$

(3 marks)
[N1998 P3 Q11]

7 Use your calculator to find the value of

$$\sqrt{47.3^2 - 9.1^2}$$

    a Write down all the figures on your calculator display.   **(2 marks)**

    b Write your answer to part **a** correct to 2 significant figures. **(1 mark)**
        [N2000 P4 Q15]

8 **a** Use your calculator to find the value of

$$5.43 \times \sqrt{18 - 6.67}$$

    Write down all the figures on your calculator display.   **(2 marks)**

    b Give your answer to part **a** correct to 2 decimal places.   **(1 mark)**
        [N1999 P4 Q6]

9 Use your calculator to work out the value of

$$\frac{\sqrt{12.3^2 + 7.9}}{1.8 \times 0.17}$$

    Give your answer correct to 1 decimal place.   **(3 marks)**
        [S2000 P4 Q12]

10 **a** Multiply out

$$t^2(t^3 - t^4)$$ **(2 marks)**

    b Multiply out and simplify

$$3(2a + 6) - 2(3a - 6)$$ **(2 marks)**

    c Simplify

$$\frac{12a^2b}{4ab}$$ **(1 mark)**
        [S2000 P3 Q20]

11 Use the formula

$$A = \tfrac{1}{4}c \sqrt{4a^2 - c^2}$$

    to calculate the value of A given that

    $c = 7.23$ and $a = 8.76$.

    Give your answer correct to 1 decimal place.   **(3 marks)**
        [S1995 P4 Q18]

12

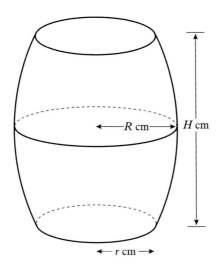

The volume, V, of the barrel is given by the formula

$$V = \frac{\pi H(2R^2 + r^2)}{3000}$$

$\pi = 3.14$, $H = 60$, $R = 25$ and $r = 20$.

Calculate the value of V.

Give your answer correct to 3 significant figures. **(3 marks)**

[N1997 P3 Q17]

13 a Calculate the value of

$$\frac{5.6(7.4 + 3.4)}{5 - 3.11}$$

(3 marks)

b Use your answer to part **a** to write down the values of

i $\dfrac{5 - 3.11}{5.6(7.4 + 3.4)}$

ii $\dfrac{50 - 31.1}{5.6(0.74 + 0.34)}$ **(3 marks)**

[N1995 P4 Q14]

14 In this question you **must** use your calculator and you **may** write down any stages in your calculation.

Evaluate $\dfrac{(14.08 - 2.003) \times 1.2}{6.3 - 2.01}$ **(3 marks)**

[S1994 P4 Q24]

13 Graphs: moving on

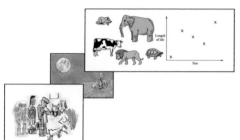

You need to know about:

- using time
- working with distances, speeds and time
- travel graphs
- conversion graphs and step graphs
- sketching graphs
- gradients of lines

Time can be written using the 24 hour clock or using a.m. and p.m.

5.35 a.m. is the same as 05:35   21:30 is the same as 9.30 p.m.

You use the 24 hour clock and the **DMS** key to put times into your calculator.

Remember these: 30 min = 0.5 h, 15 min = 0.25 h, 6 min = 0.1 h.

Use the triangle to help you remember these formulas.

$$\text{Speed} = \frac{\text{Distance}}{\text{Time}} \quad \text{Time} = \frac{D}{S} \quad \text{Distance} = S \times T$$

Travel graphs   **Travel graphs** are used to show distance and time.

The graph shows Mia's journey to the library and back.

The first part of the graph shows Mia driving away from her house.

She drives 12 km in 15 minutes.

15 minutes = 0.25 hour

Speed = Distance ÷ time = 12 ÷ 0.25 = 48 km/h

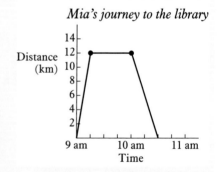

Mia's journey to the library

The horizontal part of the graph shows that Mia is not moving. This is when she is in the library.
She is in the library for 45 minutes.

The last part of the graph shows Mia driving home. This line is not as steep as the line in the first part. This shows that Mia drives home more slowly than when she was driving to the library.

Average speed = total distance ÷ total time

Total distance = 24 km   Total time = 1.5 h

The average speed for the whole of Mia's journey = 24 ÷ 1.5 = 16 km/h

The graph shows the costs for first class mail.
It is called a **step graph**.
This type of graph has some points joined up
but there are also gaps in it.
The lines look like a series of steps.

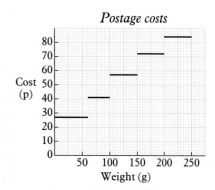

Postage costs

A **conversion graph** is a graph that you can
use to change from one unit to another.
This graph converts between miles and
kilometres.

Follow the blue line on the graph
17 miles = 27 km
Follow the red line on the graph
10 km = 6 miles

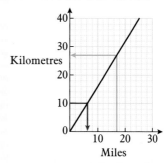

The **gradient** measures how steep a line or curve is.
The gradient of a straight line is the same all the way along.
The gradient of a curve changes.

This container is filled with water at a
constant rate. The sketch graph shows how the
height of the water changes with respect to
time.

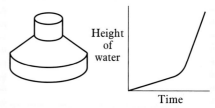

Look for these features when describing or sketching graphs that model real situations.

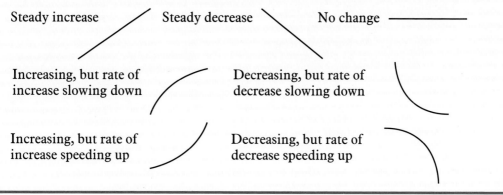

Steady increase   Steady decrease   No change

Increasing, but rate of   Decreasing, but rate of
increase slowing down   decrease slowing down

Increasing, but rate of   Decreasing, but rate of
increase speeding up   decrease speeding up

1 This is how Janine spends Saturday morning.

9:00	Wakes up, has breakfast and dresses
10:13	Catches the bus to her friend's house in Sussex Street
10:48	Arrives at Sussex Street and gets off the bus
11:08	Arrives at her friend's house
11:55	Leaves her friend's house

   a How long is the bus journey from Janine's house to her friend's house?

   b When Janine arrives at Sussex Street, she walks to her friend's house. How long does this take her?

   c The distance from the second bus stop to Janine's friend's house is $\frac{2}{3}$ mile.
Work out the average speed for this part of the journey.

   d Janine catches a bus home at 12:29.
The return journey takes the same time as the outward journey.
Write down the time that she arrives at the bus stop near her home.

2 **a** Draw a conversion graph to change from pounds (£) into dollars ($).
£1 will buy $1.40.

   b Use your graph to convert £5 into dollars.

   c Use your graph to convert $4.90 into pounds.

3 **a** A train travels 150 miles in 2 h 15 min.
Calculate the average speed of the train in mph.

   b A bus journey is 2 h 10 min. The bus travels at an average speed of 36 mph.
Find the length of the journey.

4 Meher is out in her car.
The graph shows how far away from home she is one afternoon.

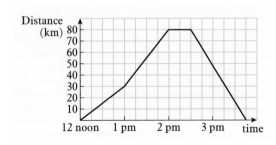

   a How fast is Meher travelling between noon and 1 p.m?
Give your answer in km/h.

   b How fast is Meher travelling between 1 p.m. and 2 p.m?
Give your answer in km/h.

   c Explain what is happening between 2 p.m. and 2.30 p.m.

   d What is Meher's speed on her return journey? Give your answer in km/h.

1 Alan leaves home at 3 p.m. to go to Bruce's house, 200 km away, and drives straight there. At the same time, Bruce leaves his house to go to Alan's.

a At what time does Alan pass Bruce? **(1 mark)**

b What happened to Bruce between 4 p.m. and 5 p.m.? **(1 mark)**

c What is Alan's average speed? **(2 marks)**

d What is Bruce's average speed for the first part of his journey? **(2 marks)**

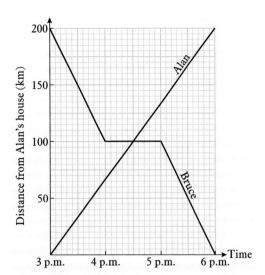

a Alan passes Bruce where the graphs cross, at 4.30 p.m. **1 mark**

b Between 4 p.m. and 5 p.m. Bruce is stationary (he has stopped). **1 mark**

A common incorrect answer is to say that Bruce has constant speed.

c Alan's average speed $= \dfrac{\text{distance}}{\text{time}} = \dfrac{200\ \text{km}}{3\ \text{h}} = 66\frac{2}{3}\ \text{km/h}$

1 mark **1 mark**

d Bruce's average speed $= \dfrac{\text{distance}}{\text{time}} = \dfrac{100\ \text{km}}{1\ \text{h}} = 100\ \text{km/h}$

1 mark **1 mark**

2 The diagram shows a water tank.

The empty tank is slowly filled with water at a constant rate. Sketch a graph to show the relationship between the volume, V cm³, of water in the tank and the depth, d cm, of water in the tank. **(3 marks)**

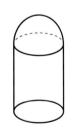

The graph should have three clear features:

AB should be a straight line from the origin. **1 mark**

BC should be a curve. **1 mark**

C is where the curve should finish horizontally. **1 mark**

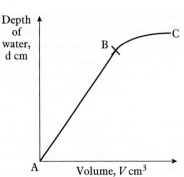

1 In the College Games, Michael Jackson won the 200 metres race in a time of 20.32 seconds.

Calculate his average speed in metres per second. Give your answer correct to 1 decimal place. **(2 marks)**

[S1998 P4 Q19]

2 On Monday, Gareth drove from Swindon to Newcastle.
The distance was 325 miles.

He left Swindon at 08:00.
He arrived in Newcastle at 14:30.

a Work out Gareth's average speed. **(3 marks)**

On Tuesday, Gareth left Newcastle at 10:00 to drive back to Swindon.
He drove for 160 miles at an average speed of 64 miles per hour.

He stopped at a Service Station for one hour, before completing the journey.

He arrived in Swindon at 16:30.

b Calculate Gareth's average speed from the Service Station to Swindon. **(3 marks)**

[N1999 P4 Q8]

3 Car P and car Q travel from Amfield to Barton.
Car P averages 10 kilometres for each litre of petrol.
It needs 45 litres of petrol for this journey.
Car Q averages 4 kilometres for each litre of petrol.
Work out the number of litres of petrol car Q needs for the same journey. **(3 marks)**

[N1999 P3 Q15]

4 Elizabeth went for a cycle ride.
The distance–time graph shows her ride.

She set off from home at 12:00 and had a flat tyre at 14:00.
During her ride, she stopped for a rest.

a i At what time did she stop for a rest?

ii At what speed did she travel after her rest? **(3 marks)**

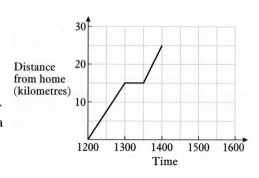

It took Elizabeth 15 minutes to repair the flat tyre.
She then cycled home at 25 kilometres per hour.

b Complete the distance–time graph to show this information. **(3 marks)**

[S2000 P4 Q8]

5 Jon cycled a distance of 18 km from Guildford to Cranleigh.
The graph shows Jon's cycle ride.
On the way, Jon stopped to buy a drink at a shop.

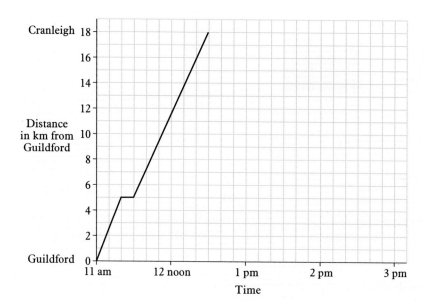

a i Write down the distance of the shop from Guildford.

  ii Write down the time at which Jon stopped.

  iii For how long did he stop?   **(3 marks)**

Jon stayed in Cranleigh for lunch.
He left Cranleigh at 1:30 p.m.
He cycled back to Guildford at a steady speed.
He reached Guildford at 3 p.m.

b On the grid, complete the graph of Jon's journey.   **(2 marks)**

c Work out the steady speed at which he cycled back to
Guildford.   **(2 marks)**

[N1998 P3 Q5]

14 Trigonometry

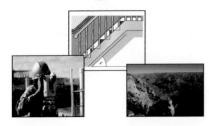

You need to know about:

- the ratios sin, cos and tan
- finding an angle in a right-angled triangle
- finding a side in a right-angled triangle

Look at this **right-angled** triangle.
The sides are labelled for angle a.

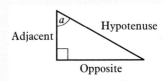

$$\sin a = \frac{\text{Opp}}{\text{Hyp}} \qquad \cos a = \frac{\text{Adj}}{\text{Hyp}} \qquad \tan a = \frac{\text{Opp}}{\text{Adj}}$$

Some people remember **SOHCAHTOA** which comes from the first letters of sin equals Opposite divided by Hypotenuse, cos equals Adjacent divided by ...

Example Find the angle x in this triangle.

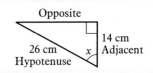

The lengths that you know are Adj and Hyp.
Only the cos ratio has Adj and Hyp, so

$$\cos x = \frac{14}{26}$$

Make sure that your calculator is working in degrees.

Key in 2nd F cos (1 4 ÷ 2 6) = to give $x = 57.421\ldots$
Always write the full answer down before rounding the angle to 1 dp.

$x = 57.4°$ (1 dp)

Example Find the length of the side marked k.

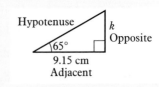

You know Adj and need to find the Opp.
Only the tan ratio has Opp and Adj in it, so

$$\tan 65° = \frac{k}{9.15}$$

Multiply both sides of the equation by 9.15 to give $k = 9.15 \times \tan 65° = 19.6222\ldots$ cm
Always write the full answer down before rounding the length to 3 sf.

$k = 19.6$ cm (3 sf)

Sometimes you need to split an **isosceles triangle** into two right-angled triangles before you solve the problem.
The base length and the top angle are both halved.

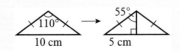

1 Find the angles marked with letters. Give each of your answers to the nearest degree.

a

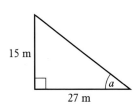

c

b

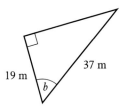

d

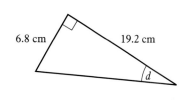

2 Find the sides marked with letters. Give each of your answers to 3 sf.

a

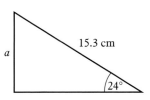

c

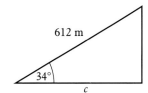

b

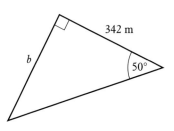

d

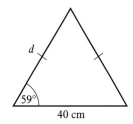

3 Jemba is 3 m from the base of a tree. He measures the angle between the ground and the top of the tree. It is 49°. Find the height of the tree to the nearest centimetre.

4 An equilateral triangle has sides of length 8 cm.
Calculate the perpendicular height of the triangle. Give your answer to 3 sf.

5 Lisa is in a department store. She uses the escalator to reach the first floor.
The escalator makes an angle of 28° with the ground floor.
The distance between the ground floor and the first floor is 10 m.
Calculate the length of the escalator. Give your answer to 3 sf.

1 Find x.

Give your answer to 3 significant
figures. **(3 marks)**

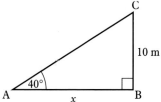

$$\tan = \frac{\text{opposite}}{\text{adjacent}}$$

$$\tan 40° = \frac{10}{x}$$

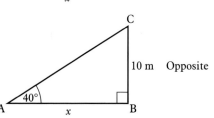

The length x is at the bottom of this fraction.
This is a special case of tangent where it is easier
to use a different angle. The angle at C is $180 - 90° - 40° = 50°$.

$$\tan 50° = \frac{x}{10}$$ ←——— *The x is now on the top (much easier).*

1 mark

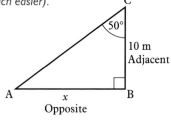

$$10 \tan 50° = x$$ **1 mark**

So $x = 10 \times 1.191\ 75 = 11.9175$
$= 11.9\ \text{m (3 sf)}$

1 mark

Show the value of tan 50°. *Always show the accurate answer before rounding.*

2 This isosceles triangle ABC has
AB = AC = 8 cm and angle
ABC = angle ACB = 35°.

Calculate the area of the triangle.

Give your answer correct to 3 significant
figures. **(5 marks)**

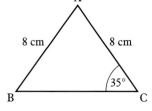

To find the area you need to find the length of the base and the height y.

$$\sin 35° = \frac{y}{8}$$
$$y = 8 \times \sin 35° = 8 \times 0.5736 = 4.5886$$
$$\quad\quad \textbf{1 mark} \quad\quad\quad \textbf{1 mark}$$

$$\cos 35° = \frac{x}{8}$$
$$x = 8 \times \cos 35° = 8 \times 0.819\ 15 = 6.5532$$
$$\quad \textbf{1 mark} \quad\quad\quad \textbf{1 mark}$$

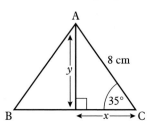

Area $= \frac{1}{2}$ base $\times$ height
$\quad = x \times y = 6.5532 \times 4.5886 = 30.07 = 30.1\ \text{cm}^2$ (to 3 sf) **1 mark**

1 Angle Q = 90°
Angle P = 32° and
PR = 2.6 metres.

Calculate the length of QR.

Give your answer in metres,
correct to 3 significant
figures.   **(3 marks)**
[N1999 P4 Q15]

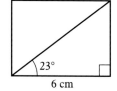

2.6 m

32°

Diagram **NOT**
accurately drawn.

2 The diagram represents a
rectangle which is 6 cm long.

A diagonal makes an angle of
23° with a 6 cm side.

Calculate the length of a
diagonal.

Give your answer correct to 3 significant figures.   **(3 marks)**
[N1998 P3 Q21]

23°

6 cm

Diagram **NOT**
accurately drawn.

3

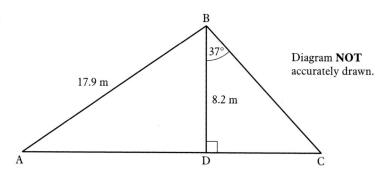

Diagram **NOT**
accurately drawn.

B

37°

17.9 m

8.2 m

A   D   C

In the diagram
AB = 17.9 m, BD = 8.2 m, angle CBD = 37° and angle BDC = 90°.
ADC is a straight line.

a Calculate the length of DC.
Give your answer, in metres, correct to 3 significant figures.

(3 marks)

b Calculate the size of angle DAB.
Give your answer correct to 1 decimal place.   **(3 marks)**
[N1997 P3 Q18]

4

Windy
Cragg

5.2 km

Diagram **NOT**
accurately drawn.

$x°$

Walton
Scree

Hill Top   6.8 km

The diagram shows three places, which are on the same horizontal plane.

Windy Cragg is 5.2 km due North of Hill Top.

Walton Scree is 6.8 km due East of Hill Top.

a Calculate the distance from Walton Scree to Windy Cragg.
Give your answer correct to 1 decimal place.   **(3 marks)**

b Calculate the size of the angle marked $x°$ in the diagram.
Give your answer correct to 1 decimal place.   **(3 marks)**

The distance of 5.2 km has been rounded to 1 decimal place.

c Write down the minimum distance it could be.   **(2 marks)**

[S1995 P3 Q13]

5

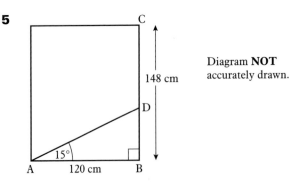

Diagram **NOT**
accurately drawn.

148 cm

D

15°

A   120 cm   B

AB and BC are two sides of a rectangle.

AB = 120 cm and BC = 148 cm.

D is a point on BC.

Angle BAD = 15°.

Work out the length of CD.

Give your answer correct to the nearest centimetre.   **(4 marks)**

[S2000 P4 Q22]

6

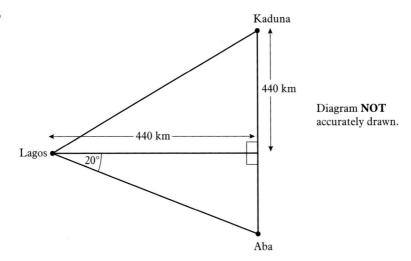

The diagram is part of a map showing the positions of three Nigerian towns. Kaduna is due North of Aba.

a Calculate the direct distance between Lagos and Kaduna.
Give your answer to the nearest kilometre. **(2 marks)**
b Calculate the distance between Kaduna and Aba.
Give your answer to the nearest kilometre. **(3 marks)**
[S1996 P4 Q14]

7

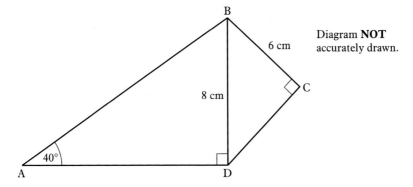

ABCD is a quadrilateral.
Angle BDA = 90°, angle BCD = 90°, angle BAD = 40°.
BC = 6 cm, BD = 8 cm.

a Calculate the length of DC. Give your answer correct to 3 significant figures. **(3 marks)**
b Calculate the size of angle DBC. Give your answer correct to 3 significant figures. **(3 marks)**
c Calculate the length of AB. Give your answer correct to 3 significant figures. **(3 marks)**
[N2000 P4 Q22]

15 Algebra: changing form

You need to know about:

- collecting like terms
- multiplying out brackets
- factorising

Collecting terms means adding and subtracting terms that have exactly the same letters in them.

Example Simplify these by collecting terms where possible.

a $p + p + p + p$

c $5x^2y - 3x^2y + x^2y$

b $4a^2 + 4ab - a^2 + 5ab$

d $4r^2s + 5rs^2$

a Adding $4\,p$s together gives 4 lots of p.

$$p + p + p + p = 4 \times p = 4p$$

b The terms with a^2 can be collected together.
So can the terms with ab.
You cannot collect the a^2s and the abs together

$$4a^2 + 4ab - a^2 + 5ab = 3a^2 + 9ab$$

c The terms all involve x^2y so they can all be collected.

$$5x^2y - 3x^2y + x^2y = 3x^2y$$

d Both terms involve r and s and 'squared' but the power 2 is on a different letter in each term. These terms **cannot** be collected.

To **multiply out a single bracket**, each term inside the bracket must be multiplied by the term outside the bracket.

Example Multiply out these brackets.

a $5(2a + 3)$

b $y^2(4y - 1)$

c $5h(2h + 7 - g^2)$

a To work out $5(2a + 3)$, multiply the $2a$ and the 3 by 5.

$$5(2a + 3) = 5 \times 2a + 5 \times 3 = 10a + 15$$

b In this part remember that $y^2 \times y$ gives y^3.

$$y^2(4y - 1) = y^2 \times 4y - y^2 \times 1 = 4y^3 - y^2$$

c $5h(2h + 7 - g^2) = 5h \times 2h + 5h \times 7 - 5h \times g^2 = 10h^2 + 35h - 5g^2h$

Notice that the letters in $5g^2h$ are written in alphabetical order.

To **multiply out two brackets** each term inside the second bracket must be multiplied by each term inside the first bracket. You can use the word **FOIL** to help you do this.

Example   Multiply out $(a + 3)(a - 4)$.

(1) Multiply the two **F**irst terms together: $\quad (a + 3)(a - 4) \qquad a^2$
(2) Multiply the two **O**utside terms together: $\quad (a + 3)(a - 4) \qquad -4a$
(3) Multiply the two **I**nside terms together: $\quad (a + 3)(a - 4) \qquad 3a$
(4) Multiply the two **L**ast terms together: $\quad (a + 3)(a - 4) \qquad -12$

So $(a + 3)(a - 4) = a^2 - 4a + 3a - 12 = a^2 - a - 12$

To **factorise** you need to insert brackets. To do this you look for common factors.

Example   Factorise   **a** $4w + 20$ **b** $3x^2 - 5x$ **c** $15m + 12m^3$

a   4 and 20 both have a factor of 4.
   $4w + 20 = 4(w + 5)$

b   3 and 5 do not have a common factor. x^2 and x both have a factor x.
   $3x^2 - 5x = x(3x - 5)$

c   15 and 12 both have a factor of 3. m and m^3 both have a factor of m.
   $15m + 12m^3 = 3m(5 + 4m^2)$

Sometimes two brackets are needed.

Example   Factorise   **a** $x^2 + 10x + 21$ **b** $x^2 + 3x - 10$

a $x^2 + 10x + 21$ The brackets will be $(x + ?)(x - ?)$.
The two missing numbers at the ends of the brackets **add** together to give 10 and **multiply** together to give 21. The numbers are 3 and 7.
So $x^2 + 10x + 21 = (x + 3)(x + 7)$

b $x^2 + 3x - 10$ The brackets will be $(x + ?)(x - ?)$.
The negative sign before the 10 means that the two missing numbers at the ends of the brackets **subtract** to give 3. They **multiply** together to give 10. The numbers are 5 and -2.
So $x^2 + 3x - 10 = (x + 5)(x - 2)$

An expression written in the form $x^2 - a^2$ is called the **difference of two squares**.
The difference of two squares can be factorised like this: $x^2 - a^2 = (x + a)(x - a)$
$25a^2 - d^2$ is the difference of two squares since $25a^2 - d^2$ can be written $(5a)^2 - (d)^2$.
So $25a^2 - d^2 = (5a + d)(5a - d)$

1 Simplify these by collecting terms.

   a $2s + 3s + 5s + 7s$ **f** $2ab - 4cd + 3ab - 6cd$

   b $16t + 5t - 3t - 8t$ **g** $4x^2 + 6x^2 - 2x^2$

   c $4a + 12b - 3a - 6b$ **h** $3y^2 + 4y^2 - 2y^2$

   d $2st + 9st$ **i** $6x^2 + 4y^2 - 2x^2 - 3x^2$

   e $4mn + 3mn - nm$ **j** $6cd^2 + 3cd^2 - 5c^2d$

2 Multiply out these brackets.

   a $4(x + 2)$ **d** $-5(3x + 7)$ **g** $y^2(y^2 + 3y - 2)$

   b $3(2x - 1)$ **e** $x(x - 6)$ **h** $ab(a + b)$

   c $4(3x + 5)$ **f** $x^2(x + 9)$ **i** $6cd(c + 2d)$

3 Multiply out these brackets and simplify.

   a $(x + 1)(x + 4)$ **e** $(4x + 3)(x + 8)$ **i** $(7x - 3)(2x - 1)$

   b $(x + 6)(x - 5)$ **f** $(2x + 7)(x - 9)$ **j** $(4x + 5)(2x - 3)$

   c $(x - 5)(x - 9)$ **g** $(3x + 5)(2x + 1)$ **k** $(5x - 1)(6x - 7)$

   d $(x - 7)(x - 8)$ **h** $(2x - 5)(5x - 2)$ **l** $(4x - 11)(3x - 5)$

4 Factorise each of these.

   a $6a + 4$ **e** $3y^3 + y^2 - 2y$ **i** $x^2 - 10x + 21$

   b $18t - 12$ **f** $14y^2 + 2y$ **j** $x^2 + 4x - 45$

   c $ab - a^2$ **g** $x^2 + 11x + 30$ **k** $x^2 - 64$

   d $3cd - 6c^2$ **h** $x^2 + 7x + 12$ **l** $x^2 - 25$

5 A rectangle has a length of $(5x - 2)$ cm.
The breadth of this rectangle is $(3x + 7)$ cm.

   a Find an expression for the perimeter of this rectangle.
      Simplify your answer.

   b Find an expression for the area of this rectangle.

6 A triangle has sides of length $(3x + 4)$ cm, $(2x - 3)$ cm and $(3x + 1)$ cm.

   a Find an expression for the perimeter of this triangle.
      Simplify your answer.

   b The perimeter is 42 cm. Write down an equation in x.
      Solve your equation.

   c Write down the lengths of the three sides of the triangle.

1 Factorise completely.

   a $2ax + 4ay$ **(2 marks)**

   b $x^2 + 5xy + 6y^2$ **(2 marks)**

   a *There are two terms, so we are looking for general factors only. Check terms carefully, since there may be more than one factor. Here there are two factors:* a *and* 2.

     $2ax + 4ay = 2a(x + 2y)$ **1 mark for 2($ax + 2ay$) or a(2$x + 4y$)**
                                              1 mark for correct answer

   b $x^2 + 5xy + 6y^2$ *needs to be put into two brackets,* ( )( ).

     $x^2 + 5xy + 6y^2 = (x + ?y)(x + ?y)$

     The missing numbers must be factor pairs of 6, i.e. 6 and 1 or 3 and 2.

     3 + 2 = 5, so use 3 and 2.

     $x^2 + 5xy + 6y^2 = (x + 2y)(x + 3y)$ **1 mark for each bracket**

2 A shop sells two types of lollipops.
The shop sells big lollipops at 80p each and small lollipops at 60p each.
Henry buys x big lollipops.

   a Write down an expression, in terms of x, for the cost of Henry's lollipops.   **(1 mark)**

Lucy buys r big lollipops and t small lollipops.

   b Write down an expression, in terms of r and t, for the total cost of Lucy's lollipops.   **(1 mark)**

The cost of g big lollipops and 2 small lollipops is £10.80.

   c Write this as an equation in terms of g.   **(2 marks)**

   a *One lollipop costs 80p;* x *lollipops will cost* x × 80p   *80x pence.*
                                                  1 mark

   b *Big lollipops cost 80p, and Lucy has* r *of these, so the cost is* r × 80p *or 80r pence.*
     Small lollipops cost 60p, so t *of these cost* t × 60 *or 60t pence.*
     Add to find the total cost: (80r + 60t) *pence*   **1 mark**

   c g *big lollipops cost* g × 80p *or 80g pence.*
     2 small lollipops cost 2 × 60p = 120 *pence*
     The total cost is (80g + 120) *pence*
     So (80g + 120) *pence* = £10.80   **1 mark**

     You have pence on the left of the equation, pounds on the right.

     You need to write the whole equation in terms of the same units (pence):

     So   80g + 120 = 1080   **1 mark**

  (£10.80 = 1080p)

1 **a** **i** Simplify $x + x + x$

  ii Simplify $2a + 4b + a - 2b$

  iii Expand $3(a + 2)$ **(3 marks)**

b Expand and simplify

  $2(x - 1) + 3(2x + 1)$ **(2 marks)**

c Expand and simplify

  $(x + 3)(2x - 1)$ **(2 marks)**

d Factorise completely

  $6a^3 - 9a^2$ **(2 marks)**

e Evaluate

  5^{-2} **(1 mark)**

  [S2001 P3 Q22]

2 **a** Simplify

  i $\dfrac{p^6}{p^2}$ **ii** $q^3 \times q$ **iii** $(4x^3)^2$ **(3 marks)**

b Factorise completely

  $9x^2y - 6xy^3$ **(2 marks)**

  [S1999 P4 Q17]

3 **a** Factorise

  $2x + 8y$ **(1 mark)**

b Factorise completely

  $3ac^2 - 6ac$ **(2 marks)**

c Factorise

  $x^2 - 9x + 18$ **(2 marks)**

  [N1999 P4 Q18]

4 **a** Expand and simplify

  $4(x + 3) + 3(2x - 3)$ **(2 marks)**

b Expand and simplify

  $(2x - y)(3x + 4y)$ **(3 marks)**

  [N2000 P4 Q16]

5 **a** Expand and simplify

$$(2x + 1)(x - 3)$$ **(2 marks)**

b Factorise completely

$$2t^2 + 4t$$ **(1 mark)**

[N1998 P4 Q18]

6 **a** Simplify

$$x^3 \times x^5$$ **(1 mark)**

b Simplify

$$y^6 \div y^2$$ **(1 mark)**

c Simplify

$$\frac{8w^7}{2w^2 \times w^3}$$ **(2 marks)**

[N2000 P3 Q21]

7 Simplify

   i $a + a + a + a$ **ii** $4b + 2c + 3b - 6c$ **(3 marks)**

[S2000 P4 Q3]

8 This rule is used to work out take home pay.

> take home pay = hours worked $\times$ hourly rate − deductions

Mary's hourly rate was £5.
Her deductions were £7.
Her take home pay was £68.
Work out the number of hours she worked. **(3 marks)**

[S2000 P4 Q4]

9 **a** Expand and simplify

$$(x + 5)(x - 3)$$ **(2 marks)**

b Factorise completely

$$6a^2 - 9ab$$ **(2 marks)**

[S2000 P4 Q20]

16 Statistics: about average

You need to know about:

- the mean, mode and median
- finding the three averages from a frequency table
- estimating the mean for grouped data
- finding the modal group
- estimating the range for grouped data
- moving averages

There are three types of average.

To find the **mean** of a set of data: (1) Find the total of all the data values.
(2) Divide the total by the number of data values.

The **mode** is the most common data value. It is sometimes called the **modal value**.

To find the **median** of a set of data: (1) Put all the data values in order of size.
(2) The median is the middle value. If there are two values in the middle you add them together and divide by 2.

You can find the three averages from a **frequency table**.

Example   The table shows the number of pieces of fruit eaten by each of 30 pupils in a day.

Find: **a**   the mode
b   the mean
c   the median

number of pieces	frequency
0	5
1	10
2	9
3	6

a   The modal number of pieces is the number with the highest frequency. The mode is 1 piece of fruit.

b   Mean $= \dfrac{\text{total number of pieces of fruit}}{\text{total frequency}} = \dfrac{0 \times 5 + 1 \times 10 + 2 \times 9 + 3 \times 6}{5 + 10 + 9 + 6}$

$= \dfrac{46}{30} = 1.53$ pieces of fruit (3 sf)

c   The median is the middle term.
To find the term number that you need: (1) add 1 to the number of terms
(2) divide by 2.

$30 + 1 = 31$ and $31 \div 2 = 15.5$ so here the median is the $15\frac{1}{2}$th value.
Find the 15th value in the table by counting down the frequency column.
$5 + 10 = 15$ so the 15th value is 1 piece of fruit. The 16th value is 2 pieces of fruit.
Median $= (1 + 2) \div 2 = 1.5$ pieces of fruit.

If the data in a frequency table is **grouped** you can only **estimate** the mean.

Example Sam records the time it takes 30 pupils each to eat an apple. The table shows her data.

Time, t (minutes)	frequency
$0 \leqslant t < 3$	2
$3 \leqslant t < 6$	14
$6 \leqslant t < 9$	8
$9 \leqslant t < 12$	6

  a Estimate the mean time.

  b Estimate the range of the data.

  c Write down the modal group.

  d Write down the group that contains the median.

a You use the mid-value of each group to estimate the mean.
The mid-values are $(0 + 3) \div 2, (3 + 6) \div 2$ and so on.

$$\text{Estimate for the mean} = \frac{1.5 \times 2 + 4.5 \times 14 + 7.5 \times 8 + 10.5 \times 6}{30} = 6.3 \text{ minutes}$$

b An estimate for the range is the highest possible value − the lowest possible value
= 12 − 0 = 12 minutes

c The modal group is the group with the highest frequency. This is $3 \leqslant t < 6$.

d The median is the $(30 + 1) \div 2 = 15\frac{1}{2}$th value. This is in the group $3 \leqslant t < 6$.

A **moving average** uses a few data values at a time in order to establish a trend in the data.

For a **4-point moving average**:

  (1) Work out the mean of the first 4 values.

  (2) Remove the first value and use the 5th value to give the next mean.

  (3) Now remove the 2nd value and use the 6th value to find the mean.

  (4) Carry on like this until you run out of data values.

For a 3-point moving average you use 3 data values at a time. You can also use any other number of points.

By plotting the moving average on a graph, a line of best fit can be drawn through these values to show the trend of the data. This line is called a trend line.

The graph shows a company's profits in each quarter of the year over a period of 3 years. A 4-point moving average has been used as there are 4 quarters in each year.
The **first average** is for quarters 1, 2, 3 and 4. This average is plotted between quarters 2 and 3.
The **second average** is for quarters 2, 3, 4 and 1.
It is plotted between quarters 3 and 4.
The trend line shows what is happening to the company's profits.

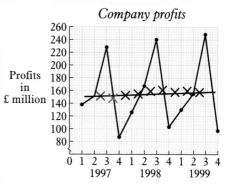

Company profits

1 Rupert is word-processing his mathematics coursework. He records the number of errors he makes on each page. These are the numbers of errors that he recorded.

   29 16 61 24 27 30 26 23 26

   a Write down the modal number of errors.
   b Find the median number of errors.
   c Calculate the mean number of errors to the nearest whole number.
   d Write down the value that best represents this data. Explain your answer.

2 The local hockey team records the number of goals it scores each week. The table shows the results for the 2000 season.

Number of goals	0	1	2	3	4
Frequency	3	4	7	6	5

   a Write down the modal number of goals.
   b Find the median number of goals.
   c Calculate the mean number of goals to the nearest whole number.

3 Josh measures the heights of the children in his swimming class. The table gives his measurements to the nearest centimetre.

Height in cm	101–110	111–120	121–130	131–140	141–150
Number of children	3	2	4	7	2

   a Calculate an estimate for the mean height of Josh's swimming class. Give your answer to the nearest centimetre.
   b Write down the modal group for these heights.

4 The mean of the numbers x, $x + 5$ and $x + 4$ is 12. Find the value of x.

5 Miss Ahmed's class has 33 pupils.

   When this class takes a test Amanda is absent.

   The mean score for the rest of the class is 68.5

   When Amanda takes the test, Miss Ahmed decides not to tell Amanda her result. She tells her that the mean for the whole class is now exactly 69.

   How many marks did Amanda score on the test?

1 The table shows the number of items sold each quarter by a company for the two years 2000 and 2001.

| | Quarter | | | |
Year	1	2	3	4
2000	97	120	122	98
2001	101	124	126	97

The graph shows this information, and the first two 4-point moving averages.

Calculate the three remaining 4-point moving averages and plot them on the graph.   **(3 marks)**

Note that the points are plotted in the middle of each range:

e.g.   *1   2 ▲ 3   4*

plotted at 2.5

The remaining 4-point moving averages are:

$(122 + 98 + 101 + 124) \div 4 = 111.25$
$(98 + 101 + 124 + 126) \div 4 = 112.25$
$(101 + 124 + 126 + 97) \div 4 = 112.0$
▲

It is important to show these calculations.

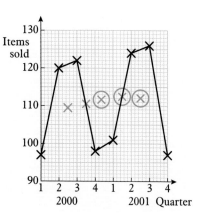

1 mark for method
1 mark for at least two calculations
1 mark if all correct

2 a A class took a test. The mean mark of the 20 boys in the class was 17.4.
The mean mark of the 10 girls in the class was 13.8.
Calculate the mean mark for the whole class.   **(2 marks)**
  b 5 pupils in another class took the test.
Their marks, written in order, were 1, 2, 3, 4 and x.
The mean for these marks is equal to twice the median of the five marks.
Calculate the value of x.   **(3 marks)**

a $\text{Mean} = \dfrac{\text{total marks for class}}{30 \text{ pupils}}$

You first need to find the total marks for the whole class.
The mean boy's mark was 17.4, so the total of the boy's marks is $17.4 \times 20 = 348$.
The mean girl's mark was 13.8, so the total of the girl's marks is $13.8 \times 10 = 138$.
    1 mark

The total for the class (30 pupils) is $348 + 138 = 486$
The mean for the class is $486 \div 30 = 16.2$.   **1 mark**
  b The median mark (the middle one) is 3, so twice the median is 6.   **1 mark**

$\text{Mean} = \dfrac{1 + 2 + 3 + 4 + x}{5} = 6$ **1 mark**

So $1 + 2 + 3 + 4 + x = 6 \times 5$
$10 + x = 30$
$x = 20$ **1 mark**

95

1 The number of goals scored by a netball team in 11 matches were

   15, 12, 17, 9, 12, 23, 16, 14, 12, 13, 16.

   a Find the mode of the number of goals scored. **(1 mark)**

   b Find the median number of goals scored. **(2 marks)**
   [N1999 P3 Q1]

2 The diagram shows a target.

Billy fires at the target ten times.
The frequency table gives information
about his scores.

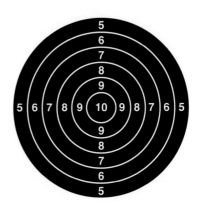

Score	Frequency
5	2
6	1
7	3
8	1
9	2
10	1

   a Work out his total score. **(2 marks)**

The target is a circle.
The diameter of the circle is 50 cm.

   b Work out the area of the circle.
     Give your answer, in cm², correct to 3 significant figures. **(2 marks)**
   [S2000 P4 Q9]

3 20 students took part in a competition.
   The frequency table shows information about the points they scored.

Points scored	1	2	3
Frequency	9	4	7

Work out the total number of points scored by the 20
students. **(2 marks)**
   [N2000 P3 Q10]

4 Some students took a mental arithmetic test.

Information about their marks is shown in the frequency table.

Mark	Frequency
4	2
5	1
6	2
7	4
8	7
9	10
10	3

a Work out how many students took the test.   (1 mark)

b Write down the modal mark.   (1 mark)

24 students had a higher mark than Caroline.

c Work out Caroline's mark.   (1 mark)

d Find the median mark.   (2 marks)

e Work out the range of the marks.   (2 marks)

[N1998 P3 Q6]

5 Sybil weighed some pieces of cheese.

The table gives information about her results.

Weight (w) grams	Frequency
$90 < w \leqslant 94$	1
$94 < w \leqslant 98$	2
$98 < w \leqslant 102$	6
$102 < w \leqslant 106$	1

Work out an estimate of the mean weight.   (4 marks)

[S2000 P3 Q18]

17 Round and round

You need to know about:

- the names of parts of a circle
- finding the circumference
- finding perimeters
- dimensions
- metric and imperial units of length

Circumference

The **circumference** of a circle is the distance around the edge of the circle.

Circumference = $\pi \times$ diameter

This is often written $C = \pi d$

π (said as pie) is a special number.

To find the value of π, key in **π** on your calculator.

You should get 3.141 592 6 ... but the decimal part of π carries on forever.

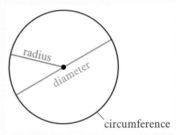

Example

Find the circumference of a circle with radius 8 cm.

Diameter = $2 \times$ radius so $d = 2 \times 8 = 16$ cm

$C = \pi d = \pi \times 16 = 50.3$ cm to 3 sf.

Perimeter

The **perimeter** of a shape is the distance around the edge of the shape.

For a circle the perimeter is the circumference.

Semi-circle

A **semi-circle** is half of a circle.

Quadrant

A **quadrant** is a quarter of a circle.

Example

Find the perimeter of this shape.

The shape is a square and a quadrant.

The blue part of the perimeter is a quarter of the circumference of a circle with radius 5 cm.

The circumference of a circle with radius 5 cm is $\pi \times 10 = 31.415\ 926\ 54 ...$ cm.

Blue perimeter = $31.415\ 926\ 54 ... \div 4 = 7.853\ 981 ...$ cm

Red perimeter = $5 + 5 + 5 + 5 = 20$ cm

Total perimeter = $7.853\ 981 ... + 20 = 27.9$ cm to 3 sf.

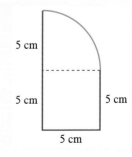

You can give the circumference of a circle in terms of π.

Circumference $= \pi d = \pi \times 8 = 8\pi \text{ cm}$

This has the advantage that the answer is exact as you haven't rounded the answer from a calculator.

8 cm

Dimension	The **dimension** of a formula is the number of lengths that are multiplied together.
Constant	A **constant** has no dimension, it is just a number. 4, 8, 12 and π are all constants.

Length has **one** dimension.

Any formula for length can only have constants and **one** length per term.

Area has **two** dimensions.

Any formula for area can only have constants and **two** lengths multiplied together per term.

Volume has **three** dimensions.

Any formula for volume can only have constants and **three** lengths multiplied together per term.

$C = \pi d$ is a formula for length.

π is a constant.
d is a length.

$A = \pi r^2$ is an area formula.

π is a constant.
$r^2 = r \times r$ which is length $\times$ length.

$V = \pi r^2 h$ is a volume formula.

π is a constant
$r^2 h = r \times r \times h$ which is
length $\times$ length $\times$ length.

Metric units of length	The **metric units of length** are millimetres (mm), centimetres (cm), metres (m) and kilometres (km).

$$1 \text{ cm} = 10 \text{ mm} \quad 1 \text{ m} = 100 \text{ cm} \quad 1 \text{ km} = 1000 \text{ m}$$

Imperial units of length	The **imperial units of length** are inches (in), feet (ft), yards (yd) and miles (m).

$$1 \text{ foot} = 12 \text{ inches} \quad 1 \text{ yard} = 3 \text{ feet} \quad 1 \text{ mile} = 1760 \text{ yards}$$

To **convert between imperial and metric units** you need to know these conversions:

8 km is about 5 miles   1 metre is about 39 inches   2.5 cm is about 1 inch

Example	Change these to the units given.

    a 4.5 m to inches   **b** 126 miles to kilometres

    a 4.5 m is about 4.5×39 inches $= 175.5$ inches.

    b You need to divide by 5 to find the number of groups of 5 miles, then multiply by 8.
        126 miles is about $126 \div 5 \times 8 = 201.6$ km.

1 Change each of these to the units given.
  a 23 cm to mm   **d** 0.76 m to mm   **g** 3 yards 2 feet to feet
  b 0.56 m to cm   **e** 7596 m to km   **h** 6 miles to yards
  c 0.342 km to m   **f** 15 feet to inches   **i** 36 feet to yards

2 **a** The distance from Chester to Southampton is about 200 miles.
  Give this distance in kilometres.
  b Rosalind is 5 feet 6 inches tall. Give her height in metres.

3 In this question a, b and c are lengths.
  Write down the dimensions of each of these expressions.
  a b **c** abc **e** $ab + bc$ **g** a^2b
  b $3ab$ **d** $2a + 3b$ **f** $b^2 + c^2$ **h** πabc

4 **a** A circle has a radius of 4.5 cm. Find the circumference of the circle.
  Give your answer to 1 dp.
  b A circle has a circumference of 178 cm. Find the diameter of the circle.
  Give your answer to 3 sf.
  c Find the exact perimeter of a circle with a radius of 9 cm.

5 Katie is making a lampshade. The top of the
lampshade is a circle of radius 8 cm.
The bottom of the lampshade is a circle of radius
21 cm.
She attaches a frill around the two circular edges.
  a Calculate the total length of frill that she needs
  to buy.
  b The frill is sold in metre lengths only. The cost
  of 1 m is £3.72. Calculate the cost of the frill.

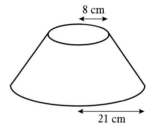

6 Find the exact perimeter of each of these shapes.

  a
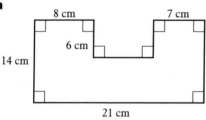

  c
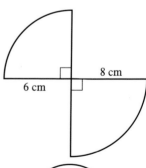

  b
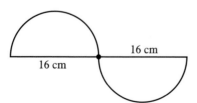

  d
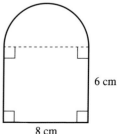

These questions would appear on a non-calculator paper.

1

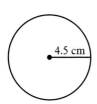

This circle has a radius of 4.5 cm.

a Find the length of the circumference of the circle.
   Give your answer as a multiple of π. **(2 marks)**

b Write your answer to part **a** in millimetres. **(1 mark)**

a Circumference = $\pi \times$ diameter   *You are expected to remember this formula.*
   diameter = $2 \times$ radius = 2×4.5
   So C = $\pi \times 2 \times 4.5$ ◄───── **1 mark**
                                     You have to do the calculation 2×4.5.
   C = 9π centimetres **1 mark**
                          Leave as a multiple of π.

b 10 mm = 1 cm   *You are expected to remember this.*
   so 9π becomes $9\pi \times 10 = 90\pi$ millimetres **1 mark**

2 Chris is 12 cm taller than Steve.
   Their heights add up to 307 cm.

a How tall is Steve in centimetres? **(2 marks)**

b How tall is Steve in inches? **(2 marks)**

Sarah is 123 cm tall.

c Estimate Sarah's height in feet.
   Give your answer to the nearest foot. **(2 marks)**

a $307 - 12 = 295$ cm **1 mark**
   295 cm $\div 2 = 147.5$ cm **1 mark**

b 1 inch is about 2.5 cm, or 2 inches is about 5 cm. **1 mark**

   $\dfrac{29.5}{5)147.5}$ So Steve is $29.5 \times 2 = 59$ inches tall. **1 mark**

c 1 foot is about 30 cm. **1 mark**
   123 cm is nearly 120 cm and $4 \times 30 = 120$
   so Sarah's height is about 4 feet. **1 mark**

1 A circle has a radius of 32 cm.

Work out the circumference of the circle.
Give your answer correct to the nearest centimetre. **(2 marks)**
[N2000 P4 Q12]

2

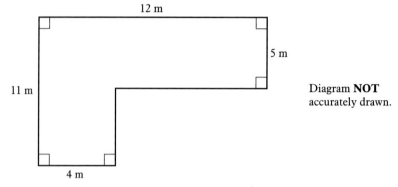

12 m

5 m

11 m

Diagram **NOT**
accurately drawn.

4 m

This diagram shows the plan of a floor.
Work out the perimeter of the floor. **(2 marks)**
[S2001 P3 Q11]

3 Here are some expressions.

$\pi r^2 l$	$2\pi r^2$	$4\pi r^3$	$abrl$	$\dfrac{abl}{r}$	$3(a^2 + b^2)r$	πrl

The letters r, l, a and b represent lengths. π, 2, 3 and 4 are numbers that have no dimensions.
Three of the expressions represent volumes.
Tick the boxes (✓) underneath these three expressions. **(3 marks)**
[S1998 P3 Q16]

4 Here are 3 expressions.

Expression	Length	Area	Volume	None of these
$3rl$				
$\dfrac{2(r + l)^2}{h}$				
$\dfrac{4\pi r^4}{3l}$				

r, l and h are lengths.
π, 2, 3 and 4 are numbers and have no dimension.

Put a tick in the correct column to show whether the expression can be used for length, area, volume or none of these. **(3 marks)**
[S2000 P3 Q26]

5 There are 27 wall tiles in a pack.
Only full packs of tiles are sold.

Barry needs 200 tiles.

a How many full packs of tiles
must he buy?   (**2 marks**)

Each tile is a rectangle 20 cm by 15 cm.

b Work out the area of one
tile.   (**1 mark**)

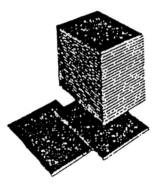

Navdeep wants to tile a wall.
The wall is a rectangle 3 metres by 2.4 metres.

c Work out the number of tiles she needs to cover the wall
completely.

(**3 marks**)
[S 2000 P4 Q1]

6

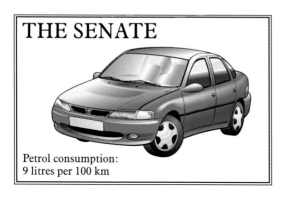

THE SENATE

Petrol consumption:
9 litres per 100 km

1 km = $\frac{5}{8}$ mile.   1 gallon = 4.54 litre.

Change 9 litres per 100 km into miles per gallon.   (**4 marks**)
[N1998 P4 Q13]

18 Pythagoras' theorem

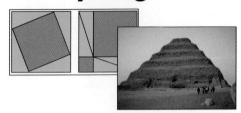

You need to know about:

- using Pythagoras' theorem
- Pythagorean triples
- finding the distance between two points
- the angle in a semi-circle

| **Pythagoras' theorem** | Pythagoras' theorem says that, in any right-angled triangle, the area of the square on the hypotenuse is equal to the sum of the areas of the squares on the other two sides. |

Example

Find the unknown blue area in this diagram.

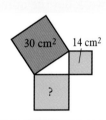

The red area is the sum of the two blue areas, so

blue area = 30 − 14
$$= 16 \text{ cm}^2$$

Example

Find the length of the hypotenuse of this triangle.

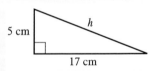

Start by saying that you are using the theorem: Using Pythagoras' theorem
Put the lengths into the formula: $h^2 = 5^2 + 17^2$
Work out the squares: $= 25 + 289$
Add the two numbers: $= 314$
Now take the square root: $h = 17.7 \text{ cm to 1 dp}$

Example

Find the length of the missing side in this triangle.

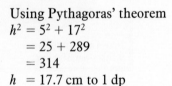

Start by saying that you are using the theorem: Using Pythagoras' theorem
Put the lengths into the formula: $14^2 = x^2 + 12^2$
Work out the squares: $196 = x^2 + 144$
Find x^2: $196 - 144 = x^2$
   $x^2 = 52$
Now take the square root: $x = 7.21 \text{ cm to 2 dp}$

Pythagorean triple	When three whole numbers work in Pythagoras' theorem, the set of three numbers is called a **Pythagorean triple**.	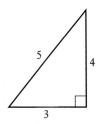

3, 4 and 5 is a Pythagorean triple.

So are these:

5, 12 and 13   8, 15 and 17   7, 24 and 25

Using square roots

Example   Find the exact length of the hypotenuse of this triangle.

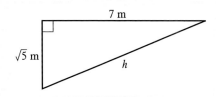

Leave your answer as a square root if you are asked for an **exact** answer or if you are not allowed to use a calculator.

Using Pythagoras' theorem
$$h^2 = (\sqrt{5})^2 + 7^2$$
$$= 5 + 49$$
$$= 54$$
$$h = \sqrt{54}\text{ m}$$

You can use Pythagoras' theorem to find the **distance between two points** given their co-ordinates.

Example   Find the distance between A(**1**, **5**) and B(**6**, **2**)

By Pythagoras' theorem
$$(AB)^2 = 3^2 + 5^2$$
$$= 9 + 25$$
$$= 34$$
$$AB = 5.83 \text{ units to 3 sf}$$

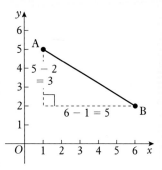

Angle in a semi-circle	The **angle in a semi-circle** is the angle made by joining both ends of a diameter of a circle to a point on the circumference. The **angle in a semi-circle** is 90°.	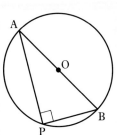

AB is the diameter of the circle with centre O.
The angle APB is 90°.
This means that you can use Pythagoras' theorem in triangle APB.

1   Find the length of the missing side in each of these triangles.
    Give your answers to 1 dp.

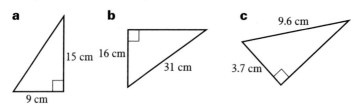

a   **b**   **c**   9.6 cm

15 cm   16 cm
                31 cm   3.7 cm

9 cm

2   Find the lengths of the sides marked with letters. Give exact answers.

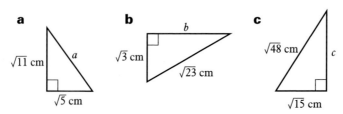

a   **b** b **c**

$\sqrt{11}$ cm a $\sqrt{3}$ cm $\sqrt{48}$ cm c
                    $\sqrt{23}$ cm
$\sqrt{5}$ cm $\sqrt{15}$ cm

3   Find the distance between the two points A(3, 5) and B(7, 8).

4   Find the length marked with a letter in each of these. Give your answers to 1 dp.

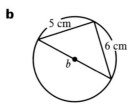

a   **b**
   12 cm a 5 cm
                                  6 cm
      16 cm b

5   Find the height of an equilateral triangle of side 20 cm. Give your answer to 1 dp.

6   Use Pythagoras' theorem to find the value of x.

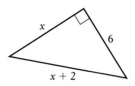

x 6

$x + 2$

7   A boat sails 5 nautical miles due north from a port P. It then sails 7 nautical miles
    due west. How far is the boat from its starting point?

8   Raana is at the top of a waterchute.
    The height of the chute is 10 m.
    The horizontal distance across the
    bottom of the chute is 15 m.
    How far does Raana slide down the chute?

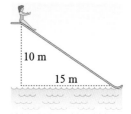

10 m

15 m

Question **1** would appear on a non-calculator paper.

1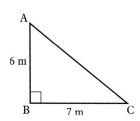

Find the length AC. **(3 marks)**

Use Pythagoras:

$$AC^2 = AB^2 + BC^2$$
$$AC^2 = 6^2 + 7^2$$ **1 mark:** *Pythagoras stated, numbers substituted.*
$$AC^2 = 36 + 49$$ **1 mark:** *Squares worked out.*
$$AC^2 = 85$$ *It is not enough to leave the answer as for AC^2.*
so $\quad AC = \sqrt{85}$ cm **1 mark**

*Since you do not have a calculator, leave the answer as a square root. Do **not** attempt to estimate the square root ($\sqrt{85}$) unless you are told to do so.*

2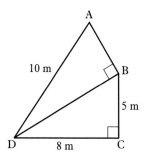

Find length AB.
Give your answer correct to
3 significant figures.

(5 marks)

You will need to find length DB first, using the lower triangle.

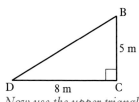

$$DB = \sqrt{8^2 + 5^2}$$
$$= \sqrt{64 + 25}$$ *It is important that you*
$$= \sqrt{89}$$ **1 mark** *keep the **accurate** value*
$$DB = \sqrt{89}$$ *of $\sqrt{89}$. Do **not** round off*
$$= 9.433\,98 \text{ m}$$ **1 mark** *at this stage.*

Now use the upper triangle.

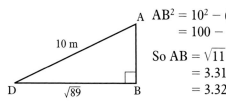

$$AB^2 = 10^2 - (\sqrt{89})^2$$ **1 mark** *You will only get an*
$$= 100 - 89$$ *accurate answer if you use*
an accurate equivalent for
So $AB = \sqrt{11}$ **1 mark** *$\sqrt{89}$ such as 9.43398.*
$$= 3.3166$$ *A rounded number (e.g.*
$$= 3.32 \text{ (to 3 sf) m}$$ **1 mark** *9.43) would give you an*
inaccurate answer.

107

1

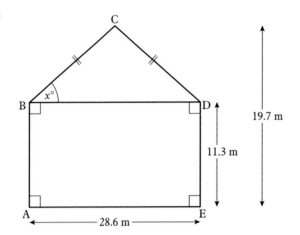

Diagram **NOT** accurately drawn.

The diagram represents the frame for part of a building.

BC and CD are equal in length.
BD and AE are horizontal.

a Write down the special mathematical name for the triangle BCD. **(1 mark)**

b Work out the area of triangle BCD. **(2 marks)**

c Calculate the length BC.
Give your answer correct to 3 significant figures. **(3 marks)**

d Calculate the size of the angle marked $x°$.
Give your answer correct to 1 decimal place. **(3 marks)**

[N1998 P4 Q16]

2

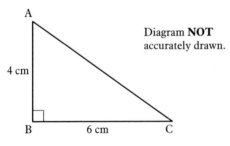

Diagram **NOT** accurately drawn.

ABC is a right-angled triangle.

AB = 4 cm,   BC = 6 cm.

Calculate the length of AC.
Give your answer in centimetres, correct to 3 significant figures. **(3 marks)**

[S2001 P4 Q16]

3

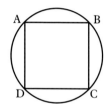

Diagram **NOT** accurately drawn.

A, B, C and D are four points on the circumference of a circle.
ABCD is a square with sides 20 cm long.

Work out the diameter of the circle.
Give your answer correct to 3 significant figures. **(4 marks)**

[N1998 P3 Q16]

4

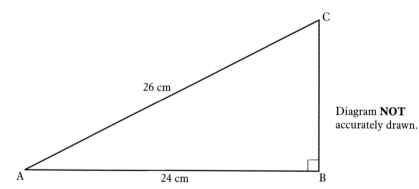

Diagram **NOT** accurately drawn.

In the diagram, triangle ABC is right-angled at B.
AB = 24 cm and AC = 26 cm.

Calculate the length of BC. **(3 marks)**

[N1995 P3 Q18]

5

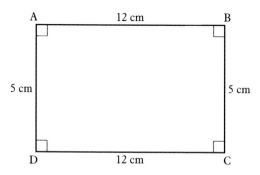

Diagram **NOT** accurately drawn.

Calculate the length of the diagonal AC of the rectangle ABCD which
has length 12 centimetres and width 5 centimetres. **(4 marks)**

[N1996 P3 Q17]

19 The power of graphs

You need to know about:

- graphs of straight lines
- quadratic graphs
- cubic graphs
- graphs involving $\dfrac{1}{x}$

The equation of a **straight line** can be written as
$y = mx + c$.
m is the gradient of the line.
c is called the y intercept. It is the point where the
line crosses the y axis.

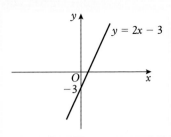

The equation of this straight line is $y = 2x - 3$
The gradient of the line is 2.
The line crosses the y axis at -3.

If the number in front of the x term is negative the line
slopes downwards.

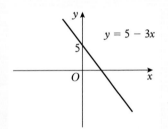

The equation of this line is $y = 5 - 3x$.
The gradient of the line is -3.
The line crosses the y axis at 5.

Quadratic

A **quadratic** equation or formula has an x^2 term in it. It can also
have x and number terms in it. It cannot have other powers of x,
such as x^3 or $\dfrac{1}{x}$. Graphs of quadratic equations are curves.

To draw the graph of $y = x^2 + 2x - 3$ you can
draw a table like this.

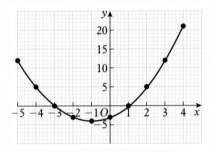

x	-5	-4	-3	-2	-1	0	1	2	3	4
x^2	25	16	9	4	1	0	1	4	9	16
$+2x$	-10	-8	-6	-4	-2	0	2	4	6	8
-3	-3	-3	-3	-3	-3	-3	-3	-3	-3	-3
y	12	5	0	-3	-4	-3	0	5	12	21

Plot the points $(-5, 12)$, $(-4, 5)$ and so on. Join the points with a smooth curve.

If the x^2 term in a quadratic is negative, the graph is turned upside down.
This is the graph of $y = 4 - x^2$

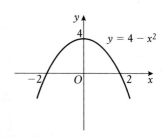

To find the values of x where the curve cuts the x axis put $y = 0$ in $y = 4 - x^2$:

$0 = 4 - x^2$

$x^2 = 4$ so $x = 2$ or -2

The two points are $(2, 0)$ and $(-2, 0)$.

Cubic

A **cubic** equation or formula has an x^3 in it. It can also have x^2, x and number terms.

It cannot have other powers of x, such as x^4, $\frac{1}{x}$ or $\frac{1}{x^2}$.

The graph of a cubic equation is also a curve but is different from a quadratic.
A cubic equation must look like one of these.

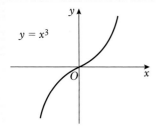

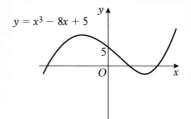

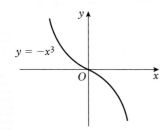

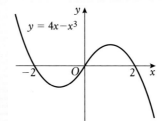

You also need to recognise the curve $y = \frac{1}{x}$.
This is called a **reciprocal graph**.
These are the values of y for positive values of x.

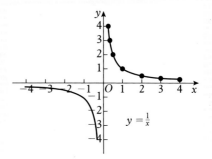

x	$\frac{1}{4}$	$\frac{1}{3}$	$\frac{1}{2}$	$\frac{2}{3}$	$\frac{3}{4}$	1	2	3	4
y	4	3	2	$\frac{3}{2}$	$\frac{4}{3}$	1	$\frac{1}{2}$	$\frac{1}{3}$	$\frac{1}{4}$

For negative values of x the values of y are the same but have a negative sign.
There is **no value of y for $x = 0$** since $1 \div 0$ is impossible.
The curve has two parts which do not meet.

1 For each of these equations:

    i Draw a suitable table and fill in the values for x and y.

    ii Draw a set of axes that fits the values in your table.

    iii Draw the graph of the equation.

    a $y = 3x + 1$ **b** $y = \frac{1}{2}x + 4$ **c** $y = 2x - 4$

2 **a** Copy and complete this table for $y = 2x^2 + x - 5$.

    b Draw axes with x from -3 to 3 and y from -5 to 20.

    c Draw the graph of $y = 2x^2 + x - 5$.

    d Use your graph to write down the equation of the line of symmetry.

x	-3	-2	-1	0	1	2	3
$+2x^2$						8	
$+x$						2	
-5						-5	
y	10					5	

3 **a** Copy and complete this table for $y = -x^3 + 2x + 6$.

    b Draw axes with x from -2 to 3 and y from -15 to 10.

    c Draw the graph of $y = -x^3 + 2x + 6$.

x	-2	-1	0	1	2	3
$-x^3$	8			-1		
$+2x$	-4			$+2$		
$+6$	$+6$			$+6$		
y	10			$+7$		

4 Match each of these equations with its graph.

    a $y = 3x + 1$ **c** $y = x^2 + 4x + 2$ **e** $y = -\frac{1}{x}$

    b $y = x^3 + 1$ **d** $y = -2x + 1$ **f** $y = -2x^2 + 5x - 7$

(1)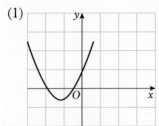

(3)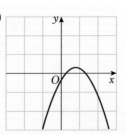

(5)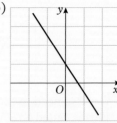

(2)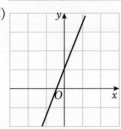

(4)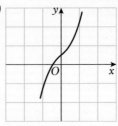

(6)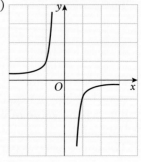

1 **a** Draw a table of values for the graphs $y = x^3 - 4x$ and $y = \dfrac{1}{x}$ for $-3 \leqslant x \leqslant 3$. **(3 marks)**

   b Draw the graphs of $y = x^3 - 4x$, and $y = \dfrac{1}{x}$ for $-3 \leqslant x \leqslant 3$. **(3 marks)**

a

x	-3	-2	-1	0	1	2	3
x^3	-27	-8	-1	0	1	8	27
$-4x$	12	8	4	0	-4	-8	-12
y	-15	0	3	0	-3	0	15

2 marks

x	-3	-2	-1	-0.5	-0.1	0	0.1	0.5	1	2	3
$y = \frac{1}{x}$	-0.33	-0.5	-1	-2	-10	$-$	10	2	1	0.5	0.33

1 mark

b

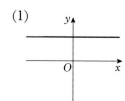

1 mark for points
1 mark for smooth curve.

You will need to round off the decimals since you can only plot to a certain degree of accuracy.

1 mark for both parts drawn.

2 The diagrams are sketches of six graphs.

(1)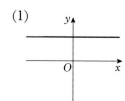

(2)

(3)

(4)

(5)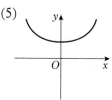

(6)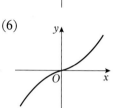

Three of the sketches are graphs of these functions:
a $y = -x^2 + 2$ **b** $y = 2$ **c** $y = x^3$

Write down the number of the graph for each function. **(3 marks)**

a (2): $-x^2$ *means an 'upside down' parabola.*   **1 mark**
b (1): *A horizontal straight line crossing the y axis at 2.*   **1 mark**
c (6): *This graph has the shape of a cubic graph.*   **1 mark**

1 a Complete the table of
values for $y = 2x^2$

x	-3	-2	-1	0	1	2	3
y	18				2	8	

(2 marks)

b On the grid draw the graph of $y = 2x^2$

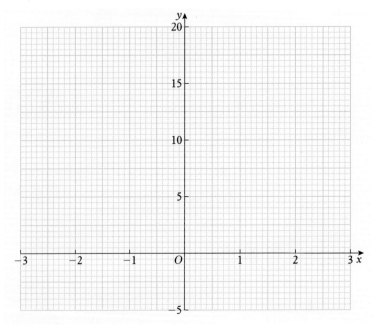

(2 marks)

c Use your graph to find
i   the value of y when $x = 2.5$,
ii the values of x when $y = 12$.

(2 marks)
[S2001 P3 Q18]

2

A

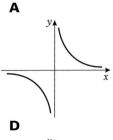

B

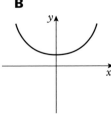

C

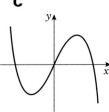

D

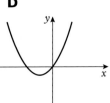

E

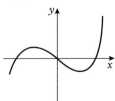

F

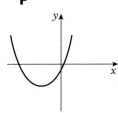

Each of the equations in the table represents one of the graphs **A** to **F**.
Write the letter of each graph in the correct place in the table.

Equation	Graph
$y = x^2 + 3x$	
$y = x - x^3$	
$y = x^3 - 2x$	
$y = x^2 + 2x - 4$	
$y = \dfrac{4}{x}$	
$y = x^2 + 3$	

(3 marks)
[N1998 P4 Q17]

3 **a** Complete the table of values for $y = x + \dfrac{1}{x}$

x	0.2	0.4	0.6	0.8	1	2	4	5
y	5.2				2		4.25	5.2

(2 marks)

b On the grid draw the graph of $y = x + \dfrac{1}{x}$

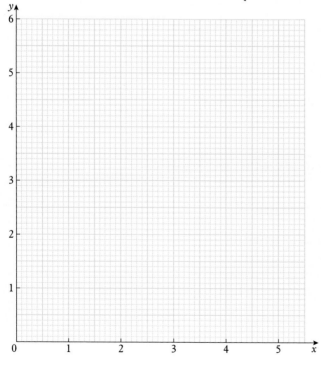

(2 marks)

c Use your graph to find estimates for the solutions of the equation

$$x + \frac{1}{x} = 5$$

(2 marks)
[N2001 P4 Q21]

20 Simultaneous equations

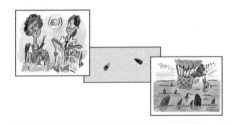

You need to know about:

- using graphs to solve simultaneous equations
- using algebra to solve simultaneous equations
- changing the subject of a formula

| **Simultaneous equations** | When you solve two equations at the same time you are solving **simultaneous equations**. |

Example

Solve the following simultaneous equations by drawing graphs.

$$y = 2x - 2$$
$$y = x + 1$$

Draw the graphs of $y = 2x - 2$ and $y = x + 1$.

The co-ordinates of the point of intersection of the two line give the solution to the simultaneous equations.
The solution is $x = 3, y = 4$.

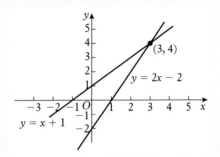

You can also solve simultaneous equations **using algebra**.

Example Solve this pair of simultaneous equations:

$$5a + 2b = 4$$
$$2a - b = 7$$

Number the equations

$$(1) \quad 5a + 2b = 4$$
$$(2) \quad 2a - b = 7$$

To get rid of the b terms you need to multiply (2) by 2 so that you have $2b$ in each equation.
Add to get rid of b, then find a.

$$(1) \quad\quad 5a + 2b = 4$$
$$(2) \times 2 \quad 4a - 2b = 14$$
$$\text{Adding} \quad\quad 9a = 18$$
$$a = 2$$

Use equation (1) to find b.

Put $a = 2$ in equation (1):
$$5 \times 2 + 2b = 4$$
$$2b = -6$$
$$b = -3$$
The answer is $a = 2, b = -3$.

Use equation (2) to check your answer.
$$2a - b = 4 - (-3) = 7 \checkmark$$

You can also use **substitution** to solve simultaneous equations.

Example   Solve this pair of simultaneous equations:

(1) $\qquad y = 8x - 1$
(2) $\quad 10x - 3y = -4$

Use equation (1) to substitute for y
in equation (2).
Then solve the equation.

$$10x - 3(8x - 1) = -4$$
$$10x - 24x + 3 = -4$$
$$-14x + 3 = -4$$
$$-14x = -7$$
$$x = \tfrac{1}{2}$$

Put the value of x in equation (1) to find y.

$$y = 8 \times \tfrac{1}{2} - 1$$
$$= 3$$

The solution is $x = \tfrac{1}{2}, y = 3$.

Use equation (2) to check your answer.
$$10x - 3y = 10 \times \tfrac{1}{2} - 3 \times 3$$
$$= 5 - 9 = -4 \checkmark$$

Changing the subject of a formula uses the same skills as solving an equation. Instead of getting a number as an answer you are trying to get a different letter on its own.

Example   Make ℓ the subject of the formula $T = 2\pi \sqrt{\dfrac{\ell}{g}}$.

The order of operations starting with ℓ are: divide by g, square root, multiply by 2π.

You need to reverse these in the opposite order: divide by 2π, square, multiply by g.

Divide both sides by 2π:

$$\frac{T}{2\pi} = \sqrt{\frac{\ell}{g}}$$

Square both sides:

$$\left(\frac{T}{2\pi}\right)^2 = \frac{\ell}{g}$$

Multiply both sides by g:

$$g\left(\frac{T}{2\pi}\right)^2 = \ell$$

Change sides so that ℓ is on the left:

$$\ell = g\left(\frac{T}{2\pi}\right)^2$$

1 a Draw a set of axes on squared paper.
Use values of x from -3 to 1 and values of y from -3 to 9.

b Draw the graph of $y = 3x + 6$.

c Draw the graph of $y = -x - 2$.

d Use your graphs to solve the simultaneous equations $y = 3x + 6$ and $y = -x - 2$.

2 Solve each pair of simultaneous equations.

a $3x + y = 13$
$2x - y = 2$

b $5x + 2y = -1$
$3x - y = -5$

c $5p + 4q = 22$
$p - 2q = 3$

d $6c - 2d = -9$
$5c - 4d = -4$

3 Louise buys 3 pencils and 4 biros for £7.60
Gemma buys the same pencils and the same biros but she buys 2 pencils and 3 biros for £5.60
By solving two simultaneous equations, find the cost of 1 pencil and the cost of 1 biro.

4 Make the red letter the subject of these formulas.

a $x = 4y + z$

b $t = \dfrac{5s}{6} + 8$

c $a(b^2 + c) = d$

d $de = \dfrac{ab + 2}{c}$

e $m = \sqrt{3p + r}$

f $s = \sqrt{vw + x}$

5 William is using the formula $b = \dfrac{2a - 4c^2}{3}$.

a Use the formula to find the value of b when $a = 5$ and $c = 2$.

b Rearrange the formula to make a the subject.

c Find the value of a when $b = 5$ and $c = 3$.

6 Solve these pairs of simultaneous equations by substitution.

a $3x + 2y = 13$
$y = x - 1$

b $4x - y = 13$
$y + 8 = 2x$

1

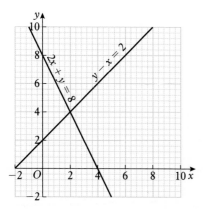

Use the graph to solve these simultaneous equations:

$$2x + y = 8$$
$$y - x = 2$$

(2 marks)

There is no need to solve the equations algebraically.
The solution is given by the point of intersection of the two graphs.

The point of intersection is at $(2, 4)$ so the solution is $x = 2, y = 4$.

1 mark for x, 1 mark for y

*Make sure you clearly write out the two solutions: **do not** leave the answer as a pair of co-ordinates.*

2   Solve these equations:

$$4x + 2y = 8 \quad (1)$$
$$2x - 5y = 10 \quad (2)$$

(4 marks)

In order to get the same number of xs in both equations it is only
necessary to multiply one of the equations throughout.

(1)	$4x + 2y = 8$	*Remember to multiply **both** sides of the*
(2) $\times 2$	$4x - 10y = 20$	*equation by the same number.*
Now subtract	$12y = -12$	$2y - (-10y) = 2y + 10y$ **1 mark**
So	$y = -1$	**1 mark**

Substitute $y = -1$ into equation (1):

$$4x + 2y = 8 \qquad \textit{Write out the equation you use.}$$

Put $y = -1$ $4x - 2 = 8$ **1 mark**

$$4x = 10$$
$$x = \tfrac{10}{4} = 2\tfrac{1}{2}$$

So $x = 2\tfrac{1}{2}$ and $y = -1$ **1 mark**

You can normally expect the solutions to simultaneous questions to be either a fraction or a negative number
in your GCSE exams.

1

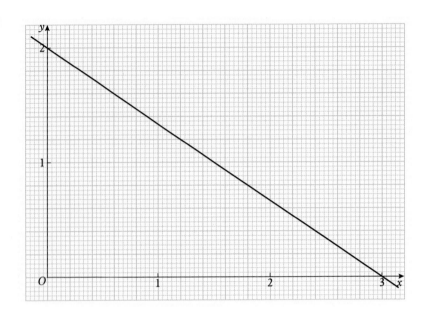

The line with equation $3y = -2x + 6$ has been drawn on the grid.

a Draw the graph of $y = 2x - 2$ on the same grid. **(2 marks)**

b Use the graphs to find the solution of the simultaneous equations

$$3y = -2x + 6$$
$$y = 2x - 2$$ **(2 marks)**

A line is drawn parallel to $3y = -2x + 6$ through the point $(2, 1)$.

c Find the equation of this line. **(2 marks)**

[S1998 P4 Q11]

2 Solve the simultaneous equations

$$4x + y = 4$$
$$2x + 3y = -3$$ **(4 marks)**

[S2001 P4 Q20]

3 Solve the simultaneous equations

$$2x + 5y = -1$$
$$6x - y = 5$$ **(4 marks)**

[N2000 P4 Q21]

4 Solve the simultaneous equations

$$2x + 6y = 17$$
$$3x - 2y = 20$$ **(4 marks)**

[S1999 P3 Q14]

5 The cost, C pounds, of a coat rack with h hooks can be worked out using the formula

$$C = 3h + 7.$$

a Work out the cost of a coat rack with four hooks. **(2 marks)**

Another coat rack costs £43.

b Use the same formula to work out the number of hooks this coat rack has. **(3 marks)**

c Make h the subject of the formula

$$C = 3h + 7.$$ **(2 marks)**

[N1999 P3 Q9]

6 **a** Solve $4x - 3 = 6$ **(2 marks)**

b Make t the subject of the formula

$$v = u + 10t$$ **(2 marks)**

[N2000 P3 Q19]

7

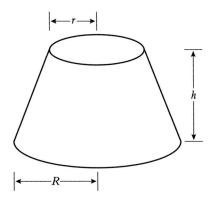

The diagram shows a solid.
The volume, V, of the solid is given by the formula

$$V = \frac{\pi h}{3}(R^2 + Rr + r^2)$$

a $h = 6.8, R = 9.7$ and $r = 5.3$

Calculate the value of V.
Give your answer correct to 3 significant figures. **(3 marks)**

b Make h the subject of the formula. **(2 marks)**

[N1998 P3 Q20]

21 Probability

You need to know about:

- sample space diagrams
- the expected number
- independent events
- mutually exclusive events

| **Sample space diagram** | A **sample space diagram** shows all the things that can happen in a probability experiment. |

Expected number = number of trials × probability

Example

a Draw a sample space diagram to show all the possible outcomes when tossing a coin and throwing a dice.
b Write down the probability of getting a head and a 6.
c The coin and dice are used 100 times.
 How many times would you **expect** to get a head and a 6?

a

		Dice					
		1	2	3	4	5	6
Coin	Head	H1	H2	H3	H4	H5	H6
	Tail	T1	T2	T3	T4	T5	T6

b $P(\text{head and } 6) = \dfrac{\text{number of outcomes of H6}}{\text{total number of outcomes}} = \dfrac{1}{12}$

c Expected number = number of trials × probability
 $= 100 \times \frac{1}{12} = 8.333\,333\,3 \ldots$

The expected number is 8 times.

| **Independent** | Two events are **independent** if the outcome of one has no effect on the outcome of the other. |

If you throw a dice and toss a coin you can get 1, 2, 3, 4, 5 or 6 on the dice and either a head or a tail with the coin.
Whatever you get on the dice has no effect on what you get with the coin.
The two events are independent.

| **Probability of independent events** | If two events A and B are **independent** then the **probability** of them both happening is called $P(\text{A and B})$.
Also $P(\text{A and B}) = P(\text{A}) \times P(\text{B})$. You **multiply** the probabilities. |

Example

Louise has to go through two sets of traffic lights on her way to work.
The probability that she has to stop at the first set is 0.4
The probability that she has to stop at the second set is 0.65
The two events are independent.
Find the probability that Louise has to stop at both sets of lights.

$$P(\text{stops at both}) = P(\text{stops at 1st set}) \times P(\text{stops at 2nd set})$$
$$= 0.4 \times 0.65$$
$$= 0.26$$

You can use independent events to find the probability of **an event happening more than once**.

Example

A dice is thrown four times. Find the probability of getting a 6 on:

a   the first throw   **b**   the first 2 throws   **c**   on all 4 throws

a $P(6 \text{ on 1st throw}) = \frac{1}{6}$

b $P(6 \text{ on 1st throw and 6 on 2nd throw}) = \frac{1}{6} \times \frac{1}{6} = \frac{1}{36}$

c $P(6 \text{ on all 4 throws}) = \frac{1}{6} \times \frac{1}{6} \times \frac{1}{6} \times \frac{1}{6} = \frac{1}{1296}$

Mutually exclusive

Events are **mutually exclusive** if they cannot happen at the same time.
When a dice is thrown it cannot show both a 5 and an even number.
This is because 5 is not an even number.
So getting a 5 and getting an even number are mutually exclusive.

Probability of mutually exclusive events

For two **mutually exclusive events** A and B, the **probability** that **either** event A or event B will occur can be found by **adding** their probabilities together.

$P(A \text{ or } B) = P(A) + P(B)$ You **add** the probabilities.

For a dice, $P(\text{getting a 5}) = \frac{1}{6}$ and $P(\text{getting an even number}) = \frac{1}{2}$.

So $P(\text{getting a 5 or an even number}) = \frac{1}{2} + \frac{1}{6} = \frac{2}{3}$

1 Two fair dice are rolled together.

   a Draw a sample space diagram to show all the possible scores.

   b Find the probability of scoring a total of 5.

   c Find the probability of getting a double.

   d Find the probability of scoring a total of 5 or getting a double.

2 The diagram shows two spinners.

 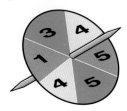

   Both spinners are spun.
   The scores on each spinner are added to give the total score.

   a Copy and complete this sample space diagram to show all the possible scores.

	1	3	4	4	5	5
1						
2						
3						
4						

   Find the probability that the score is:

   b 8   **c** 9   **d** at least 8

3 The probability that Jahangir plays golf on a Sunday is 0.75
A school term has 16 Sundays.
In this school term, how many Sundays would you expect Jahangir to play golf?

4 John and Paul have lunch at school. The probability that John has chips for
lunch is 0.71
The probability that Paul has a diet cola is 0.6. The two events are independent.
Find the probability that John has chips for lunch and Paul has a diet cola.

5 In his CD rack, Geoff has 12 classical CDs, 7 jazz CDs and 11 pop CDs.
Geoff chooses a CD at random.
Find the probability that Geoff chooses:

   a a classical CD   **c** a jazz or pop CD

   b a pop CD   **d** a classical or pop CD

1 This spinner is to be spun.

Write down the probability of getting

a a 3 on the first throw (1 mark)

b a 3 on the first two throws (1 mark)

c a 3 on the first five throws (1 mark)

a $\frac{1}{5}$ **1 mark**

b $\frac{1}{5} \times \frac{1}{5} = \frac{1}{25}$ **1 mark**

c $\frac{1}{5} \times \frac{1}{5} \times \frac{1}{5} \times \frac{1}{5} \times \frac{1}{5} = \frac{1}{3125}$ **1 mark**

2 In a game at a fair two spinners are spun together.
Each spinner is numbered 1 to 5 and each number is equally likely to occur. The game score is the sum of the two numbers shown on the spinners.

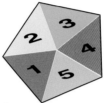 

a Complete the following table to show the possible outcomes of one throw. (2 marks)

Spinner 1

		1	2	3	4	5
	1	2	3	4	5	6
	2	3	4	5	6	7
Spinner 2	3	4	5	6	7	8
	4	5	6	7	8	9
	5	6	7	8	9	10

b What is the probability of scoring a 2 or a 3 in one turn? (2 marks)
c What is the probability of scoring 8 or more in one turn? (2 marks)
d In 200 turns, how many scores will be 8 or more? (2 marks)

a Table complete as shown in **red** above.   **1 mark: first eight correct,**
                                                 1 mark: all correct

b *There is one 2 and two 3s: 1 + 2 = 3,*
     The probability is $\frac{3}{25}$ **1 mark for 3 or 25, 1 mark if all correct**
                                  Total number of outcomes.

c There are six scores of 8 or more: $\frac{6}{25}$ **1 mark for 6 or 25,**
                                                        1 mark if all correct

d $200 \times \frac{6}{25} = 48$ *The answer is a number (as a quantity) and not a probability.*
    1 mark   **1 mark**

1 A game is played with two spinners.
  You multiply the two numbers on which the spinners land to get the score.

  Spinner A   Spinner B

  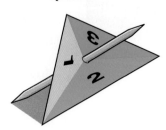   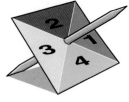

  This score is $1 \times 3 = 3$

  a Complete the table to show
    all the possible scores.
    One score has been done
    for you.

  Spinner B

×	1	2	3	4
1				
2				8
3				

  Spinner A

  b Work out the probability of getting a score of 6.   **(2 marks)**
  c Work out the probability of getting a score that is an odd number.   **(2 marks)**
                                                           [S2001 P3 Q4]

2 Tony carries out a survey about the words in a book.
  He chooses a page at random.
  He then counts the number of letters in each of the first hundred words on the page.
  The table shows Tony's results.

Number of letters in a word	1	2	3	4	5	6	7	8
Frequency	6	9	31	24	16	9	4	1

  A word is chosen at random from the hundred words.
  a What is the probability that the word will have 5 letters?   **(2 marks)**

  The book has 25 000 words.
  b Estimate the number of 5 letter words in the book.   **(2 marks)**

  The book has 125 pages with a total of 25 000 words.
  The words on each of the first 75 pages are counted.
  The mean is 192.
  c Calculate the mean number of words per page for the remaining
    50 pages.   **(3 marks)**
                                                           [S1999 P3 Q13]

3 Jack has two fair dice.
One of the dice has 6 faces numbered
from 1 to 6.
The other dice has 4 faces numbered
from 1 to 4.

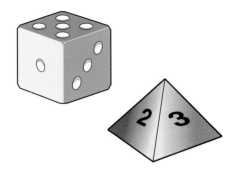

Jack is going to throw the two dice.
He will add the scores on the two dice to
get the total.

Work out the probability that he will get
i a total of 7,
ii a total of less than 5. **(4 marks)**
[S2000 P3 Q25]

4 Chris is going to roll a biased dice.
The probability that he will get a six is 0.09.
 a Work out the probability that he will **not** get a six. **(1 mark)**

Chris is going to roll the dice 30 times.
 b Work out an estimate for the number of sixes he will get. **(2 marks)**

Tina is going to roll the same biased dice **twice**.
 c Work out the probability that she will get
  i **two** sixes, **ii** **exactly one** six. **(5 marks)**
[S2000 P4 Q18]

5 The diagram shows the board for a game in a maths lesson.

FINISH	−3	−2	−1	0	+1	+2	+3	FINISH

Rules of the Game

Start with a counter on **0**.
Throw a coin.
If the coin shows heads, then move the counter one space to the right.
If the coin shows tails, then move the counter one space to the left.
The game ends when the counter reaches '**Finish**'.
Jim places a counter at **0**.
He throws a fair coin 3 times.

 a Calculate the probability that the counter will be at
  i +3, **ii** 0. **(3 marks)**

Ann places a counter at **0**.
She has a biased coin. The probability that the coin shows heads is 0.7.
Ann throws the biased coin twice.

 b Calculate the probability that her counter will be back at **0**. **(3 marks)**
[N1999 P4 Q19]

22 Standard form

You need to know about:

- standard form
- using a calculator for standard form
- solving problems in standard form without a calculator

| Standard form | A number is in **standard form** if it has two parts: |

a number between 1 and 10 multiplied by 10 to a power.

To write 59 000 in standard form, the number between 1 and 10 is 5.9

You need to **multiply** 5.9 by 10 four times to get 59 000.

So $59\,000 = 5.9 \times 10^4$ $5 . \overset{1\ 2\ 3\ 4}{9\ 0\ 0\ 0}$

You can imagine moving the decimal point four places to the right.

To write 0.004 56 in standard form, the number between 1 and 10 is 4.56

You need to divide by 10 three times to get to 0.004 56.
To show that you have to divide, put a minus in the power.

So $0.004\,56 = 4.56 \times 10^{-3}$ $\overset{3\ 2\ 1}{0\ 0\ 0\ 4} . 5\ 6$

You can imagine moving the decimal point three places to the left.

You can use a **calculator** to help with standard form.

Example   Work out $(3 \times 10^7) \div (6 \times 10^{-8})$.

Key in   **3**   **Exp**   **7**   **÷**   **6**   **Exp**   **+/−**   **8**   **=**

The answer is 5×10^{14}. Do not use the strange number sizes from the calculator display.

You must also be able to do **standard form calculations without a calculator**.
To do this you work out the number parts and the power parts separately.

Example   Work these out.

    a $(3 \times 10^4) \times (7 \times 10^6)$ **b** $(8 \times 10^4) \div (5 \times 10^{12})$

a $3 \times 7 = 21$ and $10^4 \times 10^6 = 10^{4+6} = 10^{10}$ You add the indices.
    So $(3 \times 10^4) \times (7 \times 10^6) = 21 \times 10^{10}$ but this is not in standard form.
    Notice that $21 = 2.1 \times 10$ so $21 \times 10^{10} = 2.1 \times 10^1 \times 10^{10} = 2.1 \times 10^{11}$.

b $8 \div 5 = 1.6$ and $10^4 \div 10^{12} = 10^{4-12} = 10^{-8}$ You subtract the indices.
    So $(8 \times 10^4) \div (5 \times 10^{12}) = 1.6 \times 10^{-8}$ which is the answer in standard form.

1 Work these out.
Do not use a calculator.

  a 4^2 **c** 2^4 **e** $\sqrt{64}$ **g** $\sqrt{8100}$
  b 5^3 **d** 3^5 **f** $\sqrt{10\,000}$ **h** $\sqrt{900}$

2 Write each of these as a fraction.

  a 4^{-1} **b** 5^{-2} **c** 2^{-3} **d** 10^{-2}

3 Write these numbers in standard form.

  a 1030   **c** 0.000 02   **e** 35   **g** 700 600
  b 0.087   **d** 0.7   **f** 4 million **h** 20 000

4 These numbers are written in standard form.
Write them as ordinary numbers.

  a 3.8×10^2 **b** 4.9×10^{-3} **c** 6.82×10^5 **d** 7×10^{-6}

5 Work these out. Give your answers in standard form.
Do not use a calculator.

  a $(4 \times 10^3) \times (6 \times 10^2)$ **c** $(3 \times 10^2) + (5 \times 10^3)$
  b $(1.4 \times 10^3) \div (7 \times 10^{-3})$ **d** $(5 \times 10^4) - (3 \times 10^2)$

6 Use a calculator to work these out.
Give your answer in standard form to 3 sf.

  a $(4.87 \times 10^3) \times (3.72 \times 10^4)$ **c** $(7.06 \times 10^4)^2$
  b $(6.36 \times 10^{-2}) \div (4.87 \times 10^3)$ **d** $(4.37 \times 10^2) + (3.91 \times 10^3)$

7 The table shows populations in 1981 and in 2001.

	Population in 1981	Population in 2001
Scotland	5.108×10^6	5.069×10^6
Wales	2.814×10^6	2.934×10^6
England	4.682×10^7	4.987×10^7
Northern Ireland	1.53×10^6	1.731×10^6

Give your answers as ordinary numbers to 3 sf.

a Write down the smallest population.

b For 2001, write down how many times bigger the population of Scotland is than that of Wales.

c For 1981, write down how many times bigger the population of England is than that of Northern Ireland.

d How many more people were in Wales in 2001 than in 1981?

129

1 a Write out each of the following numbers in standard form.
    i 457 170 000
    ii 0.000 000 000 656   **(2 marks)**

b Find, in standard form, the value of each of the following.
    i $(8.17 \times 10^{-4}) \times (6.54 \times 10^{-5})$

    ii $\dfrac{3.32 \times 10^4}{7.11 \times 10^{-3}}$ **(4 marks)**

a i 4.5717×10^8	**1 mark**	*Do not round off the numbers: include them all*
ii 6.56×10^{-10}	**1 mark**	*in the answer.*
b i 0.000 000 053	**1 mark**	*It is likely that your calculator may give you the*
$= 5.3 \times 10^{-8}$	**1 mark**	*answer as an ordinary decimal number. As the*
ii 4 669 479.606	**1 mark**	*question has asked for the answer in standard*
$= 4.669\,479\,606 \times 10^6$	**1 mark**	*form, you will have to change it yourself.*

2 A googol is the number 1×10^{100}.
Write, in standard form, the number that is 500 googols.   **(2 marks)**

$500 \times 1 \times 10^{100} = 5 \times 10^2 \times 1 \times 10^{100} = 5 \times 10^{100+2} = 5 \times 10^{102}$

                           1 mark   **1 mark**

3 The star Sirius is 81 900 000 000 000 km from Earth.
    a Write 81 900 000 000 000 in standard form.   **(1 mark)**

Light travels 3×10^5 km in 1 second.
    b Calculate the number of days that light takes to travel from Sirius to
    the Earth.
    Give your answer correct to 2 significant figures   **(3 marks)**

a 8.19×10^{13} **1 mark**
b $8.19 \times 10^{13} \div 3 \times 10^5 = 273\,000\,000$ seconds   **1 mark**
    $273\,000\,000 \div 60 \div 60 \div 24 = 3159.7 \ldots$ **1 mark**
                  $= 3200$ days (to 2 sf)   **1 mark**

Write down the full answer before rounding.

1 $F = \dfrac{ab}{a - b}$

Imran uses this formula to calculate the value of F.
Imran estimates the value of F without using a calculator.

   $a = 49.8$ and $b = 30.6$.

   a **i** Write down approximate values for a and b that Imran could use
         to estimate the value of F.

   ii Work out the estimate for the value of F that these
         approximations give.

   iii Use your calculator to work out the accurate value for F.

   Use $a = 49.8$ and $b = 30.6$.

   Write down all the figures on your calculator display.   **(4 marks)**

Imran works out the value of F with two new values for a and b.

   b Calculate the value of F when

   $a = 9.6 \times 10^{12}$ and $b = 4.7 \times 10^{11}$.

   Give your answer in standard form, correct to two significant
   figures.   **(3 marks)**
                                                        [S1999 P4 Q15]

2 $1 \text{ m}^3 = 220$ gallons
    $1 \text{ m}^3 = 10^6 \text{ cm}^3$

   a How many m^3 are equal to one gallon?
      Write your answer in standard form correct to 3 significant figures.
                                                               (3 marks)

The petrol tank of a small car holds 6 gallons when it is 80% full.

   b What is the capacity of the petrol tank in cm^3?
      Give your answer correct to 3 significant figures   **(3 marks)**
                                                        [S1999 P3 Q17]

3 $p = 8 \times 10^3$,
    $q = 2 \times 10^4$

   a Find the value of $p \times q$.
      Give your answer in **standard form**.   **(2 marks)**

   b Find the value of $p + q$.
      Give your answer as an **ordinary number**.   **(2 marks)**
                                                        [S2000 P3 Q21]

4 **a** Write 84 000 000 in standard form. **(2 marks)**

   b Work out

$$\frac{84\ 000\ 000}{4 \times 10^{12}}$$

Give your answer in standard form. **(3 marks)**

[S2000 P3 Q20]

5 **a i** Write the number 5.01×10^4 as an ordinary number.

   ii Write the number 0.0009 in standard form. **(2 marks)**

   b Multiply 4×10^3 by 6×10^5.
   Give your answer in standard form. **(2 marks)**

[S2001 P3 Q21]

6 $v^2 = \dfrac{GM}{R}$

   $G = 6.6 \times 10^{-11}$

   $M = 6 \times 10^{24}$

   $R = 6\ 800\ 000$

   a Calculate the value of v. Give your answer in standard form, correct to 2 significant figures. **(4 marks)**

   b Rearrange the formula $v^2 = \dfrac{GM}{R}$ to make M the subject. **(2 marks)**

[N1999 P4 Q16]

7 The mass of one electron is

   0.000 000 000 000 000 000 000 000 91 grams.

   a Write 0.000 000 000 000 000 000 000 000 91 in standard form. **(2 marks)**

   b Calculate the mass of five million electrons.

   Give your answer, in grams, in standard form. **(3 marks)**

[N1998 P4 Q12]

8 Calculate the value of

$$\frac{5.98 \times 10^8 + 4.32 \times 10^9}{6.14 \times 10^{-2}}$$

Give your answer in standard form correct to 3 significant figures.

(3 marks)
[S2001 P4 Q19]

9 The speed of light is approximately 300 000 000 m/s.

a Write 300 000 000 in standard form. **(2 marks)**

b Calculate the time, in seconds, light takes to travel 1 metre.

Give your answer in standard index form. **(2 marks)**
[N1995 P3 Q19]

10 There are approximately 150 thousand ants in a tropical ant colony.

a Write 150 thousand in standard form. **(1 mark)**

Each ant eats an average 2.4×10^{-3} kilograms of food per day.

b Calculate the total average amount of food eaten by 150 thousand ants in one day. Give your answer in kilograms. **(2 marks)**
[N1995 P4 Q18]

11 Work out the value of

$$(4.6 \times 10^{-2}) \times (8.3 \times 10^4)$$

giving your answer in standard index form. **(3 marks)**
[N1994 P4 Q16]

23 Area

You need to know about:

- estimating areas
- finding the areas of common shapes
- drawing nets
- finding surface areas
- converting area units

To **estimate the area** of an irregular shape:

(1) Count whole squares. There are 5 of these.

(2) Count squares that lie more than half inside the shape. There are 4 of these.

(3) Add the two numbers together. 5 + 4 = 9
An estimate of the area is 9 squares.

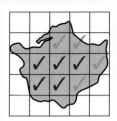

Formulas for area

Area of a rectangle
= length × width

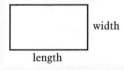

Area of a triangle
= (base × height) ÷ 2

Area of a circle
= π × radius × radius = πr^2

Area of a trapezium
= $\frac{1}{2}(a + b)h$

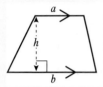

Area of a parallelogram
= base × height

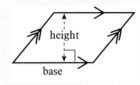

Area of a kite
= $\frac{1}{2}$(diagonals multiplied together) = $\frac{1}{2}xy$

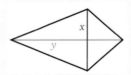

Area of a rhombus
= base × height

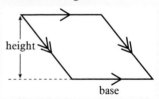

Example

Find the area of this shape.

Area of the rectangle $= 6 \times 12 = 72 \text{ cm}^2$

Area of the semi-circle $= \pi r^2 \div 2 = \pi \times 3^2 \div 2$

$= 14.1 \text{ cm}^2$ to 3 sf

Total area $= 72 + 14.1 = 86.1 \text{ cm}^2$ to 3 sf

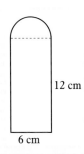

12 cm

6 cm

Net

When a solid is opened out and laid flat, the shape that you get is called a **net** of the solid.

This triangular prism gives this net

You can have more than one net for a solid.
This is also a net of a triangular prism.

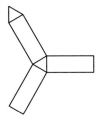

To find the surface area of a solid:

(1) sketch the net

(2) work out the area of each face

(3) find the total of all the areas.

Area of rectangles A and B $= 2 \times 8 \times 3 = 48 \text{ cm}^2$

Area of rectangles C and D $= 2 \times 8 \times 5 = 80 \text{ cm}^2$

Area of rectangles E and F $= 2 \times 3 \times 5 = 30 \text{ cm}^2$

Total surface area $= 158 \text{ cm}^2$

The diagram below shows how to convert square units.

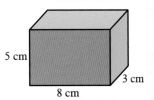

5 cm

3 cm

8 cm

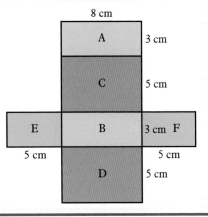

8 cm

A   3 cm

C   5 cm

E   B   3 cm F

5 cm   5 cm

D   5 cm

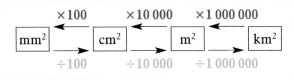

$\times 100$ $\times 10\,000$ $\times 1\,000\,000$

mm^2 cm^2 m^2 km^2

$\div 100$ $\div 10\,000$ $\div 1\,000\,000$

1 Find the area of each of these shapes.

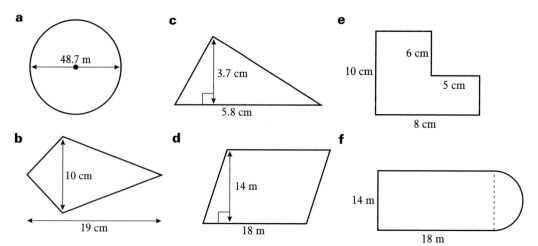

a 48.7 m

c 3.7 cm, 5.8 cm

e 6 cm, 10 cm, 5 cm, 8 cm

b 10 cm, 19 cm

d 14 m, 18 m

f 14 m, 18 m

2 A shape has an area of 520 cm².
   a If the shape is a circle, find the radius of the circle to 3 sf.
   b If the shape is a square, find the length of a side of the square to 3 sf.
   c If the shape is a rectangle of length 28.5 cm, find the width of the
      rectangle to 3 sf.

3 Work out the surface area of each of these.

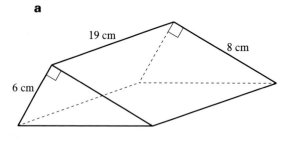

a 19 cm, 8 cm, 6 cm

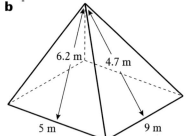

b 6.2 m, 4.7 m, 5 m, 9 m

4 This garden is a rectangle of length 14 m and
   width 12 m.
   The garden has 3 flower beds and one pond.
   The pond is a circle of diameter 4 m.
   Two flower beds are each a quarter of a circle
   of radius 3 m.
   One flower bed is a semi-circle of diameter 5 m.
   The grassed area is shown in green.

   a Find the area of the pond.

   b Find the total area of the three flower beds.

   c Find the area of the grass.

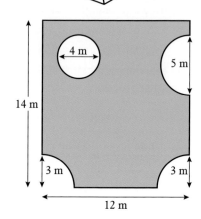

1 Find the surface area of this solid. **(5 marks)**

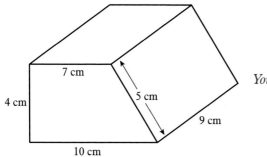

You could draw a net to help you.

Start with the end shape, which is a trapezium.
The formula for working out the area of a trapezium is on the formula sheet.

This 5 is not needed (yet).

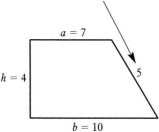

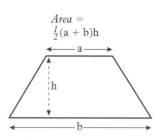

In this problem, a = 7, b = 10 and h = 4.

Area $= \frac{1}{2}(7 + 10)\,4$ **1 mark**
  $= \frac{1}{2} \times 17 \times 4 = 34\ \text{cm}^2$ **1 mark**

To find the surface area, find the area of each surface.

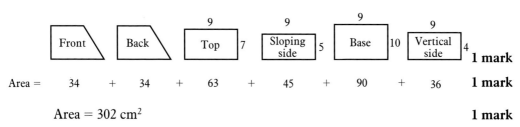

Area = 34 + 34 + 63 + 45 + 90 + 36 **1 mark**

Area = 302 cm² **1 mark**

1 The diagram shows a sketch of a triangle.

  a Work out the area of the triangle.
State the units of your answer. **(3 marks)**

  b Work out the perimeter of the
triangle. **(4 marks)**

                [S2000 P4 Q5]

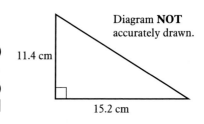

Diagram **NOT**
accurately drawn.

11.4 cm

15.2 cm

2 The diagram shows a trapezium ABCD.

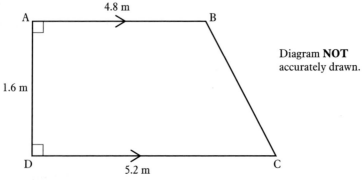

Diagram **NOT**
accurately drawn.

4.8 m

1.6 m

5.2 m

AB is parallel to DC.
AB = 4.8 m, DC = 5.2 m, AD = 1.6 m,
angle BAD = 90°, angle ADC = 90°.

Calculate the area of trapezium ABCD. **(2 marks)**
                                        [S2001 P4 Q12]

3 The radius of a circle is 5.1 m.

Work out the area of the circle.
State the units of your answer. **(3 marks)**
                    [S2001 P4 Q9]

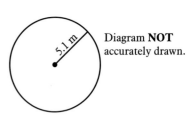

5.1 m

Diagram **NOT**
accurately drawn.

4 This diagram shows the floor plan of a room.

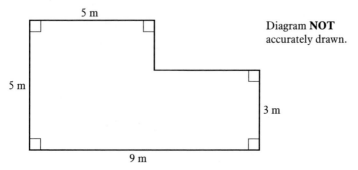

Diagram **NOT**
accurately drawn.

5 m

5 m

3 m

9 m

Work out the area of the floor.
Give the units with your answer. **(4 marks)**   [S1999 P4 Q9]

5

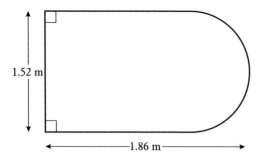

Diagram **NOT** accurately drawn.

1.52 m

1.86 m

A mat is made in the shape of a rectangle with a semicircle added at one end.

The width of the mat is 1.52 metres.

The length of the mat is 1.86 metres.

Calculate the area of the mat.

Give your answer in square metres, correct to 2 decimal places.   **(5 marks)**
[N1999 P4 Q10]

6

Shape A   Diagram **NOT** accurately drawn.   **Shape B**

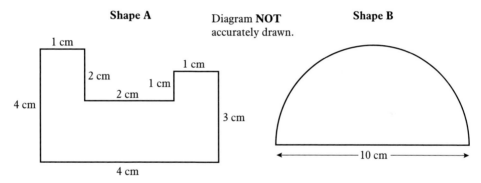

1 cm

2 cm

1 cm

1 cm

1 cm

2 cm

4 cm

3 cm

4 cm

10 cm

a Work out the area of Shape A.   **(2 marks)**

b Work out the perimeter of the semi-circle, Shape B.   **(2 marks)**
[S1998 P3 Q6]

7 The diagram shows a right-angled triangle ABC and a circle.
A, B and C are points on the circumference of the circle.
AC is a diameter of the circle.
The radius of the circle is 10 cm.
AB = 16 cm and BC = 12 cm.

Diagram **NOT** accurately drawn.

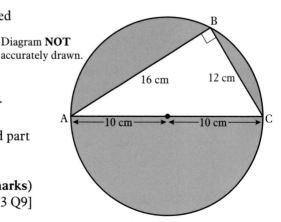

B

16 cm

12 cm

A

10 cm

10 cm

C

Work out the areas of the shaded part of the circle.

Give your answer correct to the nearest cm^2.   **(6 marks)**
[S1999 P3 Q9]

24 Pattern power

You need to know about:

- changing unfamiliar units
- number sequences
- finding formulas for number sequences

Sometimes you have to deal with units that you may not have met before.

Example

Three units of currency are used in a game: loups, cags and tows.
1 loup = 5 cags and 1 cag = 12 tows.

Convert these   **a**   2 cags to tows   **b**   720 tows to loups

a   2 cags = 24 tows   **b**   720 tows = 60 cags = 12 loups

Number sequence

A **number sequence** is a list of numbers that follow a rule.

Term

Each number in a sequence is called a **term**.

The rule for the sequence 4, 7, 10, 13, 16, 19, … is 'add 3'.

Example

The first term of a sequence is 9.
The rule is 'multiply by 2 and subtract 8'.
Write down the first four terms of the sequence.

1st term = 9
2nd term = $9 \times 2 - 8 = 10$
3rd term = $10 \times 2 - 8 = 12$
4th term = $12 \times 2 - 8 = 16$

Formula for the nth term

The **formula for the nth term** of a sequence tells you how to find the value of each term of the sequence.

Example

The formula for the nth term of a sequence is $T = 3n + 7$.

Find: **a**   the first two terms   **b**   the 80th term.

a   1st term $(n = 1) = 3 \times 1 + 7 = 10$
     2nd term $(n = 2) = 3 \times 2 + 7 = 13$

b   80th term $(n = 80) = 3 \times 80 + 7 = 247$

You can draw a sequence diagram to find **an expression for the *n*th term of a sequence**.

Example   Find an expression for the *n*th term of the sequence 9, 15, 21, 27, 33, ...

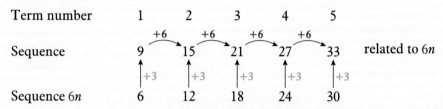

The rule is add 6 so it must be related to $6n$.
Write the sequence $6n$ underneath. Compare the two sequences.

Term number	1	2	3	4	5	

Sequence

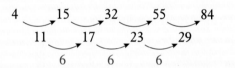

You need to add 3 to every term in $6n$ to make the sequence.
So an expression for the *n*th term of the sequence is $6n + 3$.

Some **formulas contain n^2**.

Example   Find an expression for the *n*th term of 4, 15, 32, 55, 84, ...

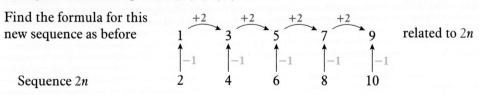

The second differences are 6 so the first part of the formula is $3n^2$.
The number in front of n^2 is half the second difference.

Term number	1	2	3	4	5

Sequence

| Value of $3n^2$ | 3 | 12 | 27 | 48 | 75 |

Look for what you need to add to get the sequence.
This gives the new sequence 1, 3, 5, 7, 9, ...

Find the formula for this new sequence as before

Sequence $2n$

The second part of the expression is $2n - 1$.
The complete expression is $3n^2 + 2n - 1$.

1   For each sequence write down the rule to get from one term to the next.

    a   4, 8, 16, 32, 64   **b**   7, 10, 13, 16, 19   **c**   18, 14, 10, 6, 2

2   The formula for the nth term of a sequence is $T = 3n + 7$.
Write down:

    a   the first four terms

    b   the 10th term

    c   the 15th term.

3   For each sequence find an expression for the nth term.

    a   10, 13, 16, 19, 22, ...   **c**   9, 15, 21, 27, 33, ...

    b   3, 8, 13, 18, 23, ...   **d**   −3, −1, 1, 3, 5, ...

4   The expression for the nth term of a sequence is $2n^2 + 3n - 1$.

    a   Find the 1st term.

    b   Find the 10th term.

5   Look at the sequence 2, 9, 18, 29, 42.
Find a formula for the nth term.

6   **a**   Copy this pattern formed from matchsticks.

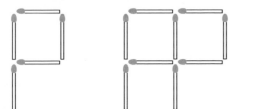 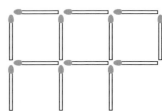

    b   Draw the next two diagrams in the pattern.

    c   Write the number of sticks in the pattern as a number sequence.

    d   Work out an expression for the nth term.

7   Which of these numbers belongs to the sequence with the nth term
$2n^2 + 3n - 8$?

    a   111   **b**   36   **c**   238

8   A sequence has the nth term given by $11 - 3n$.

    a   Find the first 4 terms.

    b   Find the 20th term.

    c   Find the term that has a value of −79.

    d   Find the term that has a value of −94.

1 There were x people on a coach.
Eight people got off.

a Write an expression for the number of people left on the coach. **(1 mark)**

There were c stamp collectors at a fair.
Each collector was given an entry pack of d stamps.

b Write an expression for the total number of stamps given to collectors on entry. **(1 mark)**

There were t people who bought an ice cream each costing 80p.

c Write down an expression, in pounds, for the total amount spent on ice creams. **(2 marks)**

a x people were on the coach and 8 got off: $x - 8$ **1 mark**

b 1 person was given d stamps, so c people were given $d \times c$ stamps: cd **1 mark**

This should be written in alphabetical order.

c One ice cream costs 80p, t ice creams will cost $t \times 80$ or $80t$ **in pence.** **1 mark**

To change to pounds you divide by 100:

$$\frac{£80t}{100}$$ **1 mark**

2 **a** **i** Write down the next two terms of the sequence.

17, 14, 11, 8, 5, …

ii Explain how you worked out your answers. **(3 marks)**

b Find, in terms of n, an expression for the nth term of the sequence. **(2 marks)**

c Find the 50th term of the sequence. **(1 mark)**

a **i** 17 $\quad$ 14 $\quad$ 11 $\quad$ 8 $\quad$ 5 $\quad$ 2 $\quad$ -1

$\quad$ -3 $\quad$ -3 $\quad$ -3 $\quad$ -3 $\quad$ -3 $\quad$ -3

1 mark for each of 2 and -1

ii *You should explain that the difference between terms is -3 and that you have continued to take 3 away.* **1 mark**

b The differences are all -3 so the rule must be related to $-3n$. **1 mark**
Compare the two sequences:

Sequence: $\qquad$ 17 $\quad$ 14 $\quad$ 11 $\quad$ 8 $\quad$ 5
Sequence $-3n$: $\quad$ -3 $\quad$ -6 $\quad$ -9 $\quad$ -12 $\quad$ -15

There is a difference of 20 between the sequences.
So the expression for the rule is $20 - 3n$. **1 mark**

c *Use your expression to find the answer.*
For $n = 50$: $20 - 3n$ becomes $20 - (3 \times 50) = 20 - 150 = -130$ **1 mark**

143

1 Sharon earns b pounds an hour.

She worked for h hours.

She also earned a bonus of c pounds.

Write down a formula for her total earnings, P pounds. **(3 marks)**

[N1999 P3 Q14]

2 A roll of wallpaper costs 4 pounds.

Joan buys w rolls of wallpaper.
The total cost is C pounds.

Write down a formula connecting C and w. **(2 marks)**

[N1998 P3 Q2]

3

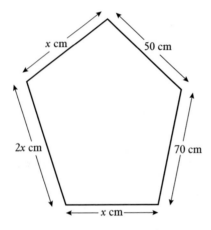

Diagram **NOT** accurately drawn.

The perimeter of the pentagon is 200 cm.

Work out the value of x. **(3 marks)**

[N1998 P4 Q11]

4 Daniel buys n books at £4 each.
He pays for them with a £20 note.
He receives C pounds change.

Write down a formula for C in terms of n. **(3 marks)**

[S2000 P4 Q10]

5 Here are the first five numbers of a simple number sequence.

$$1, \quad 5, \quad 9, \quad 13, \quad 17, \quad \ldots, \quad \ldots,$$

a Write down the next two numbers in the sequence. **(2 marks)**

b Describe, in words, the rule to continue this sequence. **(1 mark)**

c Write down, in terms of n, the nth term of this sequence. **(2 marks)**

[S1998 P3 Q4]

6 Here are the first four terms of a number sequence.

    3, 7, 11, 15

  a Write down the next two numbers in the sequence. **(2 marks)**

  b Write down an expression, in terms of n, for the nth term of the sequence. **(2 marks)**

                        [N1999 P3 Q3]

7 Here are the first five numbers of a simple sequence.

    2, 8, 14, 20, 26

Write down, in terms of n, an expression for the nth term of this sequence. **(2 marks)**

                        [S2000 P4 Q6]

8 Here are the first four terms of a number sequence.

    7, 11, 15, 19.

Write down the nth term of the sequence. **(2 marks)**

                        [S1994 P4 Q18]

9 Here are the first five terms of a number sequence.

    3, 5, 7, 9, 11.

Write down an expression for the nth term of the sequence. **(2 marks)**

                        [N1995 P3 Q14]

25 Statistics

You need to know about:

- comparing sets of data
- cumulative frequency
- box and whisker diagrams

Always use one measure of average and one measure of spread when comparing sets of data.

A small value for the range shows that the data values are **consistent**.

Example

The table shows the results of two classes in their science exam. Compare the results of the two classes.

	mean	range
class 7F	58%	42%
class 7D	61%	64%

Class 7D scored higher marks on average (61% to 58%). The lower value of the range shows that the marks for class 7F were less spread out – they were more **consistent**.

The simplest measure of spread is the **range** but this is badly affected by extreme values of data.

The **interquartile range** is a better measure of spread when there are extreme values in the data.

Example

Look at this data: 2, 2, 3, 5, 6, 8, 8, 19

Find the lower and upper quartiles and the interquartile range.

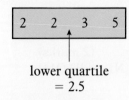

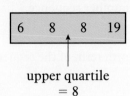

lower quartile
= 2.5

upper quartile
= 8

interquartile range
= upper quartile − lower quartile
= 8 − 2.5 = 5.5

Cumulative frequency

The **cumulative frequency** is a running total.

Cumulative frequency diagrams

A **cumulative frequency diagram** shows how the cumulative frequency changes as the data values increase. The data is shown on the horizontal axis and the cumulative frequency on the vertical axis.

You plot the upper end of each group against the cumulative frequency.

You then join the points with a straight line or curve.

You can use a cumulative frequency diagram to estimate the median and quartiles.

To get an estimate of the median: (1) divide the total cumulative frequency by 2
(2) find this point on the cumulative frequency axis
(3) draw a line across to the curve and then down
(4) read off the estimate of the median.

To get an **estimate for the lower quartile** you use the total cumulative frequency divided by 4.

For the **upper quartile** you use the total cumulative frequency divided by 4 and then multiplied by 3.

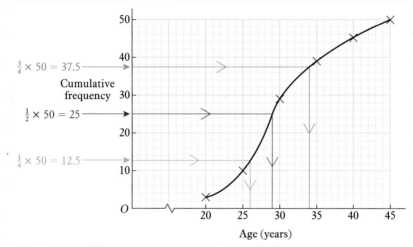

Median = 29 years   **Lower quartile** = 26 years   **Upper quartile** = 34 years

Interquartile range = $34 - 26 = 8$ years

A **box and whisker diagram** is sometimes called a **box plot**.

The box shows the middle 50% of the data. The whiskers show the extreme points of the data.

Box and whisker plot showing train journey times in minutes.

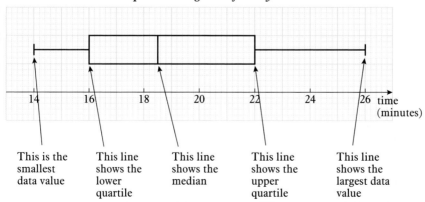

| This is the smallest data value | This line shows the lower quartile | This line shows the median | This line shows the upper quartile | This line shows the largest data value |

1 A group of 23 sixth form students compare their average weekly income from part-time jobs.
These are their earnings in pounds.

16	60	54	50	41	110	48	62	60	17	32	32
125	50	33	43	30	21	52	50	40	60	47	

a Find, to the nearest penny:
  i the mean   iii the lower quartile   v the range
  ii the median   iv the upper quartile   vi the interquartile range

b Look at the range and the interquartile range.
Write down which is the better measure of spread for this data.
Explain your answer.

2 The local hockey team is raising money for charity. As part of this, the times taken by 100 competitors to complete a simple puzzle are recorded. These are the times.

Times to complete the puzzle, x (seconds)	Number of competitors
$0 < x \leqslant 10$	4
$10 < x \leqslant 20$	6
$20 < x \leqslant 30$	15
$30 < x \leqslant 40$	35
$40 < x \leqslant 50$	32
$50 < x \leqslant 60$	8

a Draw a cumulative frequency table for the data.

b Draw a cumulative frequency curve for the data.

c Use your graph to:
  i estimate the median
  ii find the interquartile range.

3 Elspeth is planning her holiday for next year.
She looks up the temperatures for two resorts.
The table shows her results.

	Resort A	Resort B
Smallest data value	24°C	20°C
Lower quartile	26°C	24°C
Median	29°C	29°C
Upper quartile	35°C	33°C
Largest data value	39°C	36°C

a On the same diagram, draw box and whisker plots for Resort A and Resort B.

b Write a few sentences comparing the temperatures for the two resorts.

1   The ages of 500 people attending a pop concert are given in the table below.

   a   i   Complete the table by filling in the cumulative frequencies.
        ii Draw a cumulative frequency diagram for this information.   **(3 marks)**

   b Use your diagram to estimate the interquartile range   **(2 marks)**

   c Use your diagram to estimate the percentage of people who are under
        16 years of age.   **(2 marks)**

a

Age	Number of people	Age	Cumulative frequency	
$0 \leqslant A < 10$	20	$0 \leqslant A < 10$	20	
$10 \leqslant A < 20$	130	$0 \leqslant A < 20$	150	
$20 \leqslant A < 30$	152	$0 \leqslant A < 30$	302	
$30 \leqslant A < 40$	92	$0 \leqslant A < 40$	394	
$40 \leqslant A < 60$	86	$0 \leqslant A < 60$	480	
$60 \leqslant A < 80$	18	$0 \leqslant A < 80$	498	
$80 \leqslant A < 100$	2	$0 \leqslant A < 100$	500	Table completed: **1 mark**

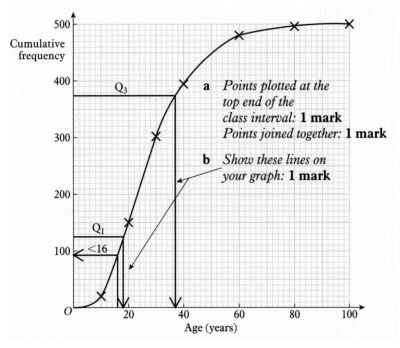

a *Points plotted at the top end of the class interval:* **1 mark**
Points joined together: **1 mark**

b *Show these lines on your graph:* **1 mark**

b Interquartile range calculated from   Q1 (lower quartile) 125 → 18
                                            Q3 (upper quartile) 375 → 37
                                            $37 - 18 = 19$ **1 mark**

c *Read off the graph from 16 years of age:* cumulative frequency of 90

                                            1 mark

$\dfrac{90}{500}$ as a percentage is $\dfrac{90}{500} \times 100 = 18\%$

                                            Show this calculation.

1 The table gives information about the ages, in years, of 100 aeroplanes.

Age (t years)	Frequency
$0 < t \leq 5$	41
$5 < t \leq 10$	26
$10 < t \leq 15$	20
$15 < t \leq 20$	10
$20 < t \leq 25$	3

a Work out an estimate of the mean age of the aeroplanes.   **(4 marks)**

b Complete the cumulative frequency table.

Age (t years)	Cumulative frequency
$0 < t \leq 5$	
$0 < t \leq 10$	
$0 < t \leq 15$	
$0 < t \leq 20$	
$0 < t \leq 25$	

(1 mark)

c On the grid, draw a cumulative frequency graph for your table.

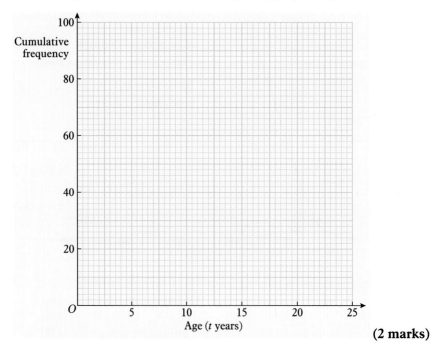

(2 marks)

d Use your graph to find an estimate of the upper quartile of the ages.
Show your method clearly.   **(2 marks)**

[N1998 P3 Q18]

2 Fred carried out a survey of the time, in seconds, between one car and the next car on a road.
His results are shown in the cumulative frequency graph on the grid below.

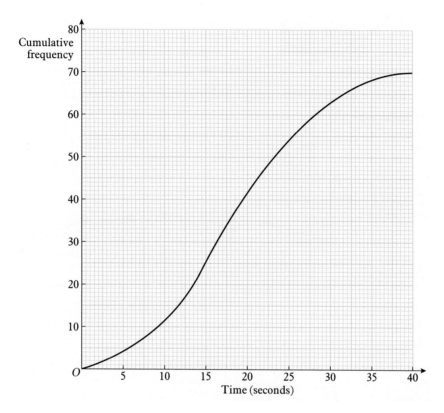

a How many cars were there in the survey?   **(1 mark)**
b Use the graph to estimate the median time.   **(2 marks)**
c Use the graph to estimate the percentage of times that were greater than 25 seconds.   **(3 marks)**

[S1999 P3 Q18]

26 Angles and bearings

You need to know about:

- finding angles
- bearings
- drawing to scale

An **acute** angle is less than 90°, an **obtuse** angle is between 90° and 180° and a **reflex** angle is bigger than 180°.

Angles on a straight line add up to 180°.

$x + 30° + y = 180°$

Angles around a point add up to 360°.

$a + 90° + b + c = 360°$

Opposite angles are equal.

$a = b$

$c = d$

Angles in a triangle add up to 180°.

$x + y + z = 180°$

Angles in a quadrilateral add up to 360°.

$a + b + c + d = 360°$

Angles and parallel lines:

$w = x = y = z$

and $a = b = c = d$

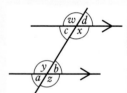

The angle in a semi-circle is a right angle.

$a = 90°$

The angle between a tangent and a radius is 90°

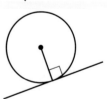

A line drawn from the centre of a circle to the mid-point of a chord is always at right angles to the chord.

There are two tangents from P to the circle. PA = PB, so triangle APB is isosceles. Triangle AOB is also isosceles.

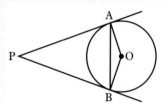

All four vertices of a cyclic quadrilateral lie on a circle. Opposite angles in a cyclic quadrilateral add up to 180°.

$a + b = 180°$

$c + d = 180°$

Angles in the same segment are equal.

Also, the angle at the centre is twice the angle at the circumference.

$a = b = c$ and

$g = 2a = 2b = 2c$

A **bearing** is an angle. Bearings are always measured clockwise starting from north.
A bearing must always have three digits. If the angle is less than 100° put a zero as
the first digit.

The bearing of B
from A means that
you are at A.
The bearing of B
from A is the red
angle.

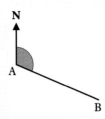

The bearing of A
from B means that
you are at B.
The bearing of A
from B is the blue
angle.

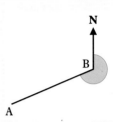

Example   **a**   Work out the bearing of Q from P.
　　　　　 b   Work out the bearing of P from Q.

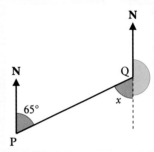

a   The bearing of Q from P is 065°.
b   The bearing of P from Q = 180° + x
　　　　　　　　　　　　　= 180° + 65°
　　　　　　　　　　　　　= 245°

It is often useful to do a scale drawing to solve bearing problems.
An accurate drawing allows you to measure both distances and bearings.

Example   A plane leaves the airport A, and flies 150 km on a bearing of 058°.
　　　　　It then flies 250 km on a bearing of 195°.
　　　　　a   Draw a scale drawing of the journey. Use a scale of 1 cm to 50 km.
　　　　　b   How far is the plane from the airport at the end of the journey?
　　　　　c   What is the bearing of the plane from the airport at this point?

a   The scale is 1 cm : 50 km. So 150 km is
represented by 3cm and 250 km is
represented by 5 cm.
b   The blue line is 3.6 cm long,
so distance = 3.6 × 50 = 180 km (2 sf).
c   360 − 20 = 340°

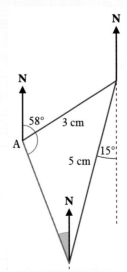

scale 1 cm to 50 km

1 **a** Write down the special name for triangle ABC.

   b Find angle x, giving a reason for your answer.

   c Find angle y, giving a reason for your answer.

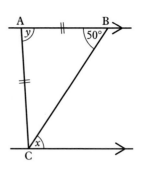

2 Find the angles marked with letters. Give a reason for each answer.

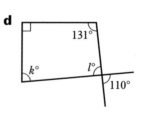

a

b

c

d

3 From Port A, a ship sails north for 10 km to B.
From B, it sails on a bearing of 070° for 8.5 km to C.
From C, it sails on a bearing of 130° for 5 km to D.

   a Make a scale drawing showing the path that the ship takes. Use a scale of 1 cm to 1 km.

   b Use your diagram to find the bearing the ship would sail on to return to the starting point at Port A.

   c Use your diagram to find the distance from D to A.

4 Calculate the angles marked with letters. Give reasons for your answers.

a

b

c

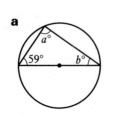

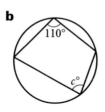

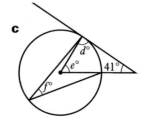

1

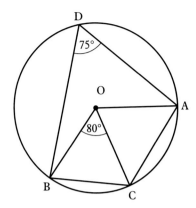

Points A, B, C and D lie on the circumference of a circle with centre O.
Angle BOC = 80°, angle BDA = 75°.

a Calculate the size of angle BAC. Give a reason for your answer.

(2 marks)

b Calculate the size of angle BCA. Give a reason for your answer.

(2 marks)

a *You need to try to link BAC to one of the given angles using a circle fact.*
The angle 80° is drawn to the centre O from points B and C.
Angle BAC is drawn to point A, also from points B and C.
Angle BAC = 40°.   **1 mark**

The reason is:
The angle at the centre (BOC = 80°) is twice the angle at the
circumference (BAC).   **1 mark**

b *Again try to link angle BCA with one of the given angles using a circle fact.*
The angle BDA is contained within the cyclic quadrilateral ABCD. BCA
is also an angle within that cyclic quadrilateral, opposite angle BDA.
BDA + BCA = 180°, giving angle BCA = 180° − 75° = 105°.
                                                            1 mark

The reason is:
Opposite angles in a cyclic quadrilateral (BDA and BCA) add up to
180°.   **1 mark**

Note: In both cases it is important that the reason is given using mathematical
language and expressions. There is always a separate mark for giving the reason.

1

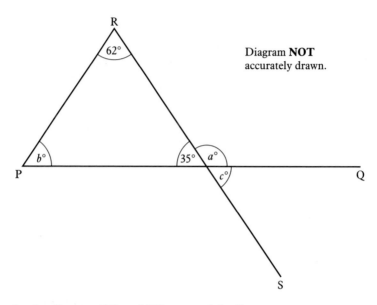

Diagram **NOT** accurately drawn.

In the diagram PQ and RS are straight lines.

a **i** Work out the value of *a*.
  ii Give a reason for your answer. **(2 marks)**
b **i** Work out the value of *b*.
  ii Give a reason for your answer. **(2 marks)**
c **i** Work out the value of *c*.
  ii Give a reason for your answer. **(2 marks)**

[S1999 P3 Q3]

2

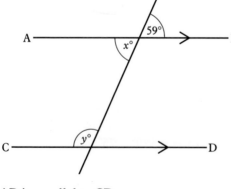

Diagram **NOT** accurately drawn.

AB is parallel to CD.

a **i** Write down the size of the angle marked *x*°.
  ii Give a reason for your answer. **(2 marks)**
b **i** Work out the size of the angle marked *y*°.
  ii Explain how you worked out your answer. **(2 marks)**

[N1998 P4 Q7]

3

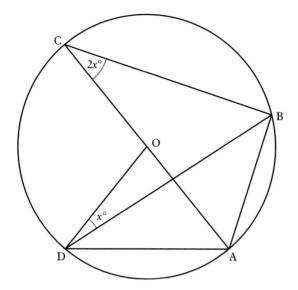

Diagram **NOT** accurately drawn.

A, B, C and D are points on the circumference of a circle centre O.

AC is a diameter of the circle.

Angle BDO $= x°$ Angle BCA $= 2x°$

Express, in terms of x, the size of

i angle BDA,   **ii** angle AOD,   **iii** angle ABD.   **(4 marks)**

[N1998 P5 Q20]

4 The diagram represents the positions of Wigan and Manchester.

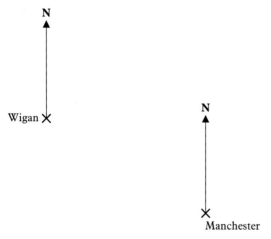

a Measure and write down the bearing of Manchester from Wigan.

(1 mark)

b Find the bearing of Wigan from Manchester.   **(2 marks)**

[S1998 P3 Q13]

27 Mainly quadratics

You need to know about:

- changing the subject
- factorising quadratics
- solving quadratic equations
- quadratic graphs

You will need the skills of factorising and multiplying out brackets to solve some 'changing the subject' problems. You need to re-arrange some formulas in which the **new subject appears twice**.

Example   Make x the subject of this formula: $5xy = 7x + c$

Get all the terms with the new subject on one side. $5xy - 7x = c$

Factorise out the new subject: $x(5y - 7) = c$

Divide by the bracket to leave x as the subject: $x = \dfrac{c}{5y - 7}$

The brackets are not needed in the fraction.

An expression like $x^2 + 3x - 28$ is called a **quadratic** expression.
When you multiply out two brackets you get a quadratic expression.
You **factorise a quadratic** by changing it back to the form with two brackets.
An equation like $x^2 + 3x - 28 = 0$ is called a **quadratic equation**.

To **solve a quadratic equation**:   (1) factorise the quadratic expression
(2) put the two brackets equal to 0
(3) solve the two simple equations.

Example   Solve $x^2 + 7x + 12 = 0$.

(1) Factorise the quadratic expression: $(x + 4)(x + 3) = 0$

The two brackets multiply to give 0 so either the 1st bracket $= 0$ or the 2nd bracket $= 0$.

It is very important that the quadratic is always equal to 0.

(2) Put the two brackets equal to 0:   either $x + 4 = 0$ or $x + 3 = 0$

(3) Solve the two simple equations: $x = -4$ or $x = -3$
These are both solutions of
$x^2 + 7x + 12 = 0$.   The solutions are $x = -4$ and $x = -3$.

Quadratic equations always have **two solutions**.

Factorising a quadratic equation allows you to draw a **sketch of the graph**.
The solution gives the values of x where the graph cuts the x axis.

Example　Sketch $y = x^2 - 5x + 6$.

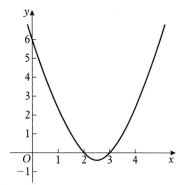

Find the points where the graph
crosses the x axis.
These are the points where $y = 0$.
To do this, solve the quadratic equal
to 0.

$$x^2 - 5x + 6 = 0$$
$$(x - 2)(x - 3) = 0$$
$$x - 2 = 0 \text{ or } x - 3 = 0$$
$$x = 2 \text{ or } x = 3$$

The graph crosses the x axis at $x = 2$
and $x = 3$.

Find the point where the curve crosses the y axis.
To do this put $x = 0$.

$$y = x^2 - 5x + 6$$
$$= 0^2 - 5 \times 0 + 6$$
$$= 6$$

You can now sketch the curve.
Quadratic curves are always **symmetrical**.
The bottom or top of the curve must be halfway between the points where
the curve crosses the x axis.
The value of x at this point is halfway between 2 and 3, that is 2.5.
Put $x = 2.5$ into $y = x^2 - 5x + 6$ to find the y co-ordinate.

$$y = x^2 - 5x + 6 = 2.5^2 - 5 \times 2.5 + 6 = -0.25.$$
The lowest point of the curve is $(2.5, -0.25)$.

When the x^2 term is negative, a quadratic graph is turned upside down.

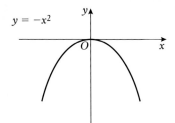

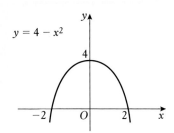

1 Multiply out these brackets.

   a $5(x + 2)$ **c** $x(2x + 1)$

   b $6(2t + 1)$ **d** $2a(3a + 2b)$

2 Factorise each of these.

   a $5x + 25$ **c** $4x^2 + 8x$

   b $26y - 8z$ **d** $16a^2 + 4a + 8b$

3 Simplify these expressions.

   a $\dfrac{5x^2}{15x^3}$ **b** $\dfrac{4a + 8}{3a + 6}$ **c** $\dfrac{15(x + 3)^2}{5(x + 3)}$

4 Make the red letter the subject of each of these formulas.

   a $a + b = 3ax - c$ **d** $s = \dfrac{w + 5}{2w}$

   b $3xy = 5x + d$ **e** $4ab + 2 = 7a + 5b$

   c $a = \dfrac{4b + 3}{2b}$ **f** $d = \dfrac{ab + c}{4b}$

5 Multiply out each of these pairs of brackets.

   a $(x + 3)(x + 5)$ **d** $(4x + 3)(2x + 1)$

   b $(x - 8)(x + 4)$ **e** $(3x - 5)(4x + 6)$

   c $(x - 3)(x - 7)$ **f** $(x + 6)^2$

6 Factorise these quadratic expressions.

   a $x^2 + 14x + 45$ **b** $x^2 + 3x - 18$ **c** $x^2 - 25$

7 Solve these quadratic equations.

   a $x^2 + x - 6 = 0$ **c** $x^2 - 5x - 14 = 0$

   b $x^2 - 5x - 36 = 0$ **d** $x^2 - 7x = 18$

8 Sketch graphs of these quadratic equations.

   a $y = x^2 - 2x - 15$ **c** $y = x^2 - x - 6$

   b $y = x^2 + x - 12$ **d** $y = x^2 - x - 2$

1   Solve: **a** $x^2 - 36 = 0$ (2 marks)

  b $x^2 - 7x = 0$ (2 marks)

  a   *Factorise:* $x^2 - 36 = 0$ becomes $(x - 6)(x + 6) = 0$ **1 mark**

  $x - 6 = 0$ or $x + 6 = 0$

  Either $x = 6$ or $x = -6$ **1 mark**

  ← *Make sure you write down both solutions.*

  b   *Factorise:* $x^2 - 7x = 0$ becomes $x(x - 7) = 0$ **1 mark**

  $x = 0$ or $x - 7 = 0$

  Either $x = 0$ or $x = 7$ **1 mark**

  ← *This solution is frequently forgotten.*

2   All lengths in this question are in metres.

A rectangular garden has a square patio of side x metres in one corner.

The remainder of the garden is lawn.

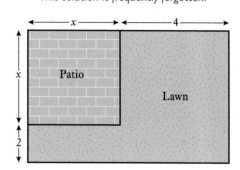

  a   Write down an expression for the longest side of the garden.   **(1 mark)**

The area of the garden is 63 m².

  b   Show that an equation for the area of the whole garden is

  $x^2 + 6x + 8 = 63$ **(3 marks)**

  c   Solve this equation to find the length, x, of the patio.   **(3 marks)**

  a $x + 4$ **1 mark**

  b   The length of the shortest side is $x + 2$.   **1 mark**

  The area of the whole garden is length × breadth $= (x + 4)(x + 2)$ **1 mark**

  Expand the brackets: $x^2 + 2x + 4x + 8$

  So $x^2 + 6x + 8 = 63$ **1 mark**

  c $x^2 + 6x + 8 - 63 = 0$

  So $x^2 + 6x - 55 = 0$ **1 mark**

  Factorise: $(x + 11)(x - 5) = 0$ **1 mark**

  Either $x + 11 = 0$ or $x - 5 = 0$

  $x = -11$ or $x = 5$

  But x is a length, and cannot have a negative value, so only one value of x is the answer.

  So $x = 5$ **1 mark**

  ← *Only one value of x must be written on the answer line*

1 **a** Expand and simplify

$(2x - 5)(x + 3)$ **(2 marks)**

   b i Factorise

$x^2 + 6x - 7$

     ii Solve the equation

$x^2 + 6x - 7 = 0$ **(3 marks)**

[S1999 P4 Q20]

2 **i** Factorise

$x^2 - 6x + 8$

   ii Solve the equation

$x^2 - 6x + 8 = 0$ **(3 marks)**

[S2001 P4 Q22]

3 **a** Solve

$$7 - \frac{3x}{2} = 11$$ **(2 marks)**

   b i Factorise

$x^2 + 4x - 12$

Hence, or otherwise,

     ii Solve

$x^2 + 4x - 12 = 0$ **(4 marks)**

[S1998 P4 Q17]

4 The diagram shows a rectangle with length
$3x + 2$ and width $2x$.
All measurements are given in centimetres.
The perimeter of the rectangle is P
centimetres.
The area of the rectangle is A square
centimetres.

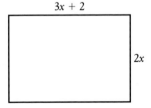

   a Write down an expression in its simplest form, in terms of x, for

     i P,   **ii** A.   **(3 marks)**

$P = 44$.

   b Work out the value of A.   **(3 marks)**

[S1999 P4 Q13]

5 The diagram shows a rectangular pond and a path.
The outside edges of the path form the rectangle ABCD.

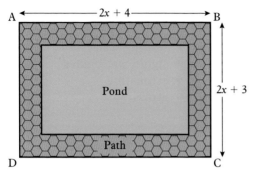

Diagram **NOT**
accurately drawn.

The length, in metres, of AB is $2x + 4$.
The length, in metres, of BC is $2x + 3$.

a Write down, in terms of x, an expression for the perimeter of the rectangle
ABCD
Write down your expression in its simplest form. **(2 marks)**

The area of the pond is 12 m^2.

b Show that the area, in m^2, of the path is $4x^2 + 14x$. **(3 marks)**

c Use the expression
$$4x^2 + 14x$$
to find the area of the path when $x = 1.2$. **(2 marks)**
[N1999 P3 Q21]

6

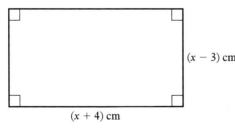

Diagram **NOT**
accurately drawn.

$(x - 3) \text{ cm}$

$(x + 4) \text{ cm}$

The length of a rectangle is $(x + 4) \text{ cm}$.
The width is $(x - 3) \text{ cm}$.
The area of the rectangle is 78 cm^2.

a Use this information to write down an equation in terms of x. **(2 marks)**
b **i** Show that your equation in part **a** can be written as
$$x^2 + x - 90 = 0$$

ii Find the values of x which are the solutions of the equation
$$x^2 + x - 90 = 0$$

iii Write down the length and the width of the rectangle. **(6 marks)**
[N2000 P3 Q24]

28 Working with errors

You need to know about:

- reading scales
- significant figures
- estimating
- errors

To read a point on a scale first work out what each division stands for.

This scale shows divisions in two different sizes

Each large division is 200 g

$$\text{200 g} \qquad \text{400 g} \qquad \text{600 g}$$

There are 10 small divisions between each large one.

Each small division stands for a weight of 200 g ÷ 10 = 20 g

The pointer is at 3 small divisions after 400 g. 400 g + (3 × 20 g) = 460 g
The weight shown by the pointer is 460 g.

To **round to any number of significant figures**:
  (1) Look at the first unwanted digit.
  (2) If it is 5, 6, 7, 8, or 9 add 1 to the last digit that you are keeping.
      If it is 0, 1, 2, 3 or 4 ignore it.
  (3) Be careful to keep the number about the right size.

428.5 to 2 sf is 430. It is not 43.
The 8 is the first unwanted digit.
This changes the 2 to a 3 when you round.

5489.06 to 1 sf is 5000. It is not 5.
The 4 is the first unwanted digit.
This does not change the 5 when you round.

The simplest way to estimate an answer is to round all the numbers to 1 sf.

Example   Estimate the answer to (23.67 + 39.021) ÷ 4.897.

              Rounding to 1 sf gives (20 + 40) ÷ 5 = 60 ÷ 5 = 12.

When you are estimating the answer to a fraction you can get a more reliable estimate using factors.

Example   Estimate the answer to $\dfrac{34.07 \times 19.265}{44.81}$.

$$\frac{35 \times 18}{45} = \frac{35 \times 18}{5 \times 9} = \frac{35}{5} \times \frac{18}{9} = 7 \times 2 = 14$$

Error   The difference between an exact answer and an estimate is called an **error**.
              Always make the error positive by taking the smaller number from the bigger one.

| **Percentage error** | The **percentage error** gives a better idea of the size of an error. |

$$\text{Percentage error} = \frac{\text{error}}{\text{exact value}} \times 100\%$$

Example

The exact value of a length is 2.41 cm. Paula measures it as 2.5 cm. Work out Paula's percentage error.

$$\text{Percentage error} = \frac{2.5 - 2.41}{2.41} \times 100\% = 3.7\% \text{ to 2 sf}$$

A length is measured as 7.5 cm to 1 dp.
The **minimum** value the exact
length can be is 7.45.
The **maximum** value the exact
length can be is 7.55.

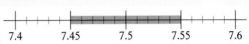

7.4   7.45   7.5   7.55   7.6

All the lengths on the red part of the scale
are rounded to 7.5 to 1 dp.

The capacity of a mug is measured
as 370 ml to 2 sf.
The **minimum** the capacity can
be is 365 ml.
The **maximum** the capacity can
be is 375 ml.

360   365   370   375   380

All the capacities on the blue part of the
scale are rounded to 370 to 2 sf.

Example

The length and width of this frame are measured to the nearest centimetre.

a Write down the minimum and maximum possible values of the length.

b Find the minimum value of the perimeter.

c Find the maximum value of the perimeter.

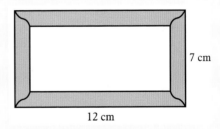

7 cm

12 cm

a Minimum value = 11.5 cm.
Maximum value = 12.5 cm.

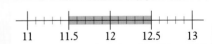

11   11.5   12   12.5   13

b To find the **minimum** value of the perimeter you use the minimum values of the length and width of the rectangle.
Minimum length = 11.5 cm   Minimum width = 6.5 cm
Minimum value of the perimeter = 11.5 + 6.5 + 11.5 + 6.5 = 36 cm

c To find the **maximum** value of the perimeter you use the maximum values of the length and width of the rectangle.
Maximum length = 12.5 cm   Maximum width = 7.5 cm
Maximum value of the perimeter = 12.5 + 7.5 + 12.5 + 7.5 = 40 cm

1 Write down the values shown by the pointers.

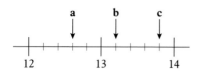 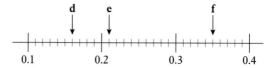

2 Round these numbers.

    a 229 to 1 sf   **c** 0.084 93 to 3 sf   **e** 0.000 058 7 to 1 sf

    b 999 to 2 sf   **d** 1.876 99 to 4 sf   **f** 350 040 to 1 sf

3 Work these out.
Write down the answer and an estimate for each one.

    a 8.93×9.8 **b** $985.88 \div 49$ **c** 0.048×0.32

4 Write down the minimum and maximum values of each number.
The accuracy of the number is given in brackets.

    a 3 g (nearest g)   **d** 5700 kg (nearest 100 kg)

    b 4.3 cm (nearest 0.1 cm)   **e** 3000 km (1 sf)

    c 54 cm (2 sf)   **f** 5.2 cm (nearest mm)

5 In each of the shapes, the lengths are correct to the nearest centimetre.
    i Write down the minimum and maximum values for each
       measurement shown.
    ii Work out the minimum and maximum perimeter.

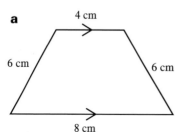 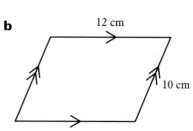

6 Joe rides to school on his bike each day. He estimates that the journey
will take him 30 minutes. The journey actually takes him 19 minutes.

    a Work out Joe's error in minutes.

    b Work out the percentage error in his estimate.
       Give your answer to 3 sf.

These questions would appear on a non-calculator paper.

1 Karen has a pencil of length 10 cm, correct to the nearest centimetre.
Write down
   a the minimum length the pencil could be
   b the maximum length the pencil could be.   **(2 marks)**

   a *Go down half a unit:* 9.5 cm   **1 mark**
   b *Go up half a unit:* 10.5 cm   **1 mark**

2 Find an estimate for $\dfrac{(4.1 \times 6.7)^2}{16.2 \times 55.8}$.   **(4 marks)**

Give your answer as a decimal, correct to 1 decimal place.

*Do **not** work out the bracket: write down the squares of the individual numbers.*

$$\frac{4.1^2 \times 6.7^2}{16.2 \times 55.8} = \frac{4^2 \times 7^2}{16 \times 56} = \frac{\cancel{16} \times \cancel{49}^{7}}{\cancel{16} \times \cancel{56}_{8}} = \frac{1 \times 7}{1 \times 8} = \frac{7}{8}$$ **2 mark**

      1 mark   Cancel   Cancel by 7

The fraction $\frac{7}{8}$ can be shown as a decimal: 0.875 or 0.9 (to 1 dp).
      1 mark

3 The length of a pole has been measured
as 1.3 m, to the nearest $\frac{1}{10}$ m.
Four poles are put together, end to end.

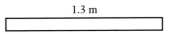

1.3 m

   a Work out the maximum total length the four poles could be.
   b Work out the minimum total length the four poles could be.
      (3 marks)

   a maximum 1.35   So $4 \times 1.35 = 5.4$ m   **1 mark**

1.3   **1 mark**

   b minimum 1.25   So $4 \times 1.25 = 5.0$ m   **1 mark**

1 **i** Write down two numbers you could use to estimate the answer to
$$793 \div 21$$
ii Work out your estimate. **(3 marks)**
[N1997 P3 Q5]

2 **a** Write down two numbers you could use to get an approximate answer to
$$41 \times 89$$ **(2 marks)**
b Work out your approximate answer. **(1 mark)**
c Work out the difference between your approximate answer and the exact answer. **(2 marks)**
[N1996 P4 Q5]

3 Jomo is going to design a circular roundabout. The roundabout will have a circumference of 7 metres.
Jomo is given three estimates for the length of the diameter of the roundabout.
The estimates are:

2.227 880 3 metres
2 metres
2.23 metres

a Give a reason why 2.23 metres is the most reasonable estimate to use. **(1 mark)**
b Explain why 2.227 880 3 metres and 2 metres are not appropriate to use. **(2 marks)**
[S1996 P4 Q10]

4 **a** Work out an estimate for
$$\frac{3.08 \times 693.89}{0.47}$$ **(3 marks)**

The length of a rod is 98 cm correct to the nearest centimetre.
b **i** Write down the maximum value that 98 cm could be.
ii Write down the minimum value that 98 cm could be. **(2 marks)**
[S2000 P3 Q19]

5 Work out an estimate for
$$\frac{88.3 \times 4.24}{72.5 - 9.87}$$ **(3 marks)**
[N2000 P3 Q12]

6 Work out an estimate for the value of

$$\frac{29.91 - 2 \times 10.03}{29.91^2 - 10.03^2}$$

Give your answer as a fraction in its simplest form. **(3 marks)**
[S2001 P3 Q16]

7 Matthew uses this formula to calculate the value of D.

$$D = \frac{a - 3c}{a - c^2}$$

a Calculate the value of D when $a = 19.9$ and $c = 4.05$.
Write down all the figures on your calculator display. **(3 marks)**

Matthew estimates the value of D without using a calculator.

b i Write down an approximate value for each of a and c that
Matthew could use to estimate the value of D.
ii Work out the estimate that these approximations give for the
value of D.
Show all your working. **(3 marks)**
[S1997 P3 Q20]

8 Karen has a pencil that has a length of 10 centimetres, correct to the
nearest centimetre.

Write down

i the minimum length the pencil could be,
ii the maximum length the pencil could be. **(2 marks)**
[S1999 P4 Q19]

9 a Calculate the area, in cm², of the circle of
diameter 12 cm.
Give your answer correct to 1 decimal
place. **(3 marks)**

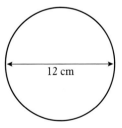

When the diameter was measured, this
measurement was rounded to 12 cm, to the
nearest centimetre.

b i Write down the minimum length, in cm, it could be.
ii Write down the maximum length, in cm, it could be. **(2 marks)**
[S1996 P4 Q15]

29 Percentages and decimals

You need to know about:

- percentages and multipliers
- finance

Multipliers can be used to help with percentage problems.

Example   Find 65% of 540 g.

Change 65% to a decimal: $65\% = \dfrac{65}{100} = 0.65$

Use 0.65 as the multiplier: 65% of 540 g = 540 × 0.65 = 351 g

VAT is charged at 17.5%. The multiplier for VAT is 0.175.

The VAT to be added to a service bill of £78.95 = £78.95 × 0.175 = £13.82 to the nearest penny.

To **decrease an amount by a percentage** the multiplier will always be between 0 and 1.

Example   The price, £34, of a game is reduced by 35%. Find the reduced price.

The reduced price is 100% − 35% = 65% of the original price so the multiplier is 0.65.

Reduced price = £34 × 0.65 = £22.10

To **increase an amount by a percentage** the multiplier will always be bigger than 1.

Example   VAT charged at 17.5% is added to a bill of £46.50
Find the total amount to be paid.

100% + 17.5% = 117.5%, so the multiplier is 1.175.

Amount to be paid = £46.50 × 1.175 = £54.64 to the nearest penny.

Sometimes you will need to **combine percentage changes**.

Example   Keith bought his classic Morgan car for £18 000. Over the next year, the value of the car went up by 8%. At the end of the year Keith damaged the car and its value dropped by 21%. Find the final value of the car.

The multiplier for the increase is 1.08
The multiplier for the decrease is 0.79
Together these give a multiplier of 1.08 × 0.79 = 0.8532
The final value of the car = £18 000 × 0.8532 = £15 357.60

You can use multipliers to **undo percentage change**.
You **divide** by the multiplier to undo a percentage change.

Example   All prices are reduced by 30% in a sale. The sale price of a TV is £591.50. Find the original price.

The multiplier is 0.7 to go from the original price to the sale price so **divide by 0.7** to go from the sale price to the original price.
Original price = £591.50 ÷ 0.7 = £845

Tax allowance   You can earn a certain amount of money before you start to pay tax.
This amount is called your **tax allowance**.

Taxable income   You take the tax allowance from what you earn to find your **taxable income**.

Example   Simon earned £8300 last year. His tax allowance was £4560 and he paid tax at the 10% rate. How much tax did Simon pay?

Taxable income = £8300 − £4560 = £3740
Tax paid = 10% of £3740 = 0.1 × £3740 = £374

You use multipliers for **compound interest**.

Example   Mira opens an investment account with £2500. The money earns 4% per year compound interest for 3 years. No money is withdrawn during this time.

a   How much will be in the account at the end of the 3 years?

b   How much compound interest will be paid?

a   1.04 is the multiplier for increasing an amount by 4%.
You multiply by **1.04** to find the amount at the end of each year.

Start	End of year 1	End of year 2	End of year 3

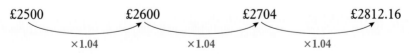

£2500   £2600   £2704   £2812.16
        ×1.04   ×1.04   ×1.04

So, for the value after **3** years, you multiply by $1.04 \times 1.04 \times 1.04 = 1.04^3$.
The value at the end of the **3** years is $£2500 \times 1.04^3 = £2812.16$.

b   To find the compound interest you subtract the original amount.
The compound interest = £2812.16 − £2500 = £312.16

1 **a** Write down the multiplier for working out 15% of an amount.
  b Work out 15% of each of these.
    Give your answers to the nearest penny where you need to round.
      i £128   **ii** £76.40   **iii** £38.59   **iv** £1460

2 Write down the multiplier for reducing an amount by:
  a 18%   **b** 24%   **c** 16.5%   **d** 73%

3 Write down the multiplier to increase an amount by:
  a 40%   **b** 17.5%   **c** 8%   **d** 110%

4 Jenny spends £540 in December on food for her family.
  a In January Jenny spends 8% less on food than in December.
    How much does she spend on food in January?
  b In February Jenny spends 7% more on food than in December.
    How much does she spend on food in February?

5 In a sale, prices are reduced by 20%.
  The sale price of a coat is £150.
  Work out the price of the coat before the sale.

6 Raj earns £25 470 in one year.
  He has a tax allowance of £6300.
  Raj pays tax at the 10% rate on the first £5000 of his taxable income.
  He pays tax at the 22% rate on the rest of his income.
  a How much tax does Raj pay at the 10% rate?
  b How much tax does he pay at the 22% rate?
  c How much tax does Raj pay altogether?

7 Julian bought an antique grandfather clock for £25 000 in January 1995.
  If it increases in value by 5% each year, how much is it worth in January 2002?
  Give your answer to the nearest penny.

8 During February, Alistair's weekly journey to work took a total of $7\frac{1}{2}$ hours.
  In March, major roadworks increased his weekly journey time by 35%.
  In April, the roadworks were completed and his March journey time was reduced by 45%.
  What was Alistair's journey time during April?
  Give your answer to the nearest minute.

1 Harold invests £800 in a bank account at 8% p.a. interest for 3 years.
He works out his interest after 3 years using a **simple** interest method.
The bank works out the interest using a **compound interest** method.
Calculate the difference between the two methods. **(6 marks)**

Simple interest: $\dfrac{£800 \times 8 \times 3}{100} = £192.00$ **1 mark for method**
1 mark for value of interest

Remember to show your method.

Compound interest:

£800 $\longrightarrow$ £864 $\longrightarrow$ £933.12 $\longrightarrow$ £1007.77 **1 mark for method**
$\times 1.08$ $\times 1.08$ $\times 1.08$ **1 mark for final amount**

Remember to show your method.

So compound interest $= £1007.77 - £800 = £207.77$ **1 mark**

Remember that £1007.77 is the final amount, so you will need to calculate the interest in a final step.

The difference between the methods is: $£207.77 - £192.00 = £15.77$ **1 mark**

2 A car cost £14 000 when it was new. Now it is worth £9100.

a Express the change in value as a fraction of its value when it was new.
Give your answer in its simplest form. **(3 marks)**

The value of another car has dropped by 20%.
Its value is now £8200

b What was its original value? **(3 marks)**

a Change in value $= £14\,000 - £9100 = £4900$ **1 mark**

Fraction $= \dfrac{£4900}{£14\,000} = \dfrac{49}{140} = \dfrac{7}{20}$
1 mark for writing fraction
1 mark for simplifying fraction

Write this down before you attempt to cancel.

b A reduction of 20% brings a value down from 100% to 80%,
so the multiplier is 0.80. **1 mark**

The original value $= \dfrac{£8200}{0.80} = £10\,250$
1 mark for writing fraction
1 mark for simplifying fraction

173

1 In a sale all the prices are reduced by 30%.
The sale price of a jacket is £28.

Work out the price of the jacket before the sale. **(3 marks)**
[N2000 P4 Q19]

2 In a sale, all the normal prices are reduced by 15%.

The normal price of a jacket is £42.
Syreeta buys the jacket in the sale.

> **SALE**
> **15% OFF**
> **all prices**

a Work out the sale price of the jacket. **(2 marks)**

In the same sale, Winston pays £15.64 for a shirt.

b Calculate the normal price of the shirt. **(3 marks)**
[S2001 P4 Q14]

3 A clothes shop has a sale.
All the original prices are reduced by 24% to give the sale price.
The sale price of a jacket is £36.86.
Work out the original price of the jacket. **(3 marks)**
[N1999 P3 Q19]

4 The price of a new television is £423.
The price includes Value Added Tax (VAT) at $17\frac{1}{2}$%.

a Work out the cost of the television **before** VAT was added. **(3 marks)**

By the end of each year, the value of a television has fallen by 12% of its value at the start of that year.
The value of a television was £423 at the start of the first year.

b Work out the value of the television at the end of the **third** year.
Give your answer to the nearest penny. **(4 marks)**
[S2000 P4 Q19]

5 A shop is having a sale. Each day, prices are reduced by 20% of the price on the previous day.

Before the start of the sale, the price of a television is £450.

On the first day of the sale, the price is reduced by 20%.

a Work out the price of the television on
   i the first day of the sale,
   ii the third day of the sale. **(5 marks)**

On the first day of the sale, the price of a cooker is £300.

b Work out the price of the cooker before the start of the sale.

(2 marks)
[N1998 P3 Q17]

6 £500 is invested for 2 years at 6% per annum compound interest.

a Work out the total interest earned over the 2 years. **(3 marks)**

£250 is invested for 3 years at 7% per annum compound interest.

b By what single number must £250 be multiplied to obtain the total amount at the end of the 3 years? **(1 mark)**
[S1998 P3 Q14]

7 Joe put £5000 in a building society savings account.
Compound interest at 4.8% was added at the end of each year.

a Calculate the total amount of money in Joe's savings account at the end of 3 years. Give your answer to the nearest penny. **(4 marks)**

Sarah also put a sum of money in a building society savings account.
Compound interest at 5% was added at the end of each year.

b Work out the number by which Sarah has to multiply her sum of money to find the total amount she will have after 3 years.

(2 marks)
[N1999 P4 Q13]

8 £5000 is invested for 3 years at 4% per annum **compound** interest.
Work out the total interest earned over the three years. **(3 marks)**
[S2001 P4 Q15]

30 Solid shapes

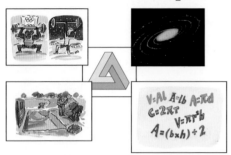

You need to know about:

- plans and elevations
- units of mass and capacity
- finding volumes
- density
- dimensions

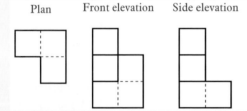

This object is made of cubes.

The **plan** is the view from above.
The **front elevation** is the view from the front.
The **side elevation** is the view from the side.

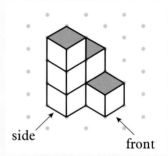

Plan   Front elevation   Side elevation

| **Metric units of mass** | The **metric units of mass** are milligrams (mg), grams (g), kilograms (kg) and tonnes (t). |

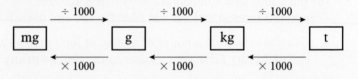

| **Metric units of capacity** | The **metric units of capacity** are millilitres (ml), centilitres (cl) and litres (l) (A capacity of 1 ml is the same as a volume of 1 cm^3.) |

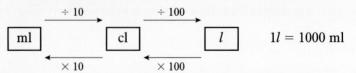

$1l = 1000$ ml

| **Imperial units of mass** | The **imperial units of mass** are ounces (oz), pounds (lb) and stones (st) |

$16\,oz = 1\,lb$ $14\,lb = 1\,st$

| **Imperial units of capacity** | The **imperial units of capacity** are pints (pt), quarts (qt) and gallons (gal). |

$$2 \, \text{pt} = 1 \, \text{qt} \quad 4 \, \text{qt} = 1 \, \text{gal} \quad 8 \, \text{pt} = 1 \, \text{gal}$$

| **Converting between metric and imperial units** | You need to know these conversions: |

1 kg is about 2.2 lb   1 l is about $1\frac{3}{4}$ pt   4.5 l is about 1 gal

The **volume of a cuboid** = length × width × height

A **prism** is a solid that is exactly the same shape and size all the way through.
The **volume of a prism** = area of cross section × length

Example   Find the volume of this prism.

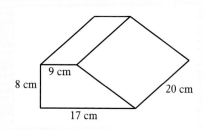

First find the area of the cross section.
The cross section is a trapezium.
Area of the trapezium = $\frac{1}{2}(9 + 17) \times 8$
                      = 104 cm^2

Volume of the prism = 104 × 20
                    = 2080 cm^3

The **volume of a cylinder** = $\pi r^2 h$ where r is the radius of the circle and h is the height.

Example   Find the volume of this cylinder.

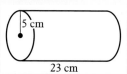

Volume = $\pi r^2 h = \pi \times 5^2 \times 23$
       = 1810 cm^3 (3 sf)

If you know the volume and length of a prism, you can work out the cross-sectional area.

Volume = Area of cross section × length $V = A \times l$

so Area of cross section = Volume ÷ length $A = \dfrac{V}{l}$

Example   The volume of this prism is 2652 cm^3.
Find the area of the cross section.

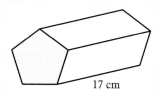

Area of cross section = 2652 ÷ 17
                      = 156 cm^2

If you know the volume and height of a cylinder, you can work out the radius.

Example   The volume of this cylinder is 400 cm³.
          Find the radius.

$$V = \pi r^2 h \text{ so } r^2 = \frac{V}{\pi h}$$

$$r^2 = \frac{400}{\pi \times 8}$$

$$= 15.915 \ldots$$

$$r = \sqrt{15.195}$$

$$= 3.99 \text{ cm (3 sf)}$$

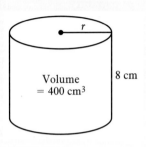

Volume = 400 cm³   8 cm

The mass of a solid is proportional to its volume.

$$\text{Density} = \frac{\text{Mass}}{\text{Volume}}$$

The units of density are g/cm³ or kg/m³.

Example   Gold has a density of 19.3 g/cm³. A gold charm weighs 57 g.
          Find the volume of the charm.

$$\text{Volume} = \frac{\text{Mass}}{\text{Density}} = \frac{57}{19.3} = 2.95 \text{ cm}^3 \text{ (3 sf)}$$

Dimension   The **dimension** of a formula is the number of lengths that are
                      multiplied together.

Constant   A **constant** has no dimension. It is just a number. 4, 8, 12 and π
                      are all constants.

Length has **one** dimension. $C = \pi d$ is a length formula.
Area has **two** dimensions. $A = \pi r^2$ is an area formula.
Volume has **three** dimensions. $V = \pi r^2 h$ is a volume formula.

Some formulas have more than one part. Each part must have the same dimension.
Look at the formula $S = 2\pi r^2 + 4\pi rh$.
Both $2\pi r^2$ and $4\pi rh$ are constant $\times$ constant $\times$ **length** $\times$ **length** so this is an area formula.

You can **cancel dimensions**.

In the formula $D = \dfrac{6x^2 y}{z}$, x, y and z are lengths.

So $D = \dfrac{\text{constant} \times \text{length} \times \text{length} \times \text{length}}{\text{length}} = \text{constant} \times \text{length} \times \text{length}$

This is a formula for area.

1 a Copy the diagram on to isometric paper.
   b Draw the plan view.
   c Draw the front elevation.
   d Draw the side elevation.

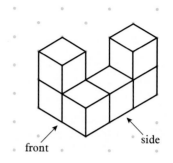

2 Change each of these to the units shown.
   a 4.8 t to kg   **c** 3.76 cl to ml   **e** 5760 g to kg
   b 53 l to cl   **d** 0.56 kg to g   **f** 489 ml to l

3 Change each of these imperial units to the metric units shown.
   a 4.4 lb to kg   **c** 2 gal to litres   **e** 6.6 lb to kg
   b $3\frac{1}{2}$ pt to ml   **d** 1.1 lb to g   **f** $2\frac{1}{2}$ gal to l

4 Change each of these to the units shown.
   a 6 lb to oz   **c** 4 st to lb   **e** 3 st 5 lb to lb
   b $7\frac{1}{2}$ lb to oz   **d** $5\frac{1}{2}$ st to lb   **f** 70 lb to st

5 Change each of these volumes into cm³.
   a 3 m³   **b** 2.8 m³   **c** 48 600 mm³

6 Aluminium has a density of 2700 kg/m³.
   The frame of a conservatory weighs 3864 kg.
   Work out the volume of the frame in m³.
   Give your answer to 3 sf.

7 Find the volumes of these shapes.
   Give your answers to 3 sf.
   a   **b**   **c**

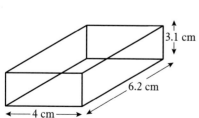
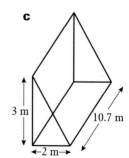

8 A cylinder has a volume of 65 cm³.
   The height of the cylinder is 7.1 cm.
   Find its radius to the nearest millimetre.

1 A skip is in the shape of a prism with cross section ABCD.
AD = 2.3 m, DC = 1.3 m, and BC = 1.7 m.
The width of the skip is 1.5 m.

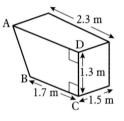

  a Calculate the area of the shape ABCD.   **(2 marks)**

  b Calculate the volume of the skip.   **(2 marks)**

  c The weight of the empty skip is 650 kg.
    The skip is full to the top with sand of density 4300 kg/m³.
    Find the total weight of the skip.   **(3 marks)**

  a *The shape is a trapezium.*
    The formula for working out the area of a trapezium is
    on the formula sheet.
    In this problem, a = 1.7, b = 2.3 and h = 1.3.

      Area $= \frac{1}{2}(1.7 + 2.3)1.3$ **1 mark**
             $= \frac{1}{2} \times 4 \times 1.3 = 2.6 \text{ m}^2$ **1 mark**

Area =
$\frac{1}{2}(a + b)h$

  b Volume = area of cross section × length (depth).

             $= 2.6 \times 1.5$ **1 mark**
             $= 3.9 \text{ m}^3$ **1 mark**

*Show what you are
going to calculate
before you do the
calculation.*

  c Weight of sand = 3.9 m³ × 4300   = 16 770 kg   **1 mark**
    add the weight of the skip: +   650 kg   **1 mark**

    Total weight of the skip   = 17 420 kg   **1 mark**

2 Here are some expressions.
The letters r and x
represent lengths.
π is a number which has
no dimension.

$\dfrac{\pi r^2}{x}$	$\pi(r + x)$	$\pi r + r$	$\dfrac{\pi r^3}{x}$	$\pi r^2 + rx$	$\pi r^4 + \pi rx$

  a Put ticks in the boxes under the **two** expressions that could represent
    areas.   **(2 marks)**

  b Put a cross in the box under the **one** expression that cannot represent a
    length, an area or a volume.   **(1 mark)**

       $\dfrac{\pi r^2}{x}$*, π(r + x) = πr + πx and πr + r are lengths.*

       $\dfrac{\pi r^3}{x}$ *and πr² + rx are areas. πr⁴ + πx has mixed dimensions.*

  a Tick $\dfrac{\pi r^3}{x}$ *and πr² + rx.*   **1 mark each**

    *Tick **only** two: any more and you could incur penalties.*

  b Cross *πr⁴ + πx.*   **1 mark**

1

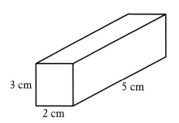

Diagram **NOT**
accurately drawn.

3 cm   5 cm

2 cm

The diagram shows a solid cuboid.

a Work out the volume of the cuboid.   **(1 mark)**

b On an isometric grid, make an accurate full size drawing of the
cuboid.   **(2 marks)**
[N2000 P4 Q1]

2

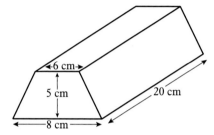

Diagram **NOT**
accurately drawn.

6 cm

5 cm   20 cm

8 cm

The diagram shows a prism.
The cross section of the prism is a trapezium.
The lengths of the parallel sides of the trapezium are 8 cm and 6 cm.
The distance between the parallel sides of the trapezium is 5 cm.
The length of the prism is 20 cm.

a Work out the volume of the prism.   **(3 marks)**

The prism is made out of gold.
Gold has a density of 19.3 grams per cm^3.

b Work out the mass of the prism.
Give your answer in kilograms.   **(2 marks)**
[N2000 P4 Q17]

3 The expressions below can be used to calculate lengths, areas or volumes of some
shapes.
The letters p, q and r represent lengths.
π and 2 are numbers and have no dimension.

Draw a circle around each of the **three** expressions that can be used to calculate
an **area**.

$$\pi(p + q) \qquad \frac{pq}{r} \qquad rq(p + q) \qquad \pi pq \qquad \frac{p^2 r}{2}$$

$$2r \qquad \frac{qr}{2} \qquad r(p + q) \qquad \frac{p^2 \pi}{r} \qquad \frac{\pi pqr}{2} \qquad \textbf{(3 marks)}$$
[S2001 P3 Q24]

31 More probability

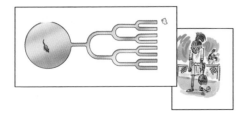

You need to know about:

- tree diagrams
- changing probabilities

You can use **tree diagrams** to show the outcomes of two or more events.

You **multiply** the probabilities along the branch.
You **add** the probabilities when more than one path is used.

Example   Jon rolls a dice three times. Find the probability that Jon gets:

    a three 4s   **b** exactly two 4s   **c** at least one 4

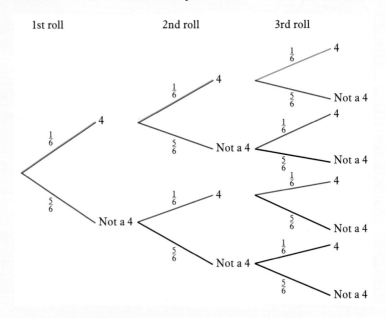

a The blue path gives three 4s.
$P(\text{three 4s}) = \frac{1}{6} \times \frac{1}{6} \times \frac{1}{6} = \frac{1}{216}$

b The three red paths give exactly two 4s.
$P(\text{exactly two 4s}) = (\frac{1}{6} \times \frac{1}{6} \times \frac{5}{6}) + (\frac{1}{6} \times \frac{5}{6} \times \frac{1}{6}) + (\frac{5}{6} \times \frac{1}{6} \times \frac{1}{6}) = \frac{15}{216}$

c The probability of at least one is the same as $1 -$ the probability of none.
$P(\text{at least one 4}) = 1 - P(\text{no 4s}) = 1 - (\frac{5}{6} \times \frac{5}{6} \times \frac{5}{6}) = 1 - \frac{125}{216} = \frac{91}{216}$

Sometimes one of the paths of a tree diagram stops before the others.

Example   Ken is taking his driving test. The probability of him passing is 0.7
If he fails, he resits the exam. Find the probability that he passes on the
third try.

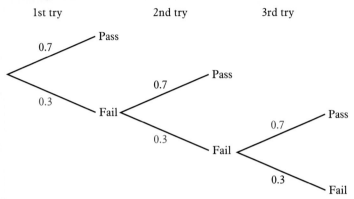

$$P \text{ (Ken passes on the 3rd try)} = 0.3 \times 0.3 \times 0.7 = 0.063$$

Probabilities can change depending on the outcome of the first event.

Example   Winston has two tennis matches to play. The probability that he wins a
match is $\frac{3}{5}$.
If Winston wins the first match the probability that he wins the second
match is $\frac{3}{4}$.
If Winston loses the first match the probability that he wins the second
match is $\frac{1}{2}$.
Use a tree diagram to find the probability that Winston

  a   wins both matches   **b**   wins only one match

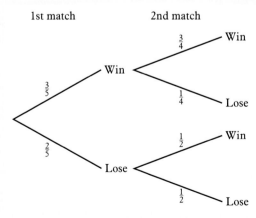

  a $P(\text{Winston wins both matches}) = \frac{3}{5} \times \frac{3}{4} = \frac{9}{20}$
  b $P(\text{Winston wins only one match}) = (\frac{3}{5} \times \frac{1}{4}) + (\frac{2}{5} \times \frac{1}{2}) = \frac{3}{20} + \frac{2}{10} = \frac{7}{20}$

1 Yasmin cycles to school each day. She passes through two sets of traffic lights.
The probability that the first set of lights is red is 0.3
The probability that the second set of lights is red is 0.2

a Copy this tree diagram to show all the possible outcomes.
Fill it in.

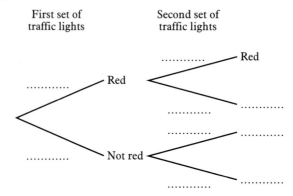

Find the probability that:

b both sets of traffic lights are red
c both sets of traffic lights are not red
d the first set of traffic lights is red but the second set is not red
e only one set of traffic lights is red.

2 Joe enjoys playing tennis and golf. He plays a tennis match and a round of golf.
The probability that he wins the tennis match is 0.7
The probability that he wins the round of golf is 0.4
Find the probability that he:

a wins at both sports   **c** wins only the game of golf
b loses at both sports   **d** wins at least one of his games

3 Trevor spins three coins.
Find the probability that he gets:

a three heads   **b** exactly two tails   **c** at least one tail

4 Cerys chooses a shirt and jacket.
The probability that she chooses a red shirt is $\frac{1}{5}$.
If she chooses a red shirt, the probability that she chooses a black jacket is $\frac{1}{3}$.
If she does not choose a red shirt, the probability that she chooses a black jacket is $\frac{3}{4}$.
Find the probability that Cerys chooses:

a a red shirt and a black jacket   **b** a black jacket

1 Every day Kevin wears either a red tie or a blue tie, each chosen at random. On any day, the probability that he will wear a red tie is $\frac{7}{10}$.
Draw a tree diagram to show the colour of Kevin's tie for Monday and Tuesday. **(2 marks)**

The probability of wearing a particular tie is $\frac{7}{10}$ for red, and therefore $\frac{3}{10}$ for blue.

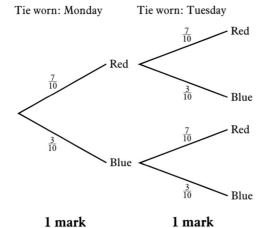

1 mark   **1 mark**

2 On an island during July, the probability that it will rain on any day is 0.2. Draw a tree diagram to show the rain for three consecutive days. **(3 marks)**

Start by dividing each event into either:
*   the probability that it will rain (0.2)*
*or   the probability that it will **not** rain (0.8)*

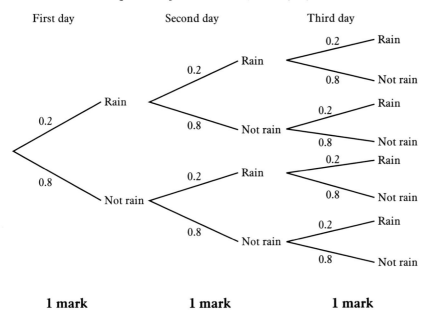

All probabilities are less than 1 (**not** whole numbers) and should be written as decimals, fractions or percentages.

1 mark   **1 mark**   **1 mark**

185

1 Sharon has 12 computer discs.
   Five of the discs are red.
   Seven of the discs are black.
   She keeps all the discs in a box.
   Sharon removes one disc at random. She records its colour and replaces it in the box.
   Sharon removes a second disc at random, and again records its colour.
   Complete the tree diagram.

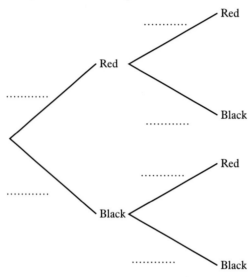

(2 marks)
[S1999 P4 Q18]

2 Esther and Nathan are going to a café for a meal.
   The probability that Esther will order a pizza is 0.8.
   The probability that Nathan will order a pizza is 0.7.
   Complete the tree diagram.

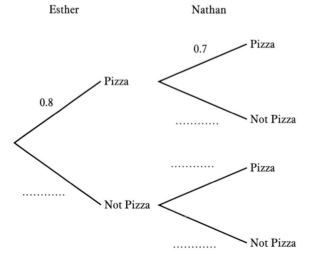

(2 marks)
[N1999 P3 Q24]

3 Helen and Joan are going to take a swimming test.
The probability that Helen will pass the swimming test is 0.95.
The probability that Joan will pass the swimming test is 0.8.
The two events are independent.

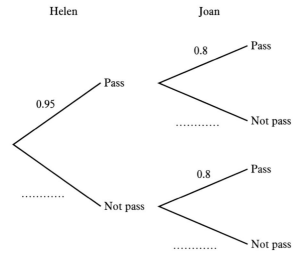

Complete the probability tree diagram.   **(2 marks)**

[N2000 P4 Q23]

4 Jason has 10 cups.
6 of the cups are Star Battle cups.
4 of the cups are Top Pops cups.
On Monday Jason picks at random one cup from the 10 cups.
On Tuesday he picks at random one cup from the same 10 cups.

Complete the probability tree diagram.

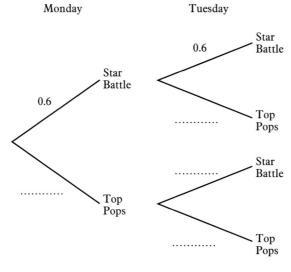

(2 marks)

[S2001 P3 Q25]

32 Inner space

You need to know about:

- congruence
- lines and planes of symmetry
- rotational symmetry
- angles in polygons
- similar triangles

Two shapes are **congruent** if they have the same size and shape.

A **line of symmetry** divides a shape into two identical halves.
Each half is a reflection of the other in the line of symmetry.
The red line in the diagram is a line of symmetry.

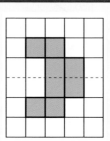

You can also have symmetry in 3 dimensions.
Instead of lines of symmetry you have planes of symmetry.
The red shading shows the planes of symmetry of this cuboid.

A shape has **rotational symmetry** if it fits on top of itself more than once as it makes a complete turn.
The **order of rotational symmetry** is the number of times that the shape fits on to itself.

For this polygon:
The blue angles are exterior angles.
The red angles are interior angles.

The sum of the exterior angles of any polygon is 360°.

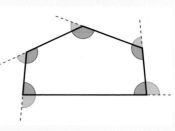

A regular polygon has all its sides equal, all the exterior angles are equal and all the interior angles are equal.

For a regular polygon:
The exterior angle = 360° ÷ number sides
The number of sides = 360° ÷ exterior angle
For this regular hexagon, exterior angle = 360° ÷ 6 = 60°

A regular polygon with n sides has n lines of symmetry and rotational symmetry of order n.
A regular octagon has 8 sides. It has 8 lines of symmetry and has rotational symmetry of order 8.

You can find the **sum of the interior angles** of any polygon.

(1) Draw the polygon.

(2) Join one vertex to all the others.
You divide the shape into triangles.
All the interior angles are now
inside one of the triangles.

(3) Count the number of triangles.
Multiply by 180° to find the total.

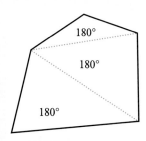

Example Find the sum of the interior angles of a pentagon.
The pentagon splits into 3 triangles.

Total = 3 × 180° = 540°

The sum of the interior angles of a pentagon is 540°.
This is true for all pentagons.

The sum of the interior angles of any polygon with n sides is $(n - 2) \times 180°$.

If two objects are **similar,** one is an enlargement of the other. They have the same shape but different sizes. All squares are similar. All circles are similar. Not all rectangles are similar.

Similar triangles have all 3 pairs of
angles equal.
The 3 pairs of sides are in the same
ratio.

Triangles ABC and FGH are similar
because BCA = GHF and CAB = HFG.
This means that two pairs of the angles
are equal so the other pair of angles
must also be equal.
The colours show the pairs of matching
angles.

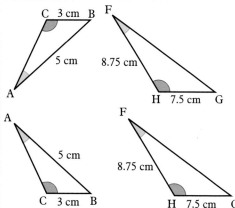

Triangle ABC can be moved so that the
equal pairs of angles are in the same position.

Going from triangle ABC to FGH

$$\text{scale factor} = \frac{GH}{BC} = \frac{7.5}{3} = 2.5$$

You can use the scale factor to find the missing lengths.

FG = 5 cm × scale factor = 5 × 2.5 = 12. 5 cm

AC = 8.75 ÷ scale factor = 8.75 ÷ 2.5 = 3.5 cm

1 Copy these shapes on to squared paper.
Shade in 6 more squares so that the red line and the blue line are both lines of symmetry.

a **b**

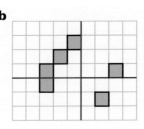

2 How many planes of symmetry are there in a
   a cuboid   **b** cube   **c** cylinder?

3 Copy the diagram.
Complete it so that it has rotational symmetry of order 4 about *C*.

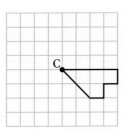

4 Copy the table. Fill it in.

Name of regular polygon	Number of sides	Size of exterior angle	Size of interior angle	Number of lines of symmetry	Order of rotational symmetry
Pentagon Hexagon Octagon Decagon					

5 Each pair of triangles are similar.
Find the missing lengths marked with letters.

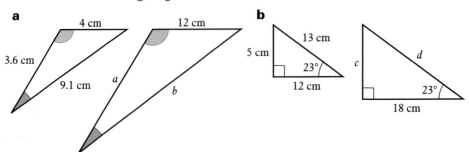

1 ABCDE is a regular polygon.
CDF and AEF are straight lines.

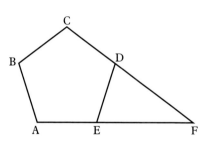

   a Write down the name given to a
polygon with 5 sides. **(1 mark)**

   b Calculate the size of an interior angle
of the polygon ABCDE. **(3 marks)**

   c **i** Explain why triangle EDF is isosceles.
      ii Calculate the size of angle EFD. **(3 marks)**

   a Pentagon   **1 mark**
   b The exterior angles of a polygon always add up to 360°.   **1 mark**
      One exterior angle of a pentagon is 360° ÷ 5 = 72°.   **1 mark**
      So the interior angle is 180° − 72° = 108°.   **1 mark**
   c **i** Angles CDE and DEA are both equal since they are both interior angles
        of a regular pentagon.
        FDE and FED are equal, since these are both exterior angles.
        So EDF is isosceles.   **1 mark**
      ii FDE = FED = 72° (from above)   **1 mark**
        EFD = 180° − 72° − 72° = 36°   **1 mark**

2 Find DB.

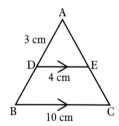

                                                           (3 marks)

Divide the diagram into two separate triangles:

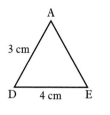 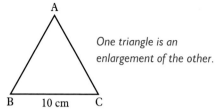

*One triangle is an
enlargement of the other.*

*To find the scale factor you match up two sides that are corresponding, and that you
know the lengths of:*

Scale factor $= \dfrac{BC}{DE} = \dfrac{10}{4} = 2.5$ *Show how you find the scale factor.*   **1 mark**

If AD = 3 cm, then AB = 3 × 2.5 = 7.5 cm   **1 mark**

So DB = AB − AD = 7.5 − 3 = 4.5 m   *Don't forget to work out the last step.*   **1 mark**

1 Draw in one plane of symmetry for each of these shapes.

i   **ii**

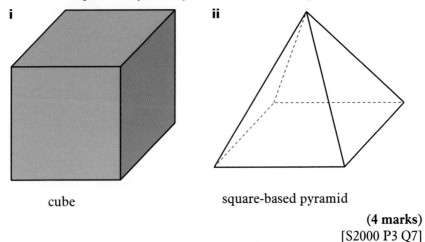

cube   square-based pyramid

(4 marks)
[S2000 P3 Q7]

2 The diagram shows a prism.

Draw one plane of symmetry of the
prism on the diagram.

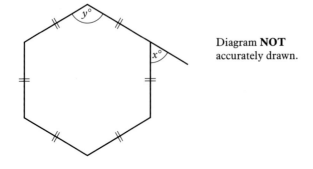

(2 marks)
[S2001 P3 Q6]

3 The diagram shows a regular hexagon.

Diagram **NOT**
accurately drawn.

a Work out the value of x.   (2 marks)
b Work out the value of y.   (1 mark)
[S2001 P3 Q13]

4

Diagram **NOT** accurately drawn.

AB : AC = 1 : 3

i Work out the length of CD.
ii Work out the length of BC. **(4 marks)**

[S1998 P3 Q15]

5

Diagram **NOT** accurately drawn.

AB is parallel to CD.
The lines AD and BC intersect at point O.
AB = 11 cm, AO = 8 cm, OD = 6 cm.
Calculate the length of CD. **(3 marks)**

[S2001 P4 Q23]

6

Diagram **NOT** accurately drawn.

BE is parallel to CD.
ABC and AED are straight lines.
AB = 6 cm, BC = 24 cm,
CD = 20 cm, AE = 3 cm.

a Calculate the length of BE. **(2 marks)**
b Calculate the length of DE. **(2 marks)**

[N2000 P3 Q18]

33 Constructions and loci

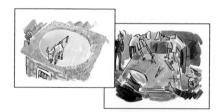

You need to know about:

- bisecting an angle and a line
- constructing angles
- constructing perpendiculars
- drawing loci

Bisecting an angle means splitting it exactly in half. All the points on the line that bisects an angle are **equidistant** from the two arms of the angle.

To bisect an angle:

Use compasses to draw the arc AB.

Put the point of your compasses on A and draw an arc.

Put the point of your compasses on B and draw another arc.

Join the vertex of the angle to where the two arcs cross.

Bisecting a line means cutting it exactly in half.
Two lines that are at right angles to each other are **perpendicular**.

To bisect a line:

Put the point of your compasses on A and draw an arc.

Put the point of your compasses on B and draw an arc.

Join the points where the arcs cross.

The line joining the points where the arcs cross is called the **perpendicular bisector** of the line.
All points on the perpendicular bisector of a line are **equidistant from the two points** at the ends of the original line.

To construct an angle of 60°:

A _____ B

Draw a line AB.

A ⌐ B

Draw an arc with the point of your compasses on A.

A ⌐ B

Put the point of your compasses where the arc crosses the line. Draw a second arc.

Join A to where the two arcs cross.

Constructing a 90° angle at a point is the same as drawing the perpendicular from a point on a line.

To construct a 90° angle at a point P:

Put the point of your compasses on P and draw an arc.

Put the point of your compasses on A and draw an arc. Do the same at B.

Join P to where the two arcs cross.

To construct the perpendicular from a point, P, to a line:

Put the point of your compasses on P and draw an arc that cuts the line in two places, A and B.

Put the point of your compasses on A first and then B and draw two arcs that cross below the line.

Join P to where the two arcs cross.

The **locus** of an object is the set of all the points that fit a certain condition.

The red line shows the locus of all points 1 cm away from the line AB.

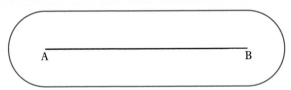

The blue line shows the locus of all points 1.5 cm from the point P.

The green shading shows the locus of all points that are less than 1.5 cm from R.
The boundary line is dotted to show it is not included.

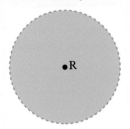

The locus of points equidistant from P and Q is the perpendicular bisector of PQ.

The locus of points equidistant from two lines AB and AC is the bisector of angle BAC.

In questions 1–4 use ruler and compasses only.

1 **a** Construct an angle of 60°.
   b Bisect this angle to show all the points that are equidistant from the two arms of the angle.

2 **a** Draw two points C and D that are 9 cm apart.
   b Join the points with a straight line.
   c Construct the perpendicular bisector of CD to show all the points that are equidistant from C and D.

3 **a** Construct this triangle.
   b Construct the perpendicular from the point Q to the line PR.

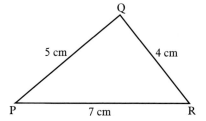

4 **a** Construct this triangle.
   b Draw the locus of a point that moves outside the triangle so that it is always 2 cm away from the edge of the triangle

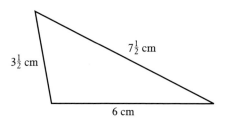

5 The diagram shows Peter's lounge and the positions of two electric sockets. Peter is vacuuming the lounge.
The vacuum lead is 10 m long.

   a Copy the diagram.
   b Draw the boundary of the region he can vacuum from socket A.
   c Draw the boundary of the region he can vacuum from socket B.
   d Use shading and a key to show the region he can vacuum from both sockets.

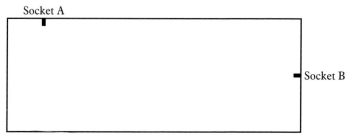

Scale: 1 cm to 2 m

These questions are to be completed using ruler and compasses only.

1 Construct accurately an equilateral triangle of side 4 cm. **(3 marks)**

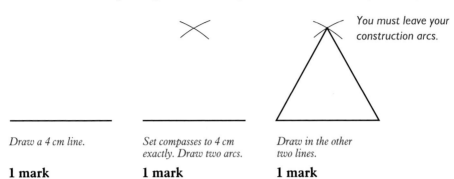

You must leave your construction arcs.

Draw a 4 cm line.

Set compasses to 4 cm exactly. Draw two arcs.

Draw in the other two lines.

1 mark **1 mark** **1 mark**

2 Construct accurately, on this diagram, the locus of points that are equidistant from OA and OB. **(2 marks)**

Set your compass to the same measurement each time.

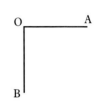

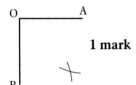 **1 mark**

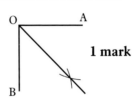 **1 mark**

You must leave in your construction lines.

3 Construct accurately, on this diagram, the locus of points that are equidistant from A and B. **(2 marks)**

Set your compass to the same measurement each time.

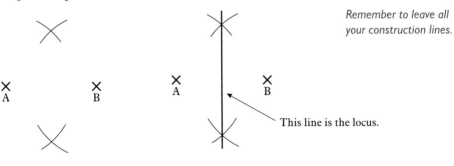

Remember to leave all your construction lines.

This line is the locus.

1 mark **1 mark**

1 Here is a sketch of a triangle.

The lengths of the sides of the triangle are 8 m, 9 m and 12 m.

Use a scale of 1 cm to 2 m to make an accurate scale drawing of the triangle.   **(3 marks)**

[S2001 P4 Q2]

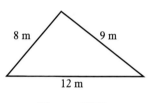

8 m   9 m

12 m

Diagram **NOT** accurately drawn.

2 In the triangle ABC,
BC = 8 cm,   angle CBA = 24°,   AB = 10 cm.

a Use the information to complete triangle ABC.
The side BC is drawn for you.

B   C   **(2 marks)**

b i Measure the size of angle BAC.
ii What mathematical name is given to angle BAC?   **(2 marks)**

[N1998 P3 Q4]

3 Draw the locus of all points which are 3 cm away from the line AB.   **(3 marks)**

[S1999 P3 Q12]

A   B

4 A treasure chest is buried on an island.
P and Q are two trees on this island.

Scale:
1 cm represents 5 m

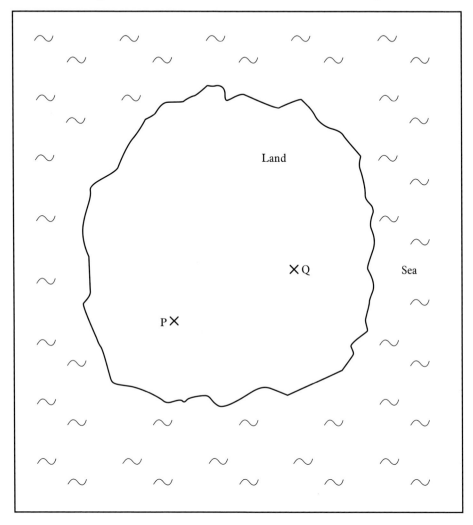

The treasure chest is buried the same distance from P as it is from Q.

a On the diagram, draw accurately the locus of points which are the same distance from P as they are from Q. **(2 marks)**

On the diagram, 1 centimetre represents 5 metres.
The treasure chest is buried 20 metres from P.

b On the diagram, draw accurately the locus which represents all the points which are 20 metres from P. **(2 marks)**

c Find the point where the treasure chest is buried. On the diagram, mark the point clearly with a T. **(1 mark)**

[N1998 P3 Q14]

34 Solving equations

You need to know about:

- drawing quadratic graphs
- using graphs to solve equations
- solving equations using trial and improvement

Use a table to help you draw quadratic curves like $y = x^2 - 3x - 1$.

x	-3	-2	-1	0	1	2	3	4	5	6
x^2	9	4	1	0	1	4	9	16	25	36
$-3x$	9	6	3	0	-3	-6	-9	-12	-15	-18
-1	-1	-1	-1	-1	-1	-1	-1	-1	-1	-1
y	17	9	3	-1	-3	-3	-1	3	9	17

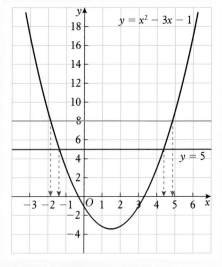

On the x axis, $y = 0$.
This means that the points where $y = x^2 - 3x - 1$ crosses the x axis are the solutions to the equation $x^2 - 3x - 1 = 0$.
The solutions are $x = -0.3$ and 3.3.

To solve the equation $x^2 - 3x - 1 = 5$ draw the line $y = 5$ onto the graph. This line is shown in red. The solutions to the equation are the x co-ordinates of the points where the line $y = 5$ cuts the curve.
The solutions are $x = -1.4$ and $x = 4.4$.

Sometimes you have to rearrange an equation to fit the graph you have drawn.

To solve the equation $x^2 - 3x - 9 = 0$ using the curve $y = x^2 - 3x - 1$ you need to rearrange the left-hand side of $x^2 - 3x - 9 = 0$ to change it to $x^2 - 3x - 1$.

The x^2 and $-3x$ terms are the same so you only need to change the number term.
Add 8 to both sides:

$$x^2 - 3x - 9 = 0$$
$$x^2 - 3x - 9 + 8 = 0 + 8$$
$$x^2 - 3x - 1 = 8$$

The left-hand side of the equation is now the same as the curve you have drawn.

Put y equal to the right-hand side, $y = 8$.
This is the line you have to draw on your graph.
Write down the x co-ordinates of the points of intersection of the curve and the line $y = 8$.
These are the solutions to the equation $x^2 - 3x - 9 = 0$.
The solutions are $x = -1.9$ and $x = 4.9$.

You can solve more complicated equations by plotting graphs.
To solve an equation using graphs:

(1) Draw graphs of both sides of the equation.

(2) Write down the x co-ordinates of the points of intersection.

Example   Solve the equation $x^2 - 3x + 4 = 3x + 2$ graphically.

   (1) Draw the graph of $y = x^2 - 3x + 4$

   (2) Draw the graph of $y = 3x + 2$

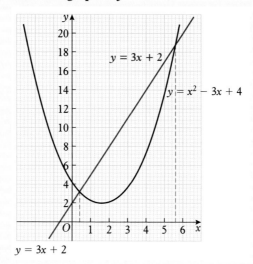

$y = 3x + 2$

The graphs intersect at $x = 0.4$ and $x = 5.6$

These values are the solutions to $x^2 - 3x + 4 = 3x + 2$

Trial and improvement is a method that can be used to solve equations.

Example   Solve $x^4 + 6x = 3100$. Give your answer to 1 dp.

Value of x	Value of $x^4 + 6x$	Bigger or smaller than 3100?	
5	655	smaller	
8	4144	bigger	
7	2443	smaller	x is between 7 and 8.
7.5	3209.062 ...	bigger	x is between 7 and 7.5.
7.4	3043.057 ...	smaller	x is between 7.4 and 7.5.
7.45	3125.227 ...	bigger	x is between 7.4 and 7.45.

This value is halfway between 7.4 and 7.5.

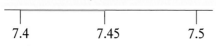

x must be somewhere in the green part of the number line. Any number in the green part rounds down to 7.4 to 1 dp.

Answer: $x = 7.4$ to 1 dp.

1 **a** Copy and complete this table for $y = x^2 - x - 6$.

x	-3	-2	-1	0	1	2	3	4
x^2			1					
$-x$			1					
-6			-6					
y			-4					

  b Use the table to draw the graph of $y = x^2 - x - 6$.
  c Use the graph to solve the equation $x^2 - x - 6 = 0$.
  d On the same axes draw the line $y = 2$.
  e Use your graphs to solve the equation $x^2 - x - 6 = 2$.
      Give your answers to 1 dp.

2 **a** Copy and complete this table for $y = x^2 - 2x - 8$.

x	-3	-2	-1	0	1	2	3	4	5
x^2			1						
$-2x$			2						
-8			-8						
y			-5						

  b Use the table to draw the graph of $y = x^2 - 2x - 8$.
  c Draw the graph of $y = x - 1$ on the same axes.
  d Use your graphs to find the solutions of the equation
      $x^2 - 2x - 8 = x - 1$.
      Give your answers to 1 dp.

3 Solve these equations using trial and improvement.
  a $x^3 - 9x = -4$ Give your answer to 2 dp.
  b $x^3 + x^2 = 861$ Give your answer to 1 dp.
  c $x^4 + 3x = 1580$ Give your answer to 1 dp.

4 Petra has drawn a graph of the equation $y = x^3 + x^2 - 3$.
  a She wants to use the graph to solve the equation $x^3 + x^2 = 7$.
      Write down the equation of the graph she should draw on the same
      axes.
  b She wants to use the graph to solve the equation $x^3 + x^2 - x = 8$.
      Write down the equation of the graph she should draw on the same
      axes.

1 The graph shown is for the function
$y = 2x^2 - x - 10$.

Use the graph to solve the equations.

a $2x^2 - x - 10 = 0$ **(2 marks)**

b $2x^2 - x - 3 = 0$ **(2 marks)**

a *$2x^2 - x - 10$ is the graph shown.*
Read off the solutions from the x axis:
$x = 2.5$ or $x = -2$ **1 mark each**

b *$2x^2 - x - 3$ is not the graph drawn, so we*
need to change the equation.
$2x^2 - x - 3 = 0$ *Subtract 7 from the left-hand side, to change*
$2x^2 - x - 10 = -7$ *this to be the same function as that drawn.*
Also subtract 7 from the right-hand side.

Read off the graph at $y = -7$: *see the green lines on the graph.*
Make sure you draw the lines you are using on the graph to show your
method.

$x = 1.5$ or $x = -1$ **1 mark each**

2 Use a trial and improvement method to find a solution to the equation
$x^3 + x = 20$.
Give your answer correct to 1 decimal place. **(4 marks)**

Try $x = 2$: $2^3 + 2 = 10$
Try $x = 3$: $3^3 + 3 = 30$ **1 mark**

A solution lies between 2 and 3.

Always show how you have
worked it out, and the
answer to the calculations.

Try $x = 2.5$: $2.5^3 + 2.5 = 18.125$
Try $x = 2.6$: $2.6^3 + 2.6 = 20.176$

A solution lies between 2.5 and 2.6, probably nearer 2.6. **1 mark**

Try $x = 2.59$: $2.59^3 + 2.59 = 19.96$ **1 mark**

The solution lies between 2.59 and 2.60

The solution is the value of x that has been used, not the value of $x^3 + x$.

So a solution, to 1 decimal place, is 2.6. **1 mark**

1   a   On the grid, draw the graph of $y = x^2 - x - 4$.
Use values of x between -2 and $+3$.

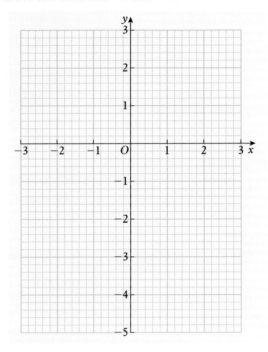

b   Use your graph to write down an estimate for
i   the minimum value of y
ii   the solutions of the equation $x^2 - x - 4 = 0$.   **(3 marks)**
[S1998 P3 Q17]

2   The equation

$$x^3 - 5x = 38$$

has a solution between 3 and 4.
Use a trial and improvement method to find this solution.
Give your answer correct to 1 decimal place.
You must show **all** your working.   **(4 marks)**
[S2000 P4 Q14]

3   A solution of the equation

$$x^3 - 9x = 5$$

is between 3 and 4.

Use the method of trial and improvement to find this solution.
Give your answer correct to 2 decimal places. You must show **all** your
working.   **(4 marks)**
[S1999 P3 Q11]

4 The graph of $y = x^3 - 2x^2 - 4x$ has been drawn on the grid below.

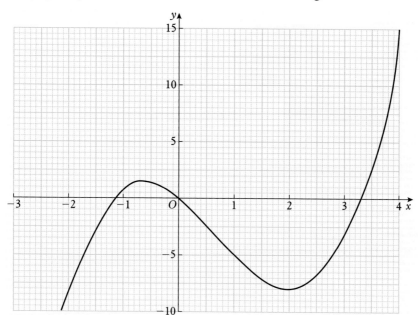

Use the graph to find estimates of the solutions to the equation

i $x^3 - 2x^2 - 4x = 0$,

ii $x^3 - 2x^2 - 4x = 1$.

(4 marks)

[S2000 P3 Q27]

5 Using trial and improvement, or otherwise, solve the equation

$$t^3 + t = 17$$

Show **all** your working and give your answer correct to 2 decimal places.

(4 marks)

[S1998 P3 Q11]

35 Using trigonometry

You need to know about:

- working in an isosceles triangle
- using trigonometry in bearings problems
- angles of elevation and depression
- finding the hypotenuse

Working in isosceles triangles

You can split an isosceles triangle into two right-angled triangles.

To find the length AB in this triangle you split the triangle into two using the red line.

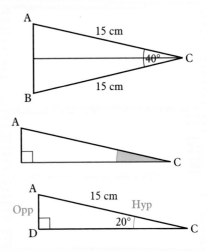

Now you have two right-angled triangles that are exactly the same.
The blue angle in each of the right-angled triangles is half of 40°.
You find the length AD using SOHCAHTOA.

$$\sin 20° = \frac{AD}{15} \text{ so } AD = 15 \times \sin 20° = 5.1303\ldots$$

AB is twice the length of AD,
so AB = 2 × 5.1303 . . . = 10.3 cm to 3 sf.

Working with bearings

Example The diagram shows the position of two lighthouses, A and B.
The bearing of B from A is 075°.
B is 35 km east of A.
How far north of A is B?

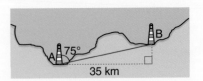

Draw a right-angled triangle to help you.
C is the point that is directly east of A and directly south of B.
So angle ACB is 90° and angle
CAB = 90 − 75 = 15°.

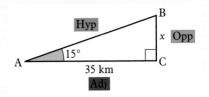

$$\tan 15° = \frac{x}{35} \text{ so } x = 35 \times \tan 15° = 9.4 \text{ km to 1 dp}$$

B is 9.4 km north of A (to 1 dp).

| **Angle of elevation** | If you are at A and you look up to a point B, the **angle of elevation of B from A** is the angle between the horizontal and the line AB. It is the angle *above* the horizontal. | 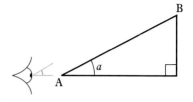 |

a is the angle of elevation of B from A.

| **Angle of depression** | If you are at P and you look down to a point Q, the **angle of depression of Q from P** is the angle between the horizontal and the line PQ. It is the angle *below* the horizontal. | 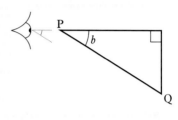 |

b is the angle of depression of Q from P.

Sometimes the **unknown length** is the **denominator**.

Finding the side *y* using SOHCAHTOA gives $\tan 58° = \dfrac{14}{y}$

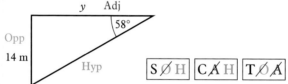

You need to make *y* the subject of the formula.
Here *y* is in the denominator so you multiply both sides by *y*.

$$y \times \tan 58° = \frac{14}{\cancel{y}} \times \cancel{y}$$

The *y*s on the right-hand side cancel.

$$y \times \tan 58° = 14$$

Now divide both sides by tan 58°.

$$y \times \frac{\cancel{\tan 58°}}{\cancel{\tan 58°}} = \frac{14}{\tan 58°}$$

Cancel tan 58° on the left-hand side.

$$y = \frac{14}{\tan 58°} = 8.748\ 17 \ldots$$

$$= 8.75 \text{ m to 3 sf}$$

You can use the formulas for sin and cos in the same way.

1   In each of these triangles, find the size of the angle marked by a letter.
Give your answers to 1 dp.

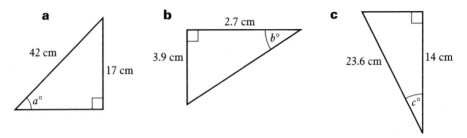

2   In each of these triangles, find the length of the side marked by a letter.
Give your answers to 3 sf.

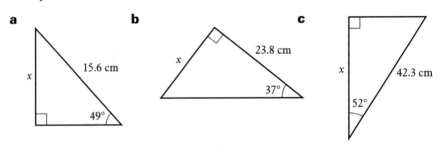

3   The diagram shows a chord in a sector of a circle.
The angle at the centre of the circle is 110°.
The radius of the circle is 15 cm.
Find the length of the chord.
Give your answer to 3 sf.

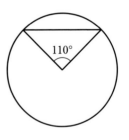

4   ABCD is a rectangle.
Find the length of DB.
Give your answer to the nearest millimetre.

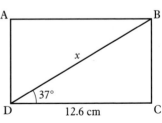

5   A ship sails 55 km from Port A on a bearing of 158°.
   a   Draw a diagram to show this information.
   b   How far east of A is the ship?
   c   How far south of A is the ship?

1 The road from village A runs due west for 5 miles to village B.
A television mast T is due south of B and 4 miles from B.
Find **a** the distance and **b** the bearing of the mast from A. **(5 marks)**

a Join A to T.
The distance AT can be found using Pythagoras' theorem:

$$AT = \sqrt{5^2 + 4^2} = \sqrt{25 + 16} = \sqrt{41} = 6.403 \text{ miles (4 sf)}$$

1 mark   **1 mark**

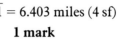
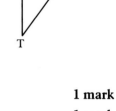

b *You need the bearing from A*

*The word 'from' tells us where to put the North line
(i.e. at A).*

*Bearings are measured clockwise from the North line.
To find the bearing you first need to find angle BAT.*

tan BAT $= \frac{4}{5}$ **1 mark**

angle BAT $= 38.7°$ **1 mark**

The bearing is $270° - 38.7° = 231.3°$.   **1 mark**

2 From the top of a 20 m tower, the angles of depression to the banks of a river are
24° and 40°.
Find the width of the river. Give your answer to 3 significant figures. **(5 marks)**

*Divide the diagram into two separate
triangles.
Use the angles of depression to find
the angles inside each of the triangles.*

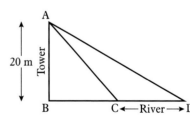

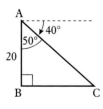
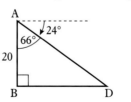

1 mark   **1 mark**

$$\tan 50° = \frac{BC}{20}$$ $$\tan 66° = \frac{BD}{20}$$

BC $= 20 \tan 50°$ BD $= 20 \tan 66°$

BC $= 20 \times 1.191\,75$ BD $= 20 \times 2.246$

BC $= 23.835$ m   **1 mark**   BD $= 44.92$ m   **1 mark**

So the width of the river, CD $=$ BD $-$ BC $= 44.92 - 23.835$

                     $= 21.085$ $= 21.1$ m (to 3 sf)   **1 mark**

1 The diagram shows the positions of three schools, P, Q and R.

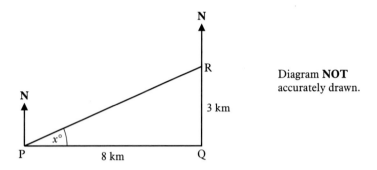

Diagram **NOT** accurately drawn.

School P is 8 kilometres due west of School Q.
School R is 3 kilometres due north of School Q.

a Calculate the size of the angle marked $x°$.
Give your answer correct to one decimal place. **(3 marks)**

Simon's house is 8 kilometres due east of School Q.

b Calculate the bearing of Simon's house from school R. **(2 marks)**

[S2001 P4 Q21]

2

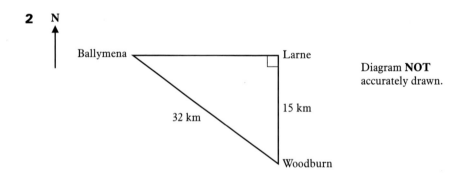

Diagram **NOT** accurately drawn.

Ballymena is due west of Larne.
Woodburn is 15 km due south of Larne.
Ballymena is 32 km from Woodburn.

a Calculate the distance of Larne from Ballymena. Give your answer in kilometres, correct to 1 decimal place. **(3 marks)**

b Calculate the bearing of Ballymena from Woodburn. **(4 marks)**

[S1998 P4 Q14]

3

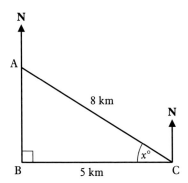

Diagram **NOT** accurately drawn.

The diagram shows the positions of three telephone masts A, B and C.

Mast C is 5 kilometres due east of Mast B.
Mast A is due north of Mast B and 8 kilometres from Mast C.

a Calculate the distance of A from B.
Give your answer in kilometres, correct to 3 significant figures. **(3 marks)**

b i Calculate the size of the angle marked $x°$.
Give your angle correct to one decimal place.
ii Calculate the bearing of A from C.
Give your bearing correct to one decimal place.
iii Calculate the bearing of C from A.
Give your bearing correct to one decimal place. **(5 marks)**
[S1999 P4 Q16]

4

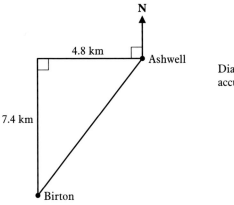

Diagram **NOT** accurately drawn.

Paul flies his helicopter from Ashwell.
He flies due west for 4.8 km.
He then flies due south for 7.4 km to Birton.
Calculate the three figure bearing of Birton from Ashwell. **(4 marks)**
[N1999 P3 Q22]

36 Inequalities

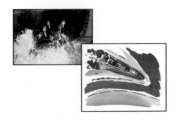

You need to know about:

- showing inequalities on a number line
- solving linear inequalities
- solving quadratic inequalities
- inequalities and graphs

You can show inequalities on a number line.

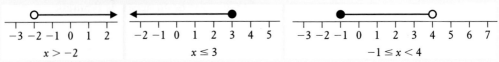

$$x > -2 \qquad\qquad x \leq 3 \qquad\qquad -1 \leq x < 4$$

You **solve inequalities** in the same way as you solve equations.

Example　　　　Solve $7 - 3x \geq 5x - 13$.

$$7 - 3x \geq 5x - 13$$

Add $3x$ to both sides:　　　　　　　　　　$7 \geq 8x - 13$

Add 13 to both sides:　　　　　　　　　　$20 \geq 8x$

Divide both sides by 8:　　　　　　　　　$2.5 \geq x$

Write this with x first:　　　　　　　　　$x \leq 2.5$

If you **multiply or divide** an inequality by a **negative number** then you must **change the direction** of the inequality sign.

Example　　　　Solve the inequality $10 - 4x > 18$.

$$10 - 4x > 18$$

Subtract 10 from both sides:　　　　　　　$-4x > 8$

Divide both sides by -4 **and** change $>$ to $<$:　　$x < -2$

Some inequalities have **three parts** to them.

Example　　　　Solve $15 < 4x + 7 < 19$.

This is the same as the two separate inequalities $15 < 4x + 7$ and $4x + 7 < 19$.
You can solve this by working on both at once.
The aim is to leave a single x in the middle of the inequality.

First remove the $+7$.　　　　　　　　　　$15 < \quad 4x + 7 \quad < 19$

To do this, subtract 7 from all three parts:　　$15 - 7 < 4x + 7 - 7 < 19 - 7$

This gives　　　　　　　　　　　　　　　$8 < \quad 4x \quad < 12$

Now divide through by 4:　　　　　　　　$\dfrac{8}{4} < \dfrac{4x}{4} < \dfrac{12}{4}$

This gives the answer　　　　　　　　　　$2 < \quad x \quad < 3$

Quadratic inequalities

When you solve $x^2 > 25$ you are looking for numbers that are more than 25 when squared.
The solution is $x < -5$ and $x > 5$.

Example   Solve the inequality $3x^2 + 10 \leq 37$.

Take away 10: $\qquad\qquad\qquad\qquad$ $3x^2 + 10 \leq 37$
Divide by 3: $\qquad\qquad\qquad\qquad$ $3x^2 \leq 27$
You are looking for numbers that $\qquad$ $x^2 \leq 9$
are less than 9 when squared. $\qquad$ $x \geq -3$ and $x \leq 3$ or $-3 \leq x \leq 3$

You can show inequalities on graphs.
A solid line shows that a boundary is included. Dotted lines are not included.

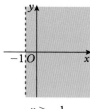 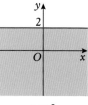 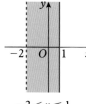 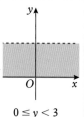

$\qquad$ $x > -1$ $\qquad\qquad$ $y \leq 2$ $\qquad\qquad$ $-2 < x \leq 1$ $\qquad\qquad$ $0 \leq y < 3$

Sometimes the lines that form the borders of the regions are not parallel to one of the axes.

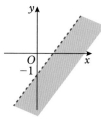 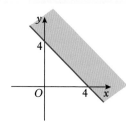 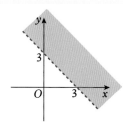

$\qquad$ $y \leq 2x - 1$ $\qquad\qquad$ $y \geq 4 - x$ $\qquad\qquad$ $x + y > 3$

Example $\qquad$ Draw a graph to show the inequality $3x + 2y \leq 12$.

First draw the boundary line on the graph.
When $x = 0$, $2y = 12$, so $y = 6$.
When $y = 0$, $3x = 12$, so $x = 4$.

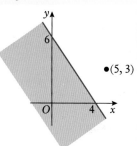

Check which side of the line is needed by checking one point.
The point $(5, 3)$ is **above** the line and
$3x + 2y = 3 \times 5 + 2 \times 3 = 21$.
21 is **not** ≤ 12 so the required region is **below** the line.

1 Write down inequalities to describe each of these.

a

c

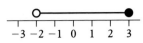

b

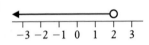

d

2 List the integers that are included in each of these inequalities.

a $2 < x \leqslant 5$

c $-1 < x < 1$

b $-3 \leqslant x \leqslant 5$

d $-5 \leqslant x < -3$

3 Solve each of these inequalities.

a $x + 5 < 9$

d $\dfrac{x}{5} - 9 > 7$

g $-7 < 14 + 9x$

b $4x - 7 \geqslant 13$

e $5x - 3 \leqslant 3x + 12$

h $9 \leqslant 3x \leqslant 27$

c $4(2x + 1) \leqslant 14$

f $6x - 13 \leqslant 42 + 11x$

i $48 < x + 10 \leqslant 63$

4 Draw graphs to show the regions defined by these inequalities.
Shade the region where each inequality is true.

a $y > 2$

b $x \leqslant 3$

c $-1 \leqslant y < 4$

5 Draw graphs to show the regions defined by these sets of inequalities.
Leave the required region unshaded.
Label each graph.

a $x \geqslant 0$ $y \geqslant 0$ $2x + 3y \leqslant 12$

b $y < 3$ $x < 4$ $3x + 5y \geqslant 15$

1 a Solve the inequality $3 \leqslant n + 4 < 6$. (**1 mark**)

  b Represent the solution set on a number line. (**1 mark**)

  c List the values of n, where n is an integer, such that $3 \leqslant n + 4 < 6$. (**1 mark**)

  a $3 \leqslant n + 4 < 6$ *In order to get* n *on its own you have to subtract 4 from each part.*

   $-1 \leqslant n < 2$ **1 mark**

  b  **1 mark**

   Make sure you use the symbols correctly, and join them with a clear, bold line.

  c *From the diagram above:*

   $n = -1, 0$ or 1 **1 mark**

2 A baker wants to buy at least 50 chocolate cakes and at least 75 apple pies.
A chocolate cake costs 50p and an apple pie costs £1.
The baker does not want to spend more than £125.
Shade regions on the grid to show these inequalities, and find the largest total number of cakes and pies that can be bought. (**6 marks**)

Let x = the number of chocolate cakes and y = the number of apple pies.
Then $x \geqslant 50$ and $y \geqslant 75$. **1 mark**
The total cost is $0.5x + 1.0y \leqslant 125$. **1 mark**
These inequalities can be drawn on the grid.

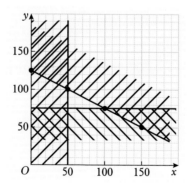

1 mark for each correct region shown

Possible solutions are shown by the vertices of the triangle:

Either 50 chocolate cakes and 100 apple pies
or   100 chocolate cakes and 75 apple pies.

The second of these has the larger total so this is the solution. **1 mark**

1 x is an integer.
Write down the greatest value of x for which $2x < 7$. **(1 mark)**
[S1997 P3 Q12]

2 x is an integer, such that $-3 < x \leqslant 2$.
List all the possible values of x. **(2 marks)**
[N1997 P4 Q13]

3 n is a whole number such that

$6 < 2n < 13$

List all the possible values of n. **(3 marks)**
[N2000 P4 Q17]

4 i Solve the inequality

$2n - 1 < n + 3$

ii List the solutions that are positive integers. **(3 marks)**
[N1996 P3 Q15]

5 y is an integer and $-2 < y \leqslant 2$.

a Write down all the possible values of y. **(2 marks)**

b i Solve the inequality $3n > -8$.

ii Write down the smallest integer which satisfies the inequality
$3n > -8$. **(2 marks)**
[N1998 P3 Q15]

6 The ingredients for one Empire Cake include 200 g of self-raising flour and one egg.
The ingredients for one Fruit Cake include 100 g of self-raising flour and three eggs.
Alphonso has 1200 g of self-raising flour and 12 eggs.
He makes x Empire Cakes and y Fruit Cakes.
Using the weight of self-raising flour available means that x and y must satisfy the inequality $2x + y \leqslant 12$.

   a Write down another inequality which x and y must satisfy, other than $x \geqslant 0$ and $y \geqslant 0$. **(1 mark)**

Use the grid below for part **b**.

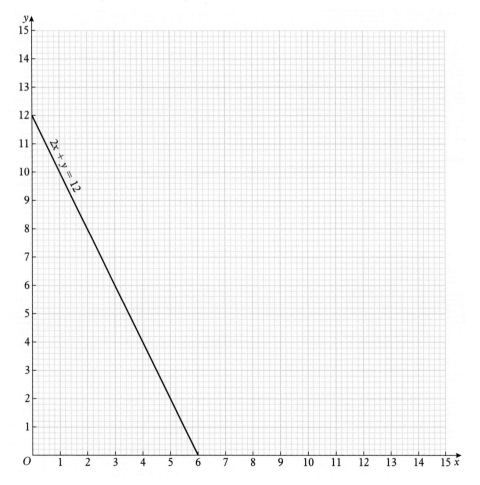

   b By drawing straight lines and shading, indicate the region within which x and y must lie to satisfy all the inequalities.
The line $2x + y = 12$ has been drawn for you. **(3 marks)**
[S1996 P3 Q25]

ANSWERS

CHAPTER 1

Questions

1 **a** **i** $\begin{pmatrix} 4 \\ 2 \end{pmatrix}$ **ii** $\begin{pmatrix} 0 \\ -4 \end{pmatrix}$ **iii** $\begin{pmatrix} 4 \\ -2 \end{pmatrix}$

b **i** **ii** **iii**

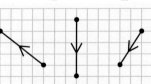

2

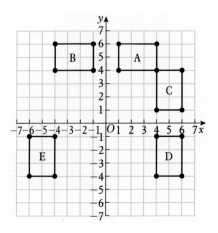

e $\begin{pmatrix} -10 \\ -5 \end{pmatrix}$

3

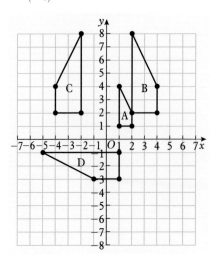

b Enlargement with centre (0, 0) and scale factor $\frac{1}{2}$.

4 **a** Rotation of 270° anticlockwise about (2, −4)
b Translation of 5 units to the right and 1 unit up
c Reflection in the line $x = 6$
d Enlargement, scale factor 4, centre (0, 6)

Exam questions

1 **a** Reflection in the y axis
b Rotation of 90° clockwise about O
2 Enlargement, scale factor $\frac{1}{3}$, centre (−5, 0)

3 **a, b**

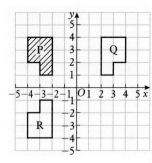

c Reflection in the x axis

4

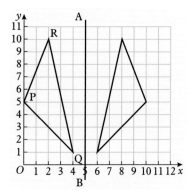

5 **a** 180° rotation about the origin
b

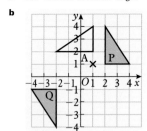

6 Triangle at (5, −3), (3, −), (2, −4)

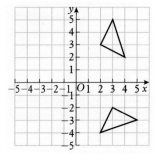

218

CHAPTER 2

Questions

1 **a** 9 tens   **d** 6 hundredths
    b 5 hundreds   **e** 2 thousandths
    c 7 units

2 **a** 01347
    b 74 301
    c $107 - 4 \times 3 = 95$

3 **a** 360   **c** 500   **e** 0.0538
    b 4500   **d** 1000   **f** 0.81

4 **a** **i** $800 \times 60 = 48\,000$
       ii   50 400

    b **i** $\dfrac{40 \times 20}{4} = 200$ **ii**   211

    c **i** $\sqrt{10 \times 4} \approx 6$ **ii**   6.49

5 **a** **i** $\dfrac{36 \times 14}{6 \times 7} = 12$

       ii   12.8

    b **i** $\dfrac{18 \times 25}{6 \times 5} = 15$

       ii   16.2

    c **i** $\dfrac{40 \times 28}{35} = 32$

       ii   33.3

6 **a** 0.4   **c** 0.625   **e** $0.41\dot{6}$
    b 0.13   **d** $0.\dot{6}$

7 **a** $\frac{9}{10}$ **c** $\frac{25}{100} = \frac{1}{4}$ **e** $\frac{23}{100}$
    b $\frac{351}{1000}$ **d** $\frac{8}{1000} = \frac{1}{125}$

8 $\frac{3}{8} = 0.375$,   0.41, $\frac{2}{5} = 0.4$, $\frac{1}{2} = 0.5$,   0.62
    Order of size is: $\frac{3}{8}$, $\frac{2}{5}$,   0.41,   0.5,   0.62

Exam questions

1 e.g. $\frac{1}{3}$, $\frac{2}{5}$, $\frac{3}{7}$

2 **a** 5
    b any number in the range 13 080–14 610

3 $\frac{1}{5}$

4 **i**   9, 2
    ii $\frac{108}{4}$ or $\frac{89}{3}$

5 **a** Answer must be less than 17.8 because it is multiplied by a number less than 1.
    b 40,   60,   300

CHAPTER 3

Questions

1

Colour	Size of angle
Red	60°
Silver	108°
Black	36°
Green	48°
White	24°
Blue	84°

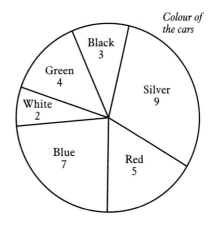

Colour of the cars

2 **a**

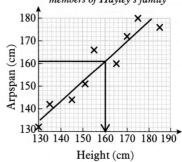

Graph to show the relationship between height and armspan of members of Hayley's family

    b Positive correlation
    d 161 cm

3

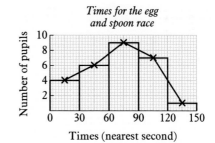

Times for the egg and spoon race

4

Stem	Leaf
4	1
5	2 4
6	4 5 6
7	3 3 4 5 8 9 9
8	2 3
9	1 1 8

4|1 means 41

Results of French test.

CHAPTER 3 (continued)

Exam questions

1   126°, 90°, 99°, 45°

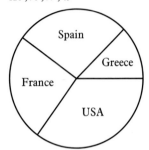

2   a

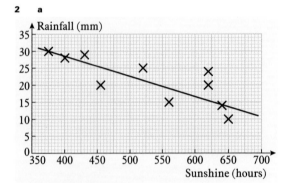

b   Relationship or negative correlation
c   Line
d   i   About 25 mm
     ii   About 570 h

CHAPTER 4

Questions

1   a   1, 3, 5, 15, 19, 45, 51, 63, 81
     b   1, 2, 4, 16
     c   14, 63
     d   2, 3, 5, 19
     e   2, 5
     f   1, 4, 16, 81, 100
     g   1, 3, 15, 45
     h   15, 45, 60

2   a $120 = 2^3 \times 3 \times 5$
     b $180 = 2^2 \times 3^2 \times 5$
     c $1485 = 3^3 \times 5 \times 11$
     d $1470 = 2 \times 3 \times 5 \times 7^2$

3   a $224 = 2^5 \times 7$
     b $1260 = 2^2 \times 3^2 \times 5 \times 7$
     c   HCF $= 2^2 \times 7 = 28$

4   a   11, 13
     b   243, 729
     c   48, 44
     d   36, 49
     e   64, 125

5   a   34
     b   25
     c   19
     d   53
     e   67
     f   130

6   a $3n + 1$
     b $7n - 2$
     c $4n + 3$
     d $-3n + 15$

7   a   7, 11, 15, 19, 23, 27
     b $4n + 3 = 43$
          $4n = 40$
          $n = 10$

Exam questions

1   i 2×5^2 ii $2^2 \times 5^4$

2   a

Pattern 4   Pattern 5

     b   14, 17, 20, 23
     c $3n + 2$ or 'add 3 each time until you get to the 12th term'. The 12th term is 38.

3   a

Pattern number 4

     b   7, 9, 11, 13, 15
     c   i   31
          ii   Add 2 each time
     d $S = 2n + 1$

4   a

Pattern number 5

     b   25, 41   c   113

5    $n + 3$

CHAPTER 5

Questions

1   a -5 e   10   i -2
     b   12   f -2 j -3.7
     c -18 g -6 k -5
     d   13   h -24 l   9

CHAPTER 5 (continued)

2   **a** $A = 14 \times 2 - 20 = 8$
     b $A = (14 \times -2) - 20 = -48$
     c $A = (14 \times 0.5) - 20 = -13$

3   **a** $P = 14.2(6 + 4.13 \times 3.43) = 286.355\,78$
     b $P = 14.2(6 + 4.13 \times (-2.81)) = -79.595\,26$
     c $P = 14.2(6 + 4.13 \times 8.17) = 564.337\,82$

4   **a** $0, 2, 4$
     b $0, -3, -6$
     c $-7.5, -5, -2.5$
     d $-128, 256, -512$

5   **a** $4 > -3$
     b $-7 > -12$
     c $-2 < 3$

6   **a**   Glasgow
     b $-12, -4, -2, 1, 3, 8$
     c $4°C$

Exam questions

1   **i** -4 **ii** -8

2   **a**   Montreal   **b** $45°C$

3   **a** $10°C$ **b** $-3°C$

4   **a** $-9°C$ **b** $13°C$

5   **a** $-4°C, -2°C, -1°C, 0°C, 1°C, 3°C, 7°C$
     b $11°C$

6   **a** -2
     b 60
     c $\frac{8}{21}$

7   **a** $-28°C$
     b $39\,000$ feet

8   **a** 7
     b $\sqrt{v^2 - 2as}$

9 -52.5

10 $\frac{5}{32}$

11 59.4

12   **a** $9°C$
      b $-2°C$

13 $97.160\,632$

CHAPTER 6

Questions

1   **a** $3b$
     b $3t - 2s$
     c $15g$
     d $6r - s$
     e $5ab$
     f $8x^2$

2   **a** $8s^2$
     b $-15t^2$
     c $40a^3$

3   **a** $4x + 24$
     b $-6x + 3$
     c $6y^2 + 4y$
     d $a^3 + a^2b$

4   **a** $2x = 6$
         $x = 3$

     b $3x = 12$
         $x = 4$
     c $x = 4$
     d $3x = 18$
         $x = 6$
     e $2x = 20$
         $x = 10$
     f $3x = -9$
         $x = -3$

5   **a** $12x + 8 = 68$
          $12x = 60$
           $x = 5$
     b $8x - 2 = 18$
          $8x = 20$
           $x = 2\frac{1}{2}$
     c $20x - 30 + 6 = 8x - 18$
           $12x = 6$
             $x = \frac{1}{2}$
     d $x = 18$
     e $20 = 2x$
          $x = 10$
     f $16 = -6x$
          $x = -2\frac{2}{3}$

6   **a**

value of x	value of x^3	
3	$3^3 = 27$	too small
4	$4^3 = 64$	too big
3.5	$3.5^3 = 42.875$	too small
3.8	$3.8^3 = 54.872$	too small
3.9	$3.9^3 = 59.319$	too big
3.85	$3.85^3 = 57.066\,625$	too small

$x = 3.9$ (1 dp)

     b

value of x	value of $x^3 + 2x$	
8	$8^3 + 2 \times 8 = 528$	too small
9	$9^3 + 2 \times 9 = 747$	too big
8.5	$8.5^3 + 2 \times 8.5 = 631.125$	too small
8.8	$8.8^3 + 2 \times 8.8 = 699.072$	too small
8.9	$8.9^3 + 2 \times 8.9 = 722.769$	too big
8.85	$8.85^3 + 2 \times 8.85 = 710.854\,125$	too small

$x = 8.9$ (1 dp)

6   **c**

value of x	value of $x^2 + \dfrac{1}{x} = 31$	
5	$5^2 + \dfrac{1}{5} = 25.2$	too small
6	$6^2 + \dfrac{1}{6} = 36.17$	too big
5.5	$5.5^2 + \dfrac{1}{5.5} = 30.43$	too small
5.6	$5.6^2 + \dfrac{1}{5.6} = 31.54$	too big
5.55	$5.55^2 + \dfrac{1}{5.55} = 30.98$	too small

$x = 5.6$ (1 dp)

CHAPTER 6 (continued)

Exam questions

1.   **a** $7x$
      b $7y - 5$
2.   **a** -2
      b $3p + 4q$
3.   **a** $4x + 3$
      b 6.5
      c 7
4.   **a** 2
      b $\frac{3}{10}$
      c -1.5
5.   **a** 5
      b -0.5
      c 0.25
6.   **a** $1\frac{1}{2}$
      b 4
      c 5.6
7. 2.9
8. 3.53
9. 2.74
10. $x = 12.5$

CHAPTER 7

Questions

1.   **a** $3:1$
      b $6:1$
      c $2:5$
      d $2:7$
      e $12:5$
      f $1:2$
2.   **a** $300:25 = 12:1$
      b $15:90 = 1:6$
      c $4:50 = 2:25$
      d $3000:200 = 15:1$
      e $40:3000 = 1:75$
      f $2000:50 = 40:1$
3.   **a** $\frac{2}{9} \times 900 = 200$ ml
      b $\frac{6}{9} \times 3000 = 2000$ ml $= 2$ litres
4.   Smallest angle $= \frac{2}{18} \times 360 = 40°$
      Other angles are $60°, 100°, 160°$
5.   Youngest child's share $= \frac{2}{30} \times 30 = £2$
      Other shares are £7, £9 and £12
6.   **a** $\dfrac{£3.12}{6} = 52\text{p}$
      b $\dfrac{480}{10} = 48\text{p}$
      c   The larger pack is better value
7.   **a** $40 \times 8 = 320$ g
      b   9 eggs
      c $\dfrac{15}{3} = 5$
8.   Costs for 100 ml are £1.135, £1.187 and £1.07.
      The 450 ml size is the best value for money.

Exam questions

1.   150 g, 120 g, 3, 135 g, 45 ml
2.   20
3.   1000 g, 1000 g, 250 g, 10, 625 g
4.   Tracey £4000, Wayne £3200
5.   **a**   9, 3, $1\frac{1}{2}$, 225 g, 15 g
      b   5 ounces
6.   £150
7.   **a**   £735
      b   £196
8.   **a**   Ruth £100, Ben £80
      b   60%

CHAPTER 8

Questions

1.   **a**   Gradient $= \dfrac{33 - 9}{12 - 4} = 3$
      b   Gradient $= \dfrac{10 - 5}{0 - 4} = -1\frac{1}{4}$
2.   **a** 5
      b 3
      c -7
3.   **a** $(0, 7)$
      b $(0, -4)$
      c $(0, 11)$
4.   **a** $y = 4x + 6$
      b $y = -2x + 3$
5.   **a** $y = 5x + 4, y = 5x + 9, y = 5x - 11, \ldots$
      b $y = 5x - 2$
6.   **a** $y = 3x + 5$
      b $y = -x - 3$
      c $y = -\frac{1}{2}x + 2$
7.   **a** $y = 3x + 5$
      b $y = -2x - 1$
      c $y = 2x - 4$

8.

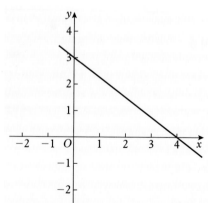

9.   Gradient $= \dfrac{19 - 7}{6 - 0} = 2$
      Line is $y = 2x + 7$

CHAPTER 8 (continued)

Exam questions

1 **a** $-3, -1, 1, 3, 5, 7$

b

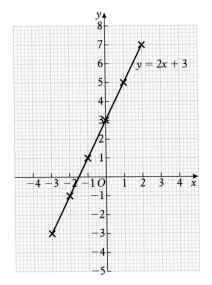

c **i** $y = 6$

 ii $x = -1.75$

2 **a** $-5, -3, -1, 1, 3, 5$

b

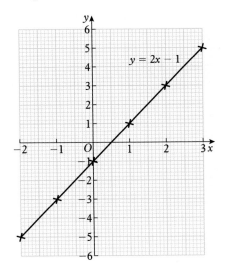

c **i** -3.8

 ii 2.4

3 **a** $-10, -7, -4, -1, 2, 5, 8$

b

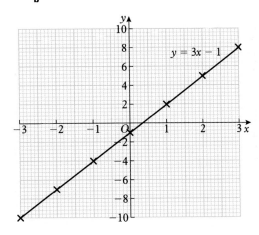

c 2.5

4 **a**

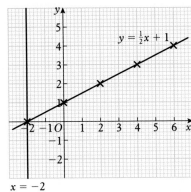

$x = -2$

b $y = 2x - 1$

CHAPTER 9

Questions

1 **a** $\frac{1}{8}$

 b $\frac{3}{8} + \frac{2}{8} = \frac{5}{8}$

 c $\frac{13}{16} - \frac{6}{16} = \frac{7}{16}$

 d $1\frac{6}{8} + \frac{1}{8} = 1\frac{7}{8}$

 e $3\frac{3}{8} - 1\frac{6}{8} = 1\frac{5}{8}$

 f $2\frac{4}{8} + 3\frac{2}{8} - 1\frac{1}{8} = 4\frac{5}{8}$

2 **a** $\frac{3}{16}, \frac{3}{8} = \frac{6}{16}, \frac{1}{2} = \frac{8}{16}, \frac{1}{4} = \frac{4}{16}$

 Order of size is $\frac{3}{16}, \frac{1}{4}, \frac{3}{8}, \frac{1}{2}$

 b $\frac{2}{3} = 66.7\%, 65\%, 0.62 = 62\%, \frac{6}{10} = 60\%$

 Order of size is $\frac{6}{10}, 0.62, 65\%, \frac{2}{3}$

CHAPTER 9 (continued)

3 **a** $\frac{2}{3} \times \frac{1}{2} = \frac{1}{3}$

  b $\frac{5}{2} \times \frac{4}{3} = \frac{20}{6} = 3\frac{1}{3}$

  c $\frac{4}{3} \div \frac{6}{5} = \frac{4}{3} \times \frac{5}{6} = 1\frac{1}{9}$

4 **a** $\frac{2}{x} = \frac{10}{5x}$

  b $\frac{20}{4x} = \frac{5}{x}$

  c $\frac{3}{2x} = \frac{15}{10x}$

5 **a** 16%

  b 0.35

  c $\frac{1}{20}$

  d 32%

6 **a** $\frac{2}{100} \times 55 = 11$

  b $\frac{1}{3} \times 75 = 25$ kg

7 30% of £36 = £10.80

8 **a** $\frac{8}{20} = \frac{2}{5}$

  b $\frac{2}{5} = 40\%$

9 **a** $480 \times \frac{30}{100} = 144, 624$

  b $150 \times \frac{25}{100} = 37.50, £112.50$

Exam questions

1 $80\%, \frac{7}{8}, \frac{8}{9}, 0.9$

2 $\frac{7}{8}, 0.8, \frac{3}{4}, 70\%$

3 $\frac{1}{4}, 0.299, 30\%, \frac{1}{3}, 0.35, \frac{2}{5}$

4 **a** **i** 0.125

    ii $12\frac{1}{2}\%$

  b £2815.75

5 60%

6 360

7 6.25p

8 £2.80

9 £14 000

10 25%

CHAPTER 10

Questions

1 $1 - 0.45 = 0.55$

2 $1 - (0.4 + 0.15) = 0.45$

3 **a** $\frac{14}{20} = \frac{7}{10}$ **b** $\frac{3}{10}$

4 **a** $\frac{13}{30}$ **c** $\frac{5}{30} = \frac{1}{6}$

  b $\frac{2}{30} = \frac{1}{15}$ **d** $\frac{9}{30} = \frac{3}{10}$

5 **a** $\frac{24}{100} = \frac{6}{25}$ **b** $\frac{10}{100} = \frac{1}{10}$ **c** $\frac{81}{100}$

6 **a** $\frac{1}{11}$ **b** $\frac{2}{11}$ **c** $\frac{5}{11}$

7 **a** $\frac{1}{6}$ **b** $\frac{2}{6} = \frac{1}{3}$ **c** $\frac{3}{6} = \frac{1}{2}$

Exam questions

1 **i** $\frac{12}{25}$ **ii** $\frac{5}{25}$

2 **a** $\frac{10}{20}$ **b** $\frac{7}{20}$

3 **i** $\frac{8}{25}$ **ii** $\frac{19}{25}$

4 0.07

5 **a** 0.1   **b** 0.7   **c** 0.15

6 **a** **i** $\frac{10}{20} = \frac{1}{2}$ **ii** 0   **iii** $\frac{7}{20}$

  b $\frac{15}{20}$

CHAPTER 11

Questions

1

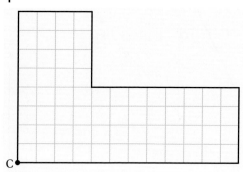

2 **a and b**

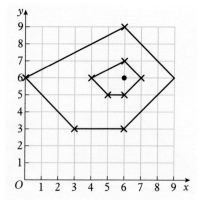

  c $(6, 7), (7, 6), (6, 5), (5, 5), (4, 6)$

3 Scale factor $= \frac{6}{4}$,
  $a = 4\frac{1}{2} \div \frac{6}{4} = 3$ cm,
  $b = 5 \times \frac{6}{4} = 7\frac{1}{2}$ cm

4 $18 \times 2.5 = 45$ cm

5 **a** $\frac{1}{5}$ km
  b $\frac{7}{5}$ km $= 1\frac{2}{5}$ km

CHAPTER 11 (continued)

6 **a**

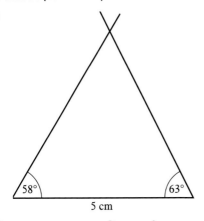

58°   5 cm   63°

b

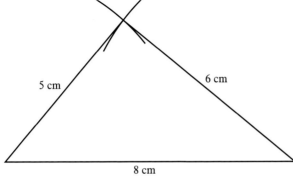

5 cm   6 cm

8 cm

Exam questions

1 **a**

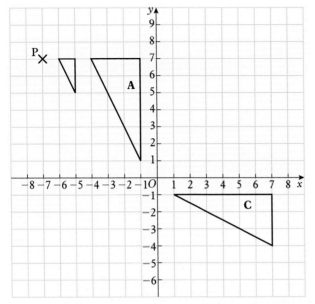

b Reflection in $y = x$

CHAPTER 11 (continued)

2 **a** 20 cm²   **b** 12, 15   **c** 9

3 **a** 2   **b, c**

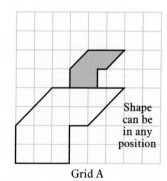

4

Shape
can be
in any
position

Grid A

CHAPTER 12

Questions

1 **a** 196 **b** 1331 **c** 23 **d** 8 **e** 729 **f** 256

2 **a** 5^3 **b** 3^2 **c** 4^4 **d** 7^5 **e** 9^6 **f** 6^4

3 **a** $\frac{1}{3}$ **c** $\frac{1}{16}$ **e** 4 **g** $\frac{3}{2}$ **i** 1 **k** 4

  b 1 **d** 5 **f** 4 **h** $\frac{1}{3}$ **j** $\left(\frac{25}{16}\right)^{-1} = \frac{16}{25}$ **l** 8

4 **a** b^8 **c** $3d^5$ **e** $12x^7$ **g** $20h^5$ **i** $10p^3q^2$ **k** $12x^3y^2$
  b c^4 **d** $2b^6$ **f** $6p^6$ **h** $12x^3y^2$ **j** $20h^2k^5$ **l** $6x^3y^4$

5 **a** $27x^6$ **b** x^2y **c** $16y^6$ **d** $2a^2b$ **e** $8a^6b^6$ **f** a^{-6} **g** $7x^3$ **h** $x^{-\frac{1}{3}}$

6 **a** $x = 4$ **b** $x = \frac{1}{2}$ **c** $x = \frac{1}{3}$ **d** $x = \frac{1}{3}$ **e** $x = \frac{1}{2}$ **f** $x = 4$

226

CHAPTER 12 (continued)

7
- **a** $35 + 4 = 39$
- **b** $12 + 12 = 24$

8
- **a** 0.5

9
- **a** 337.8

- **c** $7 - 2 = 5$
- **d** $5 + 4 = 9$
- **b** 87.9
- **b** 6314.6

- **e** $5 \times 15 = 75$
- **f** $15 + 25 = 40$
- **c** 8.0

- **g** $36 \times 4 = 144$
- **h** $4 + 24 = 28$

Exam questions

1 30
2 514.897 69 …
3 0.208 569 leading to 0.208 or 0.209
4 0.451 089
5 49.7
6 0.4075
7
- **a** 46.4163 …
- **b** 46

8
- **a** 18.277 …
- **b** 18.28

9 41.2
10
- **a** $t^5 - t^6$
- **b** 30
- **c** $3a$

11 28.845 202 69 = 28.8 to 1 dp
12 104
13
- **a** 32
- **b** **i** 0.03125
- **ii** 3.125

14 3.378

CHAPTER 13

Questions

1
- **a** 35 min
- **b** 20 min
- **c** 2 mph
- **d** 13 : 04

2
- **a**

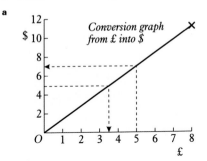

- **b** £5 = $7
- **c** $4.90 = £3.50

3
- **a** Speed $= \dfrac{150}{2.25} = 66\frac{2}{3}$ mph
- **b** Distance $= 2\frac{1}{6} \times 36 = 78$ miles
- **c** Meher is not moving
- **d** $\dfrac{80}{1\frac{1}{4}} = 64$ km/h

4
- **a** 30 km/h
- **b** 50 km/h

Exam questions

1 9.8 m per second
2
- **a** 50 mph
- **b** 55 mph

4
- **a** **i** 13 : 00
- **ii** 20 km/h

3 112.5 litres
b

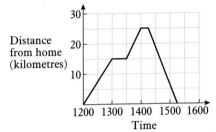

227

CHAPTER 13 (continued)

5 **a** **i** 5 km   **ii** 11:20   **iii** 10 min

b

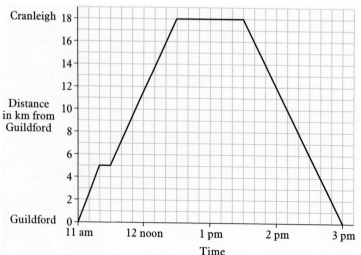

c 12 km/h

CHAPTER 14

Questions

1 **a** $\tan a = \dfrac{15}{27}$
$a = 29°$

b $\cos b = \dfrac{19}{37}$
$b = 59°$

c $\sin c = \dfrac{11.1}{39.2}$
$c = 16°$

d $\tan d = \dfrac{6.8}{19.2}$
$d = 20°$

2 **a** $\sin 24° = \dfrac{a}{15.3}$
$a = 6.22$ cm

b $\tan 50° = \dfrac{b}{342}$
$b = 408$ m

c $\cos 34° = \dfrac{c}{612}$
$c = 507$ m

d $\cos 59° = \dfrac{20}{d}$
$d = 38.8$ cm

3 $\tan 49° = \dfrac{h}{3}$
$h = 3.45$ m

4 $\sin 60° = \dfrac{h}{8}$
$h = 6.93$ cm

5 $\sin 28° = \dfrac{10}{l}$
$l = 21.3$ m

Exam questions

1 1.38 m
4 **a** 8.6 km
5 116 cm
7 **a** 5.29 cm

2 6.52 cm
  b 37.4°
6 **a** 622 km
  b 41.4°

3 **a** 6.18 m
  c 5.15 km
  b 600 km
  c 12.4 cm

b 27.3°

CHAPTER 15

Questions

1 **a** $17s$
  b $10t$
2 **a** $4x + 8$
  b $6x - 3$
3 **a** $x^2 + 5x + 4$
  b $x^2 + x - 30$
  c $x^2 - 14x + 45$
4 **a** $2(3a + 2)$
  b $6(3t - 2)$
  c $a(b - a)$

c $a + 6b$
d $11st$
c $12x + 20$
d $-15x - 35$
d $x^2 - 15x + 56$
e $4x^2 + 35x + 24$
f $2x^2 - 11x - 63$
d $3c(d - 2c)$
e $y(3y^2 + y - 2)$
f $2y(7y + 1)$

e $6mn$
f $5ab - 10cd$
e $x^2 - 6x$
f $x^3 + 9x^2$
g $6x^2 + 13x + 5$
h $10x^2 - 29x + 10$
i $14x^2 - 13x + 3$
g $(x + 6)(x + 5)$
h $(x + 3)(x + 4)$
i $(x - 7)(x - 3)$

g $8x^2$
h $5y^2$
g $y^4 + 3y^3 - 2y^2$
h $a^2b + ab^2$
j $8x^2 - 2x - 15$
k $30x^2 - 41x + 7$
l $12x^2 - 53x + 55$
j $(x + 9)(x - 5)$
k $(x - 8)(x + 8)$
l $(x - 5)(x + 5)$

i $x^2 + 4y^2$
j $9cd^2 - 5c^2d$
i $6c^2d + 12cd^2$

CHAPTER 15 (continued)

5 **a** $2(5x - 2 + 3x + 7)$ **b** $(5x - 2)(3x + 7)$
      $= 2(8x + 5)$ $= 15x^2 + 29x - 14$
      $= 16x + 10$

6 **a** $(3x + 4) + (2x - 3) + (3x + 1)$
      $= 8x + 2$
  b $8x + 2 = 42$ **c** $19\,\text{cm}, 7\,\text{cm}, 16\,\text{cm}$
      $x = 5\,\text{cm}$

Exam questions

1 **a i** $3x$ **ii** $3a + 2b$ **iii** $3a + 6$
  b $8x + 1$ **d** $3a^2(2a - 3)$
  c $2x^2 + 5x - 3$ **e** $\frac{1}{25}$
2 **a i** p^4 **ii** q^4 **iii** $16x^6$
  b $3xy(3x - 2y^2)$
3 **a** $2(x + 4y)$ **c** $(x - 3)(x - 6)$
  b $3ac(c - 2)$
4 **a** $10x + 3$ **b** $6x^2 + 5xy - 4y^2$
5 **a** $2x^2 - 5x - 3$ **b** $2t(t + 2)$
6 **a** x^8 **b** y^4 **c** $4w^2$
7 **i** $4a$ **ii** $7b - 4c$
8 15 hours
9 **a** $x^2 + 2x - 15$ **b** $3a(2a - 3b)$

CHAPTER 16

Questions

1 **a** 26
  b 16, 23, 24, 26, 26, 27, 29, 30, 61   Median = 26
  c Mean $= \dfrac{262}{9} = 29$
  d The mode or the median best represent this data. The mean is distorted by the extreme value of 61.

2 **a** 2
  b 2
  c Mean $= \dfrac{56}{25} = 2$ (nearest whole number)

3 **a** Mean height =
  $$\dfrac{(105.5 \times 3) + (115.5 \times 2) + (125.5 \times 4) + (135.5 \times 7) + (145.5 \times 2)}{18}$$
      $= 127\,\text{cm}$
  b 131–140 cm

4 $\dfrac{x + x + 5 + x + 4}{3} = 12$
              $x = 9$

5 $2277 - 2192 = 85$

Exam questions

1 **a** 12   **b** 14
2 **a** 73   **b** $1960\,\text{cm}^2$
3 38
4 **a** 29   **b** 9   **c** 6   **d** 8   **e** 6
5 98.8 g

CHAPTER 17

Questions

1 **a** 230 mm   **d** 760 mm   **g** 11 feet
  b 56 cm   **e** 7.596 km   **h** 10 560 yards
  c 342 m   **f** 180 inches **i** 12 yards
2 **a** 320 km   **b** 1.62 m
3 **a** length   **d** length   **g** volume
  b area   **e** area   **h** volume
  c volume   **f** area
4 **a** $C = \pi \times 9.0 = 28.3\,\text{cm}$
  b $d = 178 \div \pi = 56.7\,\text{cm}$
  c $18\pi\,\text{cm}$
5 **a** $\pi \times 16 + \pi \times 42 = 182.2\,\text{cm}$
  b $2 \times 3.72 = £7.44$
6 **a** 82 cm
  b $16 + 16 + (\pi \times 16) = (32 + 16\pi)\,\text{cm}$
  c $6 + 6 + 8 + 8 + (\frac{1}{4} \times \pi \times 12) + (\frac{1}{4} \times \pi \times 16)$
      $= (28 + 7\pi)\,\text{cm}$
  d $8 + 6 + 6 + (\frac{1}{2} \times \pi \times 8) = (20 + 4\pi)\,\text{cm}$

Exam questions

1 201 cm   **3** $\pi r^2 l, 4\pi r^3, 3(a^2 + b^2)r$
2 46 m   **4** Area, length, volume
5 **a** 8   **b** $300\,\text{cm}^2$ **c** 240
6 31.5–31.6 mpg

CHAPTER 18

Questions

1 **a** $\sqrt{9^2 + 15^2} = 17.5\,\text{cm}$ **c** $\sqrt{9.6^2 - 3.7^2} = 8.9\,\text{cm}$
  b $\sqrt{31^2 - 16^2} = 26.6\,\text{cm}$
2 **a** $\sqrt{11 + 5} = 4\,\text{cm}$ **c** $\sqrt{48 - 15} = \sqrt{33}\,\text{cm}$
  b $\sqrt{23 - 3} = \sqrt{20}\,\text{cm}$
3 $\sqrt{3^2 + 4^2} = 5$
4 **a** $\sqrt{16^2 - 12^2} = 10.6\,\text{cm}$ **b** $\sqrt{5^2 + 6^2} = 7.8\,\text{cm}$
5 $\sqrt{20^2 - 10^2} = 17.3\,\text{cm}$
6 $(x + 2)^2 = x^2 + 6^2$
   $x^2 + 4x + 4 = x^2 + 6^2$
         $x = 8$

7 Distance $= \sqrt{7^2 + 5^2}$
            $= 8.6$ nautical miles (1 dp)

7

5

Port P

8 Distance $= \sqrt{10^2 + 15^2} = 18.0\,\text{m}$ (1 dp)

Exam questions

1 **a** Isosceles   **c** 16.6 m
  b $120.12\,\text{m}^2$ **d** $30.4°$
2 7.21 cm   **4** 10 cm
3 28.3 cm   **5** 13 cm

CHAPTER 19

Questions

1 **a**

x	0	$-\frac{1}{3}$
y	1	0

or similar

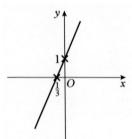

b

x	0	-8
y	4	0

or similar

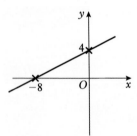

c

x	0	2
y	-4	0

or similar

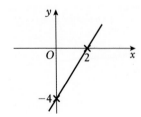

2 **a**

x	-3	-2	-1	0	1	2	3
$+2x^2$	18	8	2	0	2	8	18
$+x$	-3	-2	-1	0	1	2	3
-5	-5	-5	-5	-5	-5	-5	-5
y	10	1	-4	-5	-2	5	16

b and **c**

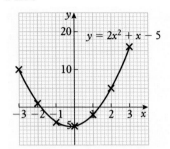

d $x = -\frac{1}{4}$

3 **a**

x	-2	-1	0	1	2	3
$-x^3$	8	1	0	-1	-8	-27
$+2x$	-4	-2	0	2	4	6
$+6$	6	6	6	6	6	6
y	10	5	6	7	2	-15

b and **c**

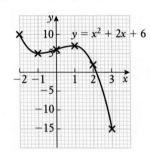

4 **a** (2) **c** (1) **e** (6)
  b (4) **d** (5) **f** (3)

Exam questions

1 **a** 18, 8, 2, 0, 2, 8, 18

b

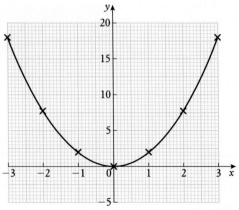

c **i** 12.5 **ii** ± 2.5

230

CHAPTER 19 (continued)

2 D, C, E, F, A, B

3 **a** 2.9, 2.27, 2.05, 2.5

b

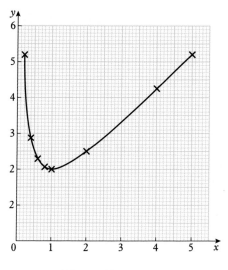

c $x = 0.21$ or $x = 4.8$

CHAPTER 20

Questions

1 **a**

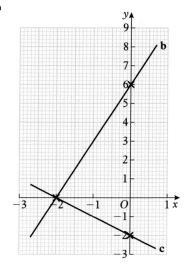

d $(-2, 0)$

2 **a** $5x = 15$ **b** $11x = -11$
  $x = 3$ $x = -1$
  $y = 4$ $y = 2$

2 **c** $7p = 28$ **d** $7c = -14$
  $p = 4$ $c = -2$
  $q = \frac{1}{2}$ $d = -1\frac{1}{2}$

3 $3p + 4b = 760$
  $2p + 3b = 560$
  $p = 40, \quad b = 160$
  1 pencil cost 40p; 1 biro cost £1.60

4 **a** $\dfrac{x - z}{4} = y$

b $6t = 5s + 48$
  $\dfrac{6t - 48}{5} = s$

c $ab^2 + ac = d$
  $b = \sqrt{\dfrac{d - ac}{a}}$

d $dec = ab + 2$
  $\dfrac{dec - 2}{a} = b$

e $\dfrac{m^2 - r}{3} = p$

f $\dfrac{s^2 - x}{v} = w$

5 **a** $b = \dfrac{10 - 4 \times 2^2}{3}$
  $= -2$

b $\dfrac{3b + 4c^2}{2} = a$

c $\dfrac{3 \times 5 + 4 \times 3^2}{2} = a$
  $a = 25\frac{1}{2}$

6 **a** $3x + 2(x - 1) = 13$
  $5x = 15$
  $x = 3$
  $y = 2$

b $4x - (2x - 8) = 13$
  $2x = 5$
  $x = 2\frac{1}{2}$
  $y = -3$

Exam questions

1 **a** line through $(0, -2)$ and $(1, 0)$
  b $x = 1.5, y = 1$
  c $3y = -2x + 7$

2 $x = 1.5, y = -2$

3 $x = \frac{3}{4}, y = -\frac{1}{2}$

4 $x = 7, y = 0.5$

5 **a** £19 **b** 12 **c** $\dfrac{C - 7}{3}$

6 **a** 2.25 **b** $\dfrac{v - u}{10}$

7 **a** 1240 **b** $h = \dfrac{3V}{\pi(R^2 + Rr + r^2)}$

CHAPTER 21

Questions

1 **a**

	1	2	3	4	5	6
1	1,1	1,2	1,3	1,4	1,5	1,6
2	2,1	2,2	2,3	2,4	2,5	2,6
3	3,1	3,2	3,3	3,4	3,5	3,6
4	4,1	4,2	4,3	4,4	4,5	4,6
5	5,1	5,2	5,3	5,4	5,5	5,6
6	6,1	6,2	6,3	6,4	6,5	6,6

  b $\frac{4}{36} = \frac{1}{9}$ **c** $\frac{6}{36} = \frac{1}{6}$ **d** $\frac{10}{36} = \frac{5}{18}$

2 **a**

	1	3	4	4	5	5
1	2	4	5	5	6	6
2	3	5	6	6	7	7
3	4	6	7	7	8	8
4	5	7	8	8	9	9

  b $\frac{4}{24} = \frac{1}{6}$ **c** $\frac{2}{24} = \frac{1}{12}$ **d** $\frac{6}{24} = \frac{1}{4}$

3 $0.75 \times 16 = 12$

4 $0.71 \times 0.6 = 0.426$

5 **a** $\frac{12}{30} = \frac{2}{5}$ **c** $\frac{18}{30} = \frac{3}{5}$

  b $\frac{11}{30}$ **d** $\frac{23}{30}$

Exam questions

1 **a**

SPINNER B

SPINNER A ×	1	2	3	4
1	1	2	3	4
2	2	4	6	8
3	3	6	9	12

  b $\frac{1}{6}$ or $\frac{2}{12}$ **c** $\frac{4}{12}$ or $\frac{1}{3}$

2 **a** $\frac{16}{100}$ **b** 4000   **c** 212

3 **i** $\frac{4}{24}$ **ii** $\frac{6}{24}$

4 **a** 0.91   **b** 3

  c i 0.0081   **ii** 0.1638

5 **a i** 0.125   **ii** 0   **b** 0.42

CHAPTER 22

Questions

1 **a** 16   **c** 16   **e** 8   **g** 90
  b 125   **d** 243   **f** 100   **h** 30

2 **a** $\frac{1}{4}$ **b** $\frac{1}{25}$ **c** $\frac{1}{8}$ **d** $\frac{1}{100}$

3 **a** 1.03×10^3 **e** 3.5×10
  b 8.7×10^{-2} **f** 4×10^6
  c 2×10^{-5} **g** 7.006×10^5
  d 7×10^{-1} **h** 2×10^4

4 **a** 380   **c** 682 000
  b 0.0049   **d** 0.000 007

5 **a** $24 \times 10^5 = 2.4 \times 10^6$
  b $0.2 \times 10^6 = 2 \times 10^5$
  c $300 + 5000 = 5300 = 5.3 \times 10^3$
  d $50\,000 - 300 = 49\,700 = 4.97 \times 10^4$

6 **a** 1.81×10^8 **c** 4.98×10^9
  b 1.31×10^{-5} **d** 4.35×10^3

7 **a** 1 530 000

  b $\dfrac{5.069 \times 10^6}{2.934 \times 10^6} = 1.73$

  c $\dfrac{4.682 \times 10^7}{1.53 \times 10^6} = 30.6$

  d $2.934 \times 10^6 - 2.814 \times 10^6 = 120\,000$

Exam questions

1 **a i** $a = 50, b = 30$
    ii 75
    iii 79.368 75
  b 4.9×10^{11}

2 **a** 4.55×10^{-3} **b** 34 100 cm^3

3 **a** 1.6×10^8 **b** 28 000

4 **a** 8.4×10^7 **b** 2.1×10^{-5}

5 **a i** 50 100   **b** 2.4×10^9
    ii 9×10^{-4}

6 **a** 7.6×10^3 **b** $\dfrac{Rv^2}{G}$

7 **a** 9.1×10^{-25} **b** 4.55×10^{-18}

8 8.01×10^{10}

9 **a** 3×10^8 **b** 3.3×10^{-9}

10 **a** 1.5×10^5 **b** 360

11 3.818×10^3

CHAPTER 23

Questions

1 **a** $\pi \times 24.35^2 = 1860$ m^2 (3 sf)

  b $\dfrac{19 \times 10}{2} = 95$ cm^2

  c $\frac{1}{2} \times 5.8 \times 3.7 = 10.73$ cm^2
  d $18 \times 14 = 252$ m^2
  e 50 cm^2
  f $14 \times 18 + \frac{1}{2} \times \pi \times 7^2 = 329$ m^2

2 **a** $\sqrt{\dfrac{520}{\pi}} = 12.9$ cm

  b $\sqrt{520} = 22.8$ cm

  c $\dfrac{520}{28.5} = 18.2$ cm

3 **a** $(19 \times 8) + (19 \times 6) + (\frac{1}{2} \times 6 \times 8 \times 2)$
    $+ (10 \times 19) = 504$ cm^2
  b $(9 \times 5) + (2 \times \frac{1}{2} \times 5 \times 6.2) + (2 \times \frac{1}{2} \times 9 \times 4.7)$
    $= 118$ m^2

4 **a** $\pi \times 2^2 = 12.57$ m^2
  b $(\frac{1}{2} \times \pi \times 3^2) + (\frac{1}{2} \times \pi \times 2.5^2) = 23.95$ m^2
  c $(12 \times 14) - 12.57 - 23.95 = 131$ m^2

Exam questions

1 **a** 86.64 cm^2 **b** 45.6 cm

2 8 m^2 **4** 37 m^2

3 81.7 m^2 **5** 2.58 m^2

6 **a** 11 cm^2 **b** 25.7 cm

7 218 cm^2

CHAPTER 24

Questions

1 **a** ×2   **b** +3   **c** −4

2 **a** 10, 13, 16, 19   **b** 37   **c** 52

3 **a** $3n + 7$ **c** $6n + 3$
      b $5n - 2$ **d** $2n - 5$

4 **a** 4   **b** 229

5 $T = n^2 + 4n - 3$

6 **a**

   b

   c 5, 9, 13, 17, 21   **d** $4n + 1$

7 **a** Yes   **b** Yes   **c** No

8 **a** 8, 5, 2, −1
   b −49
   c $-79 = 11 - 3n$
      $n = 30$
   d $-94 = 11 - 3n$
      $n = 35$

Exam questions

1 $P = hb + c$ or $P = bh + c$

2 $C = 4w$ **3** 20   **4** $C = 20 - 4n$

5 **a** 21, 25   **b** Add 4   **c** $4n - 3$

6 **a** 19, 23   **b** $4n - 1$

7 $6n - 4$ **8** $4n + 3$ **9** $2n + 1$

CHAPTER 25

Questions

1 **a** **i** $\dfrac{1133}{23} = £49.26$

   ii 16, 17, 21, 30, 32, 32, 33, 40, 41, 43, 47, 48,
      50, 50, 50, 52, 54, 60, 60, 60, 62, 110, 125
      Median = 48
   iii Lower quartile = 32
   iv Upper quartile = 60
   v Range = 109
   vi Interquartile range = 28

   b Interquartile range is a better measure of spread
      for this data.
      It excludes the extreme value of 125.

2 **a**

Time in seconds (x)	Cumulative frequency
$x \leqslant 10$	4
$x \leqslant 20$	10
$x \leqslant 30$	25
$x \leqslant 40$	60
$x \leqslant 50$	92
$x \leqslant 60$	100

b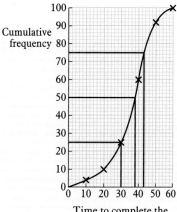

Time to complete the
puzzle, x (seconds)

   c **i** 38 seconds   **ii** $43 - 29 = 14$ seconds

3 **a**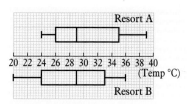

   b The median temperatures are the same.
      The ranges are almost identical: 15°C for
      Resort A, and 16°C for Resort B. The
      interquartile ranges are both 9°C. The
      temperatures are lower for Resort B than for
      Resort A. There are more higher temperatures
      for Resort A.

Exam questions

1 **a** 7.9 years
   b 41, 67, 87, 97, 100
   c

d About 11.5 or 12 years

2 **a** 70   **b** 18 seconds   **c** 22–24%

CHAPTER 26

Questions

1 **a** Isosceles **b** 50° (alternate angle to angle ABC) **c** 80° (angles in a triangle add up to 180°)

2 **a** $a° = 56°$ (angles on a straight line)
   $b° = 56°$ (base angles of an isosceles triangle are equal)
   $c° = 68°$ (angles in a triangle add up to 180°)
   b $d° = 67°$ (corresponding angles)
   $e° = 64°$ (angles in a triangle add up to 180°)
   $f° = 64°$ (corresponding angles)
   c $g° = j° = 55°$ (angles in a triangle add up to 180°)
   $h° = 55°$ (opposite angles)
   $i° = 125°$ (angles on a straight line add up to 180°)
   d $l° = 110°$ (opposite angles)
   $k° = 29°$ (angles in a quadrilateral add up to 360°)

3 **a**

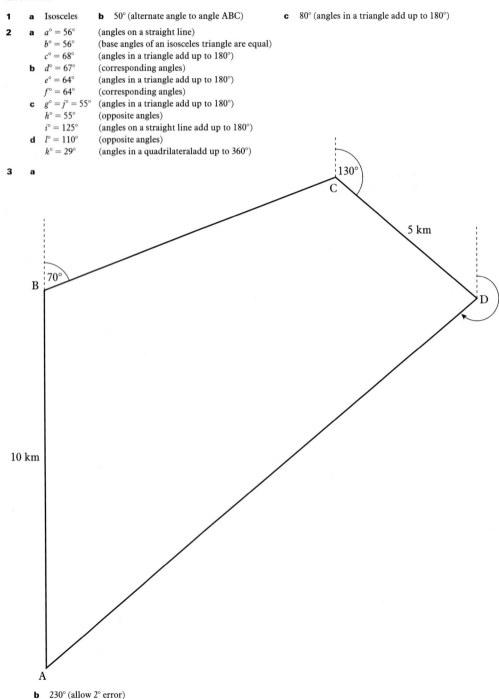

   b 230° (allow 2° error)
   c 152 km

CHAPTER 26 (continued)

4 **a** $a° = 90°$ (angles in a semi-circle)
$b° = 31°$ (angles in a triangle add up to 180°)
b $c° = 70°$ (opposite angles of a cyclic
quadrilateral add up to 180°)
c $d° = 90°$ (tangent is perpendicular to the radius)
$e° = 49°$ (angles in a triangle add up to 180°)
$f° = 24\frac{1}{2}°$ (angle at the centre is twice the angle at
the circumference)

Exam questions

1 **a** **i** $145°$ **ii** Angles on a straight line
 b **i** $83°$ **ii** Angles in a triangle
 c **i** $35°$ **ii** Vertically opposite angles
2 **a** **i** $59°$ **ii** Opposite angles
 b **i** $121°$ **ii** Interior angles
3 **a** **i** $2x$ **ii** $180 - 6x$ **iii** $90 - 3x$
4 **a** $120°$ **b** $300°$

CHAPTER 27

Questions

1 **a** $5x + 10$ **c** $2x^2 + x$
 b $12t + 6$ **d** $6a^2 + 4ab$

2 **a** $5(x + 5)$ **c** $4x(x + 2)$
 b $2(13y - 4z)$ **d** $4(4a^2 + a + 2b)$

3 **a** $\dfrac{1}{3x}$ **b** $\dfrac{4(a + 2)}{3(a + 2)} = \dfrac{4}{3}$ **c** $3(x + 3)$

4 **a** $b + c = 3ax - a$
$\quad\quad\; = a(3x - 1)$
$\dfrac{b + c}{3x - 1} = a$
 b $3xy - 5x = d$
$x(3y - 5) = d$
$x = \dfrac{d}{3y - 5}$
 c $2ab - 4b = 3$
$b(2a - 4) = 3$
$b = \dfrac{3}{2a - 4}$
 d $2sw - w = 5$
$w(2s - 1) = 5$
$w = \dfrac{5}{2s - 1}$
 e $4ab - 7a = 5b - 2$
$a(4b - 7) = 5b - 2$
$a = \dfrac{5b - 2}{4b - 7}$
 f $4bd - ab = c$
$b(4d - a) = c$
$b = \dfrac{c}{4d - a}$

5 **a** $x^2 + 8x + 15$ **d** $8x^2 + 10x + 3$
 b $x^2 - 4x - 32$ **e** $12x^2 - 2x - 30$
 c $x^2 - 10x + 21$ **f** $x^2 + 12x + 36$

6 **a** $(x + 9)(x + 5)$
 b $(x - 3)(x + 6)$
 c $(x - 5)(x + 5)$

7 **a** $(x + 3)(x - 2) = 0$
$x = -3 \text{ or } 2$
 b $(x - 9)(x + 4) = 0$
$x = 9 \text{ or } -4$
 c $(x - 7)(x + 2) = 0$
$x = 7 \text{ or } -2$
 d $x^2 - 7x - 18 = 0$
$(x + 2)(x - 9) = 0$
$x = 9 \text{ or } -2$

8 **a**

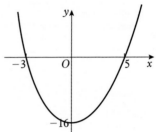

 b

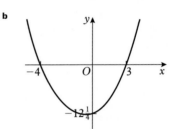

 c

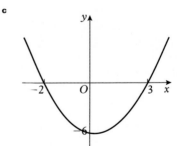

 d

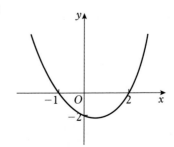

CHAPTER 27 (continued)

Exam questions

1 **a** $2x^2 + x - 15$
   b **i** $(x + 7)(x - 1)$ **ii** $x = -7$ or $x = 1$

2 **i** $(x - 4)(x - 2)$ **ii** $x = 2$ or $x = 4$

3 **a** $-\frac{8}{3}$
   b **i** $(x + 6)(x - 2)$
     ii $x = -6$ or $x = 2$

4 **a** **i** $10x + 4$ **ii** $2x(3x + 2)$
   b 112

5 **a** $8x + 14$ **b** Show   **c** $22.56\,\text{m}^2$

6 **a** $(x + 4)(x - 3) = 78$
   b **i** Show
     ii $9, -10$
     iii 13 cm, 6 cm

CHAPTER 28

Questions

1 **a** 12.6   **c** 13.8   **e** 0.21
   b 13.2   **d** 0.16   **f** 0.35

2 **a** 200   **c** 0.0849   **e** 0.000 06
   b 1000   **d** 1.877   **f** 400 000

3 **a** $9 \times 10 = 90$
     87.514
   b $1000 \div 50 = 20$
     20.12
   c $0.05 \times 0.3 = 0.015$
     0.015 36

4 **a** 2.5, 3.5   **d** 5650, 5750
   b 4.25, 4.35   **e** 2500, 3500
   c 53.5, 54.5   **f** 5.15, 5.25

5 **a** **i** 3.5, 4.5   **ii** 22 cm, 26 cm
     5.5, 6.5
     7.5, 8.5
   b **i** 11.5, 12.5   **ii** 42 cm, 46 cm
     9.5, 10.5

6 **a** 11 minutes   **b** $\frac{11}{19} \times 100 = 57.9\%$

Exam questions

1 **i** $800 \div 20$ **ii** 40

2 **a** 40×90 **b** 3600   **c** 49

3 **a** e.g. 2.23 m can be measured
   b e.g. 2 m not accurate, not near enough to 7 m.
     2.227 880 3 too accurate, cannot be measured to
     this accuracy.

4 **a** 4200   **b** **i** 98.5 cm   **ii** 97.5 cm

5 6

6 $\frac{1}{80}$

7 **a** 2.215 868 …
   b **i** $a = 20, c = 4$ **ii** 2

8 **i** 9.5   **ii** 10.5

9 **a** 113.1 cm²
   b **i** 11.5 cm   **ii** 12.5 cm

CHAPTER 29

Questions

1 **a** 0.15
   b **i** £19.20   **ii** £11.46   **iii** £5.79   **iv** £219

2 **a** 0.82   **b** 0.76   **c** 0.835   **d** 0.27

3 **a** 1.40   **b** 1.175   **c** 1.08   **d** 2.10

4 **a** $540 \times 0.92 = \pounds496.80$
   b $540 \times 1.07 = \pounds577.80$

5 $150 \times \dfrac{100}{80} = \pounds187.50$

6 **a** £500
   b $14\,170 \times 0.22 = \pounds3117.40$
   c £3617.40

7 $25\,000 \times 1.05^7 = \pounds35\,177.51$

8 $7.5 \times 1.35 \times 0.55 = 5$ hours 34 minutes

Exam questions

1 £40

2 **a** £35.70   **b** £18.40

3 £48.50

4 **a** £360   **b** £288.26

5 **a** **i** £360   **ii** £230.40   **b** £375

6 **a** £61.80   **b** 1.23

7 **a** £5755.11   **b** 1.157–1.158

8 £624.32

CHAPTER 30

Questions

1 **a** Copy of diagram
   b
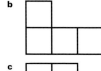
   c

   d

2 **a** 4800 kg   **c** 37.6 ml   **e** 5.760 kg
   b 5300 cl   **d** 560 g   **f** 0.489 litres

3 **a** 2 kg   **c** 9 litres   **e** 3 kg
   b 2000 ml   **d** 500 g   **f** 11.25 litres

4 **a** 96 oz   **c** 56 lb   **e** 47 lb
   b 120 oz   **d** 77 lb   **f** 5 stone

5 **a** 3 000 000 cm³   **b** 2 800 000 cm³   **c** 48.6 cm³

6 $\dfrac{3864}{2700} = 1.43\,\text{m}^3$

7 **a** $4 \times 6.2 \times 3.1 = 76.9\,\text{cm}^3$
   b $\frac{1}{2}(6.1 + 8.4) \times 16 \times 22 = 2550\,\text{m}^3$
   c $\frac{1}{2} \times 2 \times 3 \times 10.7 = 32.1\,\text{m}^3$

8 $\sqrt{\dfrac{65}{\pi \times 7.1}} = 1.7\,\text{cm}$

CHAPTER 30 (continued)

Exam questions

1 **a** 30 cm³   **b**

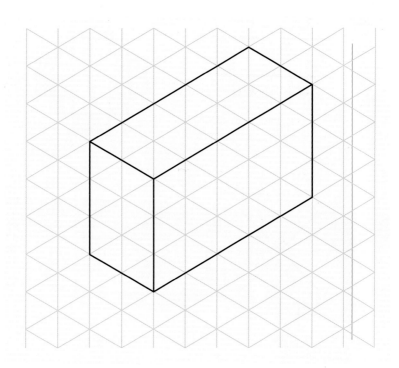

2 **a** 700 cm³   **b** 13.51 kg
3 $\pi pq, \frac{1}{2}qr, r(p+q)$

CHAPTER 31

Questions

1 **a**

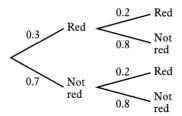

    b $0.3 \times 0.2 = 0.06$
    c $0.7 \times 0.8 = 0.56$
    d $0.3 \times 0.8 = 0.24$
    e $0.24 + 0.14 = 0.38$

2 **a** $0.7 \times 0.4 = 0.28$ **b** $0.3 \times 0.6 = 0.18$ **c** $0.4 \times 0.3 = 0.12$ **d** $1 - (0.3 \times 0.6) = 0.82$
3 **a** $\frac{1}{2} \times \frac{1}{2} \times \frac{1}{2} = \frac{1}{8}$ **b** $3 \times \frac{1}{2} \times \frac{1}{2} \times \frac{1}{2} = \frac{3}{8}$ **c** $1 - (\frac{1}{2} \times \frac{1}{2} \times \frac{1}{2}) = \frac{7}{8}$
4 **a** $\frac{1}{5} \times \frac{1}{3} = \frac{1}{15}$ **b** $\frac{1}{15} + (\frac{4}{5} \times \frac{3}{4}) = \frac{2}{3}$

Exam questions

1 LHS: $\frac{5}{12}, \frac{7}{12}$ **2** LHS: 0.2   **3** LHS: 0.05   **4** LHS: 0.4
    RHS: $\frac{5}{12}, \frac{7}{12}, \frac{5}{12}, \frac{7}{12}$ RHS: 0.3, 0.7, 0.3   RHS: 0.2, 0.2   RHS: 0.4, 0.6, 0.4

CHAPTER 32

Questions

1 **a** 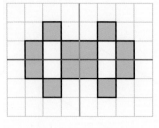 **b**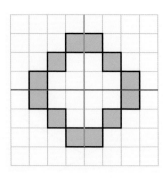

2 **a** 3
  b 6
  c infinite

3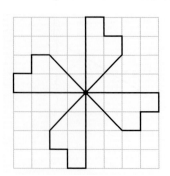

4

Name of regular polygon	Number of sides	Size of exterior angle	Size of interior angle	Number of lines of symmetry	Order of rotational symmetry
Pentagon	5	72°	108°	5	5
Hexagon	6	60°	120°	6	6
Octagon	8	45°	135°	8	8
Decagon	10	36°	144°	10	10

5 **a** $a = 3.6 \times \frac{12}{4} = 10.8$ cm
  $b = 9.1 \times \frac{12}{4} = 27.3$ cm

  b $c = 5 \times \frac{18}{12} = 7.5$ cm
  $d = 13 \times \frac{18}{12} = 19.5$ cm

Exam questions

1 **i** 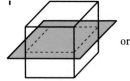 or or or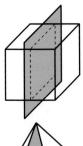

ii 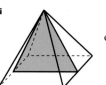 or or 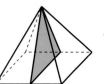 or

2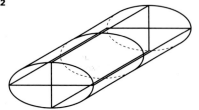

3 **a** 60° **b** 120°
4 **i** 12 cm **ii** 10 cm
5 8.25 cm
6 **a** 4 cm **b** 12 cm

CHAPTER 33

Questions

1 **a**

2 **a, b** and **c**

3

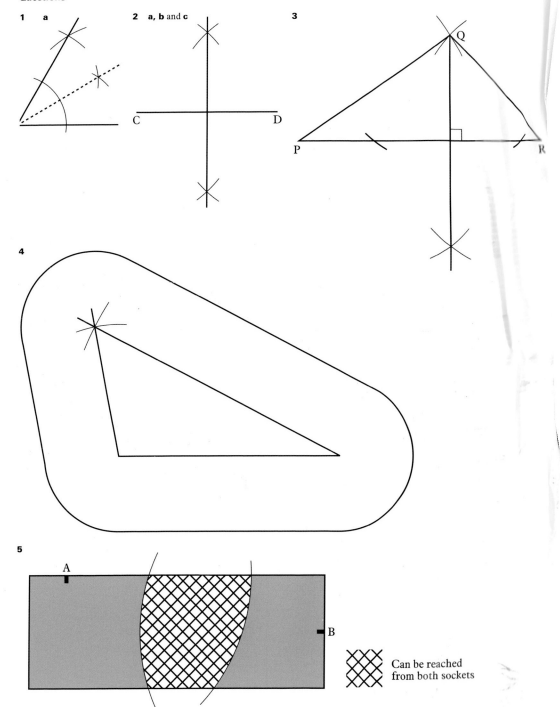

4

5

A

B

Can be reached
from both sockets

Exam questions

1

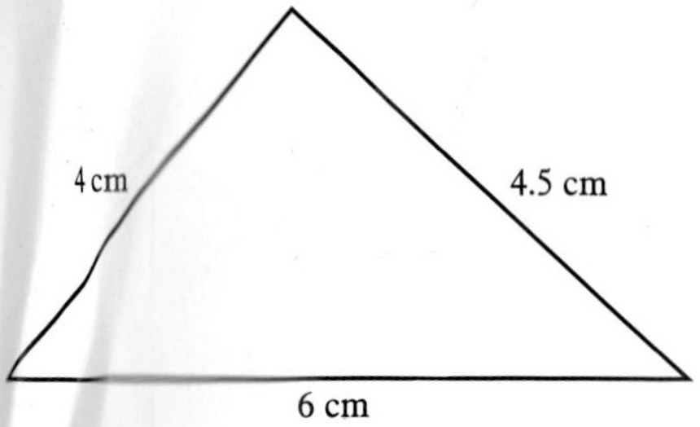

4 cm

4.5 cm

6 cm

a

A

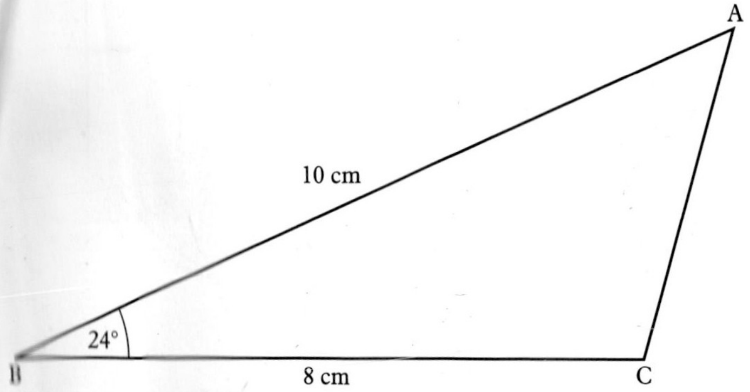

b i 50°
ii Acute

10 cm

24°

B

8 cm

C

3

3 cm

A

B

3 cm

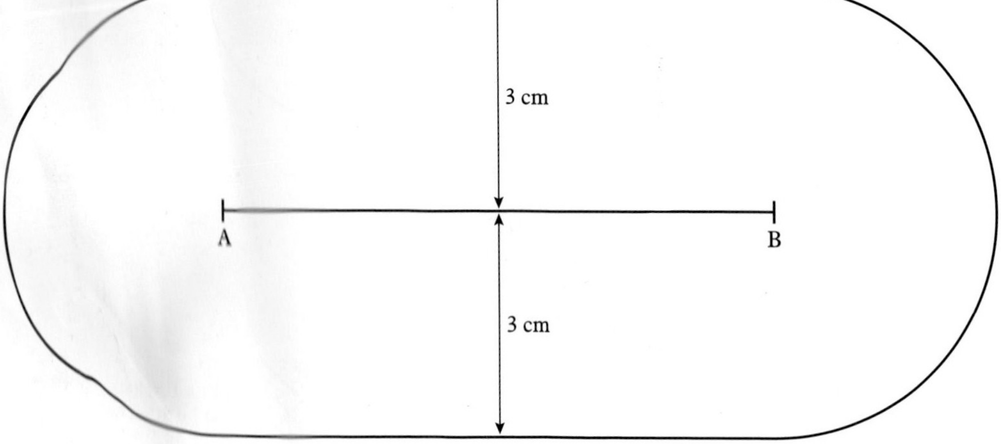